CHEATING

The Human Project and its Betrayal

CHEATING

The Human Project and its Betrayal

FRED HARRISON

SHEPHEARD WALWYN
PUBLISHERS

First published in 2026 by
Shepheard-Walwyn (Publishers) Ltd

www.shepheardwalwyn.com
www.ethicaleconomicsbooks.com

British Library Cataloguing in Publication Data
A catalogue record of this book is available
from the British Library

hardback ISBN 978-1-916517-23-3
paperback ISBN 978-1-916517-21-9
eBook ISBN 978-1-916517-22-6

Printed and bound in the USA

Contents

INTRODUCTION

4+1

Civilisation was constructed on a fraud, perpetrated in antiquity, and we are still living that nightmare. That betrayal of the human project now threatens the continued existence of humankind. We have arrived at the precipice: 4 existential crises, all of them long in the making, plus 1 that arrived in recent years. And yet, I refuse to yield to despair. The convergence of those threats, combined with the empathy and ingenuity of human beings, lead me to believe that we will pull back from extinction.

The knowledge needed to chart a new course has long been at our disposal, so that is not a problem. What is required is the determination to break from a disastrous past, so that we can restore human experience of the authentic kind. For the last five millennia, humans deviated from the path of authentic evolution, which is why we are now facing chaos.

The issue that threatens to force the convergence of the existential threats is the global economy. It is heading for collapse. On that issue, there is no time left to prevent the bust. Nonetheless, we can navigate the near future, if we adopt the correct strategy for restoring humanity on the evolutionary growth path. We can achieve this, because there is a single cause, and a single fix to the 4+1 threats.

Am I naïve? *The Times* of London invited its readers to judge. It asked: is Harrison a "crackpot or savant?"[1] I am neither. My job is to follow the money, collate the facts and connect the dots. The narrative unfolds itself. By understanding the perverse power of the culture of cheating, we can equip ourselves – materially, morally and spiritually – to diminish the dystopian world that awaits survivors if our world tips over the looming precipice.

The benefit of the *longue durée* is that – assuming we understand the inner working mechanism of the social system – the relevant patterns can be revealed. Apply the correct diagnostic theories, and we can identify the remedial policies. But, what if the global economy now heads for a protracted period of economic growth? If I am wrong, should we celebrate? Unfortunately, no. Because our world would still be challenged by the four existential crises.

Political paralysis

Law-makers are on a merry-go-round, continuously offering manifestoes with promises that, if elected, they will solve socially significant problems. They recycle failed policies which necessarily frustrate their electorates, which is why trust in democracy is at its lowest ebb.

The eco-crisis

Developing countries, according to the Basque Centre for Climate Change, could suffer losses estimated at $580bn by 2030. They will not be able to cope with the trauma of droughts, floods and fires, such as the devastation in Valencia in 2024 in which over 200 people died.

Migration

Exodus from the global south is on an alarming scale. An estimated 108 million people fled their countries in 2022, according to UNHCR Global Trends. Long-run projections for displacement runs into several billions. Many desperate people will seek refuge in Europe and the USA.

Autocracy

In the West, ideological paralysis is exploited by autocrats, who hype military adventures as solutions. The CIA warns that President Xi is preparing China to retake Taiwan by 2027.[2] In Russia, President Vladimir Putin says he is gearing up the missiles that deliver nuclear warheads.

The fifth threat is from the recent onset of the Digital Age (Ch. 13). Again, I remain convinced that we can snatch triumph from disaster, provided we shake ourselves out of the collective trauma that originated in antiquity.

HUMAN BEINGS are the greatest invention ever. We are the consequence of a purposeful creation, the product of a unique life force – the evolutionary force that created our ancestors.

Unlike our cousins, the Great Apes, our primate ancestors found a way to leave nature. To achieve that feat, they needed a chemical formula. That formula was the evolutionary force for growth (EFG), which did, indeed, deliver *Homo sapiens*. We can unravel the EFG by studying chimpanzees. They are content to work to meet their metabolic needs. Once they have filled their stomachs, they return to basking in the sun, or grooming their brothers and sisters. Our ancestors decided that they did not want to settle for that lifestyle. But the only way to grow out of nature was to work to produce more than their metabolic needs. That extra flow of energy could then be invested in bodies, minds and what became their souls. That EFG was like no other in physics. Its composition included a material content; but it also incorporated a consciousness that became the framework for a new realm in the universe: the Social Galaxy.

Without the EFG, our ancestors would still be living in close proximity to chimpanzees. Instead, they embarked on a project that knew no boundaries. So long as they worked to produce the EFG, they could realise the dream of reaching for the stars.

Economics as an intellectual discipline gave us the name for EFG: *economic rent*. I shall shorten it to Rent. We all own a share of that Rent, because we all work in cooperation to produce it. Tragically, statecraft – the kind created by the culture of cheating – deprives us of the property that we jointly own. Rent has become what economists designate as a “transfer income”. We all produce it, and it is then transferred as the exclusive property of people who give nothing in exchange.

The privatisation of the commons became the first conduit for diverting Rent into privileged pockets. That turned working people into hostages. If they agreed to pay the Rent to the Rentlords, they could continue to work to earn their wages to meet their metabolic needs, and remain alive. That model of exploitation has prevailed for five millennia. But we are now at an existential turning point. Without the restoration of justice in our financial affairs, Europe's civilisation will collapse under pressures from the coming economic crash.

Worse still: because, through colonialism, Europe's statecraft was globalised, the whole of humanity is now at risk of termination.

To grasp the truth of this thesis, we need a whole-of-history approach to diagnosing our problems. And, to heal the pathologies that abound in our midst, we must understand the metaphysics of property rights. Which is why, to comprehend what it would take to restructure statecraft today, we need an informed public debate about the origins of the scam. Most urgently, we need answers to three key questions.

First, how, back in antiquity, did the new elites repress people's resistance to cheating?

Second, how was power shaped, to immerse the cheating virus in the institutions of civilisation?

Third, how did the appropriation of Rent undermine the foundations of the civilisation model, leading to their persistent collapse?

Our search for the vital insights takes us back to the origins of the material and psycho-social legacies of ancient Egypt. The pathologies stemming from the fraud are visible every night, when we turn on the TV news. Russia sends explosive drones into nurseries to shatter children's lives; to kill their parents as they lie in their beds, blowing up the energy plants that keep families warm in winter. That is one symptom of the culture of cheating.

At the individual level, cheating in its violent form is branded as evil. During my career as a journalist, I had a professional reason to plumb the depths of that evil. I spent many hours sitting in a prison cell in the company of Ian Brady. He was raised as a fatherless child in the Gorbals, a deprived part of Glasgow. He shared with me the traumas that he experienced. As an adult, he became a serial killer of children. In cold blood, he kidnapped boys and girls off the streets in Manchester, tortured and killed them, and buried the bodies on a desolate moor.[3] In prison, he spent the remainder of his life converting books into braille for blind people; and supporting a charity for animals.

What animates such violence, both in its state-sponsored and individual forms? How do we reconcile such behaviour with what it means to be human? Why can't we banish it out of existence?

Our most ancient ancestors brought the capacity for violence out of nature. Gwen Adshead, the British psychotherapist, reminded us in her 2024 Reith Lectures that "the capacity for evil is present in all of us".[4] True, but to understand how we keep evil under control, we need to locate it in its cultural context. For, once upon a time, humans routinely ostracised cheating before it could mutate into evil forms of behaviour. What happened to change that check on the behaviour that was unbecoming of humanity?

In Part 1, I explain how the evolutionary blueprint was corrupted. Humans lost the rules of good behaviour, at the core of which was this principle:

Keep what you create, and pay for the benefits you receive.

People portrayed as primitive pagans were sophisticated, when it came to economic activity. They would not tolerate deviation from the evolutionary blueprint. If you tried to ride on other people's backs, you were ostracised; which meant you would not share in the resources reserved for the common good.

No cheating! By disallowing cheating, people were treated as equals. Thus, our ancient ancestors laboured their way out of nature, to the point where foraging was replaced by farming. And that was when things went wrong.

Cheating addresses my two major theses.

In economics, the harmonies of evolutionary growth were replaced by the rhythms of booms and busts. Today, we can trace those malign effects through the 18-year business cycle. I tested the evidence in 1983.[5] Sure enough, economic activity was dislocated by cyclical behaviour that could be predicted.

In politics, the perversion of income distribution is licensed by a statecraft designed to privilege one group of people – the owners of Rent-yielding assets. The legacies of that discrimination include institutionalised poverty, psychological despair and spiritual depletion. That, in turn, creates the space for the intrusion of evil behaviour in its many forms.

This was not what the people of the commons would have condoned, either in antiquity or in the modern era.

The archetype cheats emerged within the earliest civilisations, in Egypt and Mesopotamia. Their free riding mutated into the evil in our midst. There is a solution to this tragedy. But to restore an authentic humanity, we need to evolve the metaphysics of Rent to match our needs in the 21st century. I scope out that reform in Part 3.

At stake is our place on planet Earth. We are now confronted with pathologies rooted in a common cause – the private appropriation of our socially created Rents.

We humans are a project; a species constantly in the making. We are the architects and artisans of that project. We exercise control over it – or, rather, we *ought* to exercise control, in the way that our evolutionary ancestors intended.

We have now entered a phase in human existence that is unique. The end of the current 18-year business cycle will force the convergence of the existential threats in one big collision. We cannot be sure what will emerge out of the rubble. But there is one reason for optimism: because all of the threats are rooted in a common cause, a single, correctly applied reform to the financial system would empower us to navigate the catastrophe. And by erasing the 18-year cycle, we would re-embark on the human project.

At this eleventh hour, we must not prevaricate. Responsibility for action is on the shoulders of each and every one of us.

Fred Harrison
London
February 2026

References Introduction

1 Martina Lees (2022), "'House prices will crash in 2026'", *The Times*, July 22.

2 https://www.foxnews.com/world/china-xi-ordered-military-ready-taiwan-invasion-2027-cia-director-burns-says

3 Fred Harrison (1986), *Brady & Hindley: Genesis of the Moors Murders*, Bath: Ashgrove Press.

4 Gwen Adshead (2025), *Four Questions About Violence*, London: Faber & Faber, p. 23.

5 Fred Harrison (1983), *Power in the Land*, London: Shepheard-Walwyn.

Part 1

We Are Rent

PROLOGUE

To Be, or Not

Shakespeare expressed the choice perfectly: "To be, or not to be, that is the question". Hamlet's speech captured the essence of the dilemma faced by our primate ancestors. There was nothing in the laws of physics that would elevate the hominins out of nature. To accomplish that feat, they had to pay a price: they would have to work to produce a net flow of resources.

Hominins did not have the capacity to make a conscious choice. By instinct, they selected what turned out to be the evolutionary course of action. They cooperated to produce more than nature required for their metabolic needs. They pooled those extra resources in their bodies, minds and souls, which created the evolutionary force for growth (EFG). That formula resulted in *Homo sapiens*. Property rights, as the membrane of the system, were at the interface between people's public and private lives.

In Part 1, I explain how it all went wrong. Scientists realise that "On our present path, civilization as we know it will disappear", according to the former chief scientific advisor to the UK government.[1] Based on current thinking, there is no way to break loose from the doom loop.

The source of humanity's problems is the perversion of our net income. When it is diverted into non-social uses, Rent turns hostile to the people who work to produce it. Rent becomes the lethal power that systematically corrupts everything that defines what it means to be human – material, moral and spiritual. It packs the punch capable of delivering the killer blow against our species.

How can this one flow of income exercise such an existential threat? For the answer, we need to burrow into the history of property rights. We must understand how and why income is now allocated on an unjust basis, and how the culture of cheating shapes our behaviour. We need to deconstruct both the nature of Rent, and the social system that perverted the human commons. This interrogation begins with the Law of Increasing Net Returns.

Einstein's Theory of General Relativity explains how space-time in the universe is warped by massive objects that create the distortions which result in the pull of gravity. Rent exercises a similar thermodynamic force in the Social Galaxy. In scale and weight, it is sufficient to affect people's behaviour, *en masse*, for good or evil, depending on the prevailing possessory rights.

Assets that yield Rent are the most valuable on Earth. The most visible of those assets is land in its locational manifestation. In economics, by "land" we mean everything in the universe in its natural state, unmodified by humans. Rent, however, is a composite value. Understanding that composition is crucial, if we are to motivate people behind the mission to rescue humanity.

Two streams of value converge in the locations we occupy. One is contributed by the resources of nature. The heat of the sun adds Rental value to the beach-side locations on the Costa Brava. The second stream of Rent is generated by the services delivered by people and their public agencies. Rents are higher where there is law and order; where transport systems and welfare services meet people's needs; as well as all of the other attributes of communities that lure people to those locations. When the net values of those amenities are privatised and traded in markets, annual Rents are capitalised into a single price.

Airlines that possess landing slots over airports reap Rents. Fossil fuels, fish landed on quaysides, minerals mined out of the land – they all generate Rents. Then there are the Rents created by the highways along ocean floors that host the copper cables we need for our computers. In urban locations, Rents flow from investments in hospitals and schools; and from the military defence of the realm.

Control Rent and you control the institutions and values of society. The numbers support this assertion. Those numbers, however, are confined to the measurable real estate values in today's markets. As such, they understate the quantum of Rent in the global system. For a comprehensive assessment, we need to take account of two further considerations.

First, add the revenue collected by governments. Ultimately, *that revenue comes out of Rent.* In a 700-page book devoted to the algebra of space and time, the single most important practical insight offered by classical economics is summarised in two half-sentences. One states that, to understand the realities of the market economy, we need to combine "land values *plus* pure site taxes". Why? Because "a pure site tax falls completely on the landlord, even if levied on the tenant".[2] Translation: the tax-take from what appears to be other sources of income (wages of labour, or the interest received for the use of capital) is ultimately derived from Rent. ATCOR: all taxes come out of Rent.

Second, we need to add the deadweight losses induced by taxes levied on wages and interest. Those taxes distort behaviour and create what economists call "excess burdens". Those burdens reduce – are at the expense of – the Rent that people would otherwise produce. Excess burden comes out of Rent: EBCOR, the acronym coined by the late Mason Gaffney (1923–2020), who spent most of his working life as professor of economics in the University of California.[3]

In sheer weight and global reach, Rent eclipses all the other streams of income. The facts are documented by Savills, the London realtor with a global reach. It estimates the worldwide value of real estate at $326.5 trillion (2020). Residential property, at the top of the list, "is by far the largest real estate sector, accounting for 79% of all global real estate value" ($258.5 trillion). Savills emphasises that "real estate is more valuable than all global equities and debt securities combined, and almost four times that of global GDP. The value of all gold ever mined pales by comparison at $12.1 trillion, at just 4% the value of global property".[4]

Location is the most valuable of real estate assets. Over time, while buildings depreciate, the value of locations appreciates. In the UK, residential locations are valued at £5.4 trillion, 86% of the total value of non-produced non-financial assets. The Office of National Statistics states: "The UK's net worth reached £10.7 trillion in 2020, with land consistently being the most valuable asset in the economy. Estimated at £6.3 trillion, it accounts for nearly 60% of the UK's net worth, with households owning £4.3 trillion of that."[5]

Rent is now escalating towards the next crisis. Note the estimates and timings by Savills:

> **Our forecasts, which cover over 90% of the global market, expect turnover to increase by 7% by the end of this year [2024], reaching US$747 billion. This recovery is anticipated to gather momentum in 2025, with investment forecast to rise by 27% to US$952 billion. By 2026, global activity is expected to surpass the US$1 trillion mark.**[6]

Governments, unfortunately, are urging their financial regulators to loosen the analysis of risks associated with property. They ignore the harsh lessons of history. This renders the 18-year boom/bust cycle inevitable. The three post-war US trends are illustrated in Fig. P1.1, which terminated in the recessions of 1974, 1992 and 2010.

The end of the cycle that began in 2010 is 2028. Few politicians are as frank as the South Korean president. In late 2025, he warned that his country's property market was a bubble on the point of bursting; with the prospect of a catastrophic collapse comparable to what happened in Japan in 1992.[7]

Figure P1.1 **The US Real House Price Index**

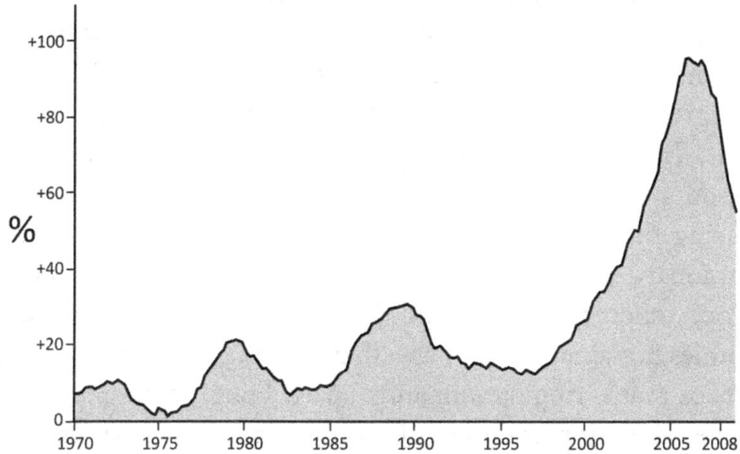

Source: CB2 10_Percentage Change in Real Home Price Index since 1890, 1970–2008

OVER THE PAST 50 years, I interrogated the nature of Rent to understand how we can erase features like poverty in the midst of plenty, and the boom/bust cycles. This effort was met with blocked ears, closed minds. So why this present attempt at communicating a philosophy that was originally developed in the salons of Paris in the 18th century? The Physiocrats were a school of philosophers who sought to guide France in the direction of an enlightened financial system that would have avoided a bloody revolution. Adam Smith in Scotland took up the cause, but was also unsuccessful. In the 19th century, John Stuart Mill in England and Henry George in America were equally frustrated in their attempts to communicate the Rent doctrine to lawmakers. In the 20th century, academicians who understood the unique nature of Rent were also ignored – people like Joseph Stiglitz and a string of Nobel Prize winners.[8]

The consequences are now visible on our television screens every night. Reporters describe the terrible effects of an angry natural world: the burning down of towns and the flooding of whole regions across continents. None of this is accidental. It is the result of a purposeful state of affairs wrapped up in wilful blindness.

Most of us seek nothing more than the freedom to work for our living, to achieve our personal aspirations, and to give our children the best possible chance in life. We cannot imagine ourselves as cheating our fellow citizens. We all own or rent locations. But, no matter how small a plot of land, that makes us complicit in the most egregious of crimes against humanity. That proposition is horrific. The size of each occupied site is just enough on which to locate a home to shelter a family. How can that be a crime? By asking that question, we embark on the most fundamental of revolutionary journeys, a revolution of the mind. Examine the evidence, follow the money, and there is a good chance – given the empathies ingrained in all of us – that we will once-and-for-all end the chaos that is ripping humanity apart. Time, however, is not on our side. The big picture reveals why we must reshape statecraft. The devil is in the detail. First, the timetable.

The laws of physics are converging with the perverted laws licensed by the culture of cheating. When the moon "wobbles" the effects are felt on Earth. Physicists report that the moon's tremors operate in cycles of 18.6 years duration. We cannot moderate those wobbles. Down on Earth, the ripples are visible in the shifts in ocean tides. NASA, America's space gazing agency, reports that the moon's cycle is about to reach the point where its wobbles will amplify the high tides on Earth.[9] This time, the moon's 18-year cycle is synchronised with the 18-year Rent cycle.

In *The Power in the Land*, I explained how Rent in its privatised form drives the business cycle in 18-year periodicities.[10] The pattern is visible in the economic record spanning hundreds of years. The 2026 peak in land prices will tip the global economy into chaos. In *Boom Bust*, I hypothesised that this cycle was due to the average 5% rate of interest that prevailed over many centuries.[11] The arc of the cycle is from recession to growth in the recovery phase, and onwards to credit-fuelled land speculation, terminating in busts that crush people's jobs and aspirations.

How credible are my warnings about the timing of the cyclical downturn following the end of the last cycle? According to the UK's Office for Budget Responsibility, there will be no downturn

Figure P1.2 **UK house prices**

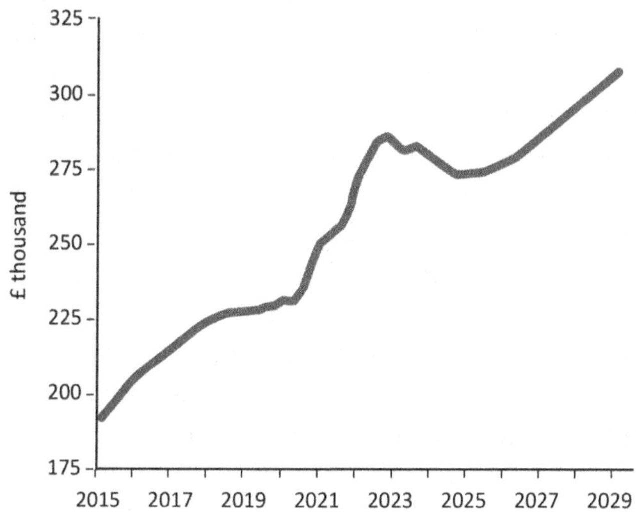

Source: OBR (2024), Economic and fiscal Outlook, October, p. 45.

in house prices in 2026, nor will there be a recession in 2028 (Fig. P1.2). In its 2024 report to Parliament, the OBR forecast continuous growth trends through to 2029.

Government forecasters and their expert advisers from academia and the think-tanks failed to anticipate recessions at the end of the three previous post-war house price cycles. I did forecast those recessions. I tried to alert UK governments with my books, and (in 1997) letters to the incumbents of Nos. 10 and 11, Downing Street, to no avail. In real time, the reader will now judge whether my forecast of an economic crisis in 2027 is robust, following the end of the house price cycle in 2026.[12]

Unlike the tidal wobbles caused by the Moon, *we can control economic wobbles on Earth*. We can level the amplitudes of boom/busts to deliver sustained economic growth, harmony in communities and peace in our minds. Governments, however, refuse to alter the Rent cycle. Why? Ultimately, law-makers owe their prime duty of care to the culture of cheating. That means everyone will pay the price, as the cycle that began in 2010 heads for its end in 2028. This time, however, we are not just faced with a recession. Civilisation is at stake.

The collision of the twin forces, from the Moon and from beneath our feet, will amplify the multitude of stresses in the Social Galaxy. Already, some coastal communities and island nations are being swamped; with governments standing helpless as vast territories disappear under water. About 40% of humanity occupies continental coasts. Pakistan and Bangladesh have had a foretaste of nature's revenge, in the devastating floods of 2022.

The economic downturn in 2028 will synchronise the existential crises. We are, as UN Secretary General António Guterres put it, "on the highway to hell".[13] He was referring to the climate crisis, which is just one of the highways. The 2030s are the crossroads for The Great Convergence of 4+1 threats to humanity.

The interventions of climate change will amplify the scale of the chaos. According to the World Meteorological Organisation, for the first time in human history we are more likely than not to exceed and sustain 1.5°C annual mean temperature by 2028.[14]

Politicians refuse to discuss the roots of the threats, because that would lead them to the remedy. Academic communities are likewise derelict, declining to examine the relevant issues in peer-reviewed journals. Why do we tolerate this state of affairs?

There *is* a single cause, *and* a single fix in the form of revisions to the tax regime. The tool for gravitating away from the existential threats is a new metric: Zero Deadweight. The UN's Net Zero carbon emissions is just one element of Zero Deadweight. We also need remedial methods that encompass personal behaviour and statecraft. In assembling the information to achieve Zero Deadweight, we expose the malevolent secret in economics: the scale of the burdens imposed on all of us by fiscal policies.

My assessment of prospects for the future rests on two hypotheses.

1. We now occupy No Man's Land. Our globalised civilisation is hostage to the pathologies of the culture of cheating. These have consigned all societies to the state of terminal decline.

2. The fiscal route to recovery is anchored in the primary codes of the evolutionary blueprint. We survive by honouring human rights aligned to the corresponding social responsibilities.

Hope is what we need. Informed hope, to enable us to navigate our way beyond the 2030s. It all depends on the fate of Rent. If we fail to conform to the basic principles of the evolutionary blueprint, our species cannot continue to exist. For, in the language of the prophets…

Ezekiel's Horsemen are saddled up. The apocalypse is coming. Every day, we observe the flooding of communities across the world. Threats of nuclear Armageddon. Unchecked migration. Ideological paralysis. Are we going to meet those threats head-on, in the fight for our existence? We have the tools: the power marshalled by our ancestors, the creative power of human fusion, which materialises in the form of Rent.

References Part 1, Prologue

1 Humanity's survival is still within our grasp – just. But only if we take these radical steps | David King | The Guardian

2 Arnold M. Faden (1977), *Economics of Space and Time: The Measure=theoretic Foundations of Social Science*, Ames, Iowa: Iowa State University Press, p.513. Emphasis in original.

3 Mason Gaffney (2009), "The Hidden Taxable Capacity of Land: Enough and to Spare", *International J. of Social Economics*. http://dx.doi.org/10.1108/03068290910947930

4 https://www.savills.com/impacts/market-trends/the-total-value-of-global-real-estate.html

5 https://www.ons.gov.uk/economy/nationalaccounts/uksectoraccounts/articles/improvingestimatesoflandunderlyingdwellingsinthenationalbalancesheetuk/2022

6 Global real estate investment: 2025 and beyond | Savills Impacts

7 South Korea faces property 'ticking bomb' as Lee backs BOK hold – The Business Times https://www.businesstimes.com.sg/property/south-korea-faces-property-ticking-bomb-lee-backs-bok-hold

8 See the list of signatories to an Open Letter to Mikhail Gorbachev, which includes William Vickrey, James Tobin, Franco Modigliani and Robert Solow. Richard Noyes (1991), *Now the Synthesis: Capitalism, Socialism & the New Social Contract*, London: Shepheard-Walwyn, pp. 225-229.

9 Philip R. Thompson *et al* (2021), "Rapid increases and extreme months in projections of US high-tide flooding", *Nat. Clim. Chang.* 11 https://doi.org/10.1038/s41558-021-01077-8

10 Fred Harrison, 2nd edn. (2021), *Power in the Land*, London: Shepheard-Walwyn.

11 Fred Harrison (2005), *Boom Bust: House Prices, Banking and the Depression of 2010*, London: Shepheard-Walwyn.

12 Among academics, few are as frank about the failings of their discipline as Angus Deaton, the Nobel prize economist who has come to realise the need to rethink the terms of his discipline. Rethinking Economics or Rethinking My Economics by Angus Deaton (imf.org) https://www.imf.org/en/Publications/fandd/issues/2024/03/Symposium-Rethinking-Economics-Angus-Deaton?utm_medium=email&utm_source=govdelivery

13 BBC interview, October 26, 2022. https://www.youtube.com/watch?v=XQXhHpGcQdw

14 https://public.wmo.int/en/media/press-release/global-temperatures-set-reach-new-records-next-five-years

CHAPTER ONE

The Act of Creation

Charles Darwin treated humans as similar to other species. We evolved through natural selection. Small genetic variations bequeathed an evolutionary advantage, yielding the ability to compete, survive and reproduce. Like other species, a branch of the primates evolved into human by *adapting* to ecological niches. Dependent on nature.

The evolution of our earliest ancestors, it turns out, was more complicated than that. And, for the sake of the survival of *Homo sapiens*, as a matter of urgency we need to unravel the forces that animated the drama that became the human project.

There was nothing like it in the universe. The laws of physics would not authorise the emergence of lifestyles that were not pre-determined by the genetic code. And nature could not incubate it, because the 2nd Law of Thermodynamics prescribes decay, decomposition. The growth of our ancestors was an affront to physics.

To become human, one branch of the primate species became the architects of their own fate. This claim offends the views of scientists who assert that human behaviour is predetermined. If they are correct, the laws of physics must have been capable of singling out one branch of the primates to behave in a unique way, enabling our earliest ancestors to choose their existence while other species conformed to the law of entropy. How plausible is it that the laws of the universe would create the conditions for one species to offend its own powers?

The order did not come from nature. Proto-humans chose to embark on a unique voyage of creativity. To do so, they deployed a dynamic system that could co-exist with, but not remain confined within, the logic of the laws of the universe. They achieved this with the aid of three elements. They combined the physics of the universe with spiritual beliefs and with their moral sensibilities. This integration of three dimensions provided the framework for the voyage of discovery that began a million years ago. That composition was possible, because they created the existential driving force. I refer to a unique stream of energy that proto-humans had to labour to produce and invest.

From the first moments of flickering self-consciousness, hominins beheld a new world. Framed by nature, but an emerging space of their creation. A sphere without boundaries if they were willing to work, to create the energy that would open up a galaxy of possibilities. They drew on the resources of that embryonic space, their emerging consciousness animated by visions that became mysterious images of forces gazing at them, the grist for what became the first spiritual narratives. Thus emerged the tools for understanding, communicating, encoding...providing the strength of purpose to sustain the project on which they were embarked. An existence that pushed against the universe of physics and genetics.

This was the origin of agency – free will. Neuro-physicists disagree, arguing that pulses from the brain precede conscious decisions to act. This, apparently, demonstrated that humans did not have free will. Their behaviour was genetically predetermined. A professor of biology and neurology at Stanford University maintains that the "sense of freely choosing is just a *post hoc* illusion, a false sense of agency".[1]

Our earliest ancestors deviated from nature's evolutionary path by creating the capacity to produce the flow of energy that would liberate them. They altered behaviour patterns by weighing risks and rewards, so that they could select the strategies that made possible the fulfilment of dreams. This yielded an evolutionary advantage transmitted, in part, through the gene pool. But, increasingly, that genetic effect was the consequence of the choices made by groups

Box 1.1 Left behind

The remains of one strand of our earliest ancestors were excavated on the Indonesian island of Flores. The bone of an arm, from 700,000 years ago, revealed that this was from the smallest human species, standing just over 3ft tall.* Palaeontologists conclude that, despite their small brains, they were skilled toolmakers who hunted elephants and rodents. In the end, however, they were isolated on their island home. The contraction in the availability of food was at the expense of their metabolic needs, which left no net resources for further growth. They lost the capacity to sustain themselves.

* Y. Kaifu *et al.* (2024), "Early evolution of small body size in *Homo floresiensis*". *Nature Communications* 15(6381). https://doi.org/10.1038/s41467-024-50649-7.

of individuals who decided not to be subservient to, dependent upon, the laws of nature. This was achieved by opting to labour to produce more than their daily metabolic needs. That additional flow of resources would be invested for future benefits.

This was a hazardous process. Something like 99% of species that ever existed are now extinct. Evolution, if it proceeds by trial and error, is a brutal form of empiricism (Box 1.1). But proto-humans had an evolutionary advantage: they developed the power to choose. In time, *other species had to adapt themselves to the unique habitats created by humans.*

The capacity to choose was required, if proto-humans were to distinguish between good and evil, aided by the emergence of the spiritual life. Self-consciousness was inspired by questions such as: who are we, how did we come to be here? The spiritual life helped to answer the existential questions. The earliest versions of the creation story drew for inspiration from the natural world. At each stage of the human project, a new creation story emerged to animate the progress to what became humanity (Box 1.2).

Box 1.2 **The spiritual life**

Our foraging ancestors drew strength from imagined creatures in nature. Then, from antiquity through to the modern Enlightenment, God appeared.

The origins story continues to evolve in the age of science. Only recently have scientists discovered that the human brain owes much to a family of genes called Notch2NL.* They believe the gene emerged through chance in our ancestors 3m to 4m years ago.** But the threefold increase in the size of the brain would not have occurred without the investment of the net resources which people chose to work to produce.

Creation stories gave direction to life, motivation to behaviour, and they continue to support the human project in the age of science.

* We Just Found a Genetic Key to Why Humans Have Such Massive Brains: ScienceAlert. https://www.sciencealert.com/big-human-brains-down-to-neuron-building-genes-notch2nl

** Clive Cookson (2024), "Scientists discover why humans have big brains", *Financial Times*, June 1.

In physics, fusion is the capacity to generate a net gain of power, delivering energy in quantities that exceed the sum of its parts. That extra energy is available to invest in the biology of life on Earth, as through the nourishing warmth exuded by the sun. Scientists in California demonstrated nature's fusion in their laboratory on December 5, 2022. Lasers fused two atoms. More energy came out than went in.

Our ancestors cracked that code long ago. By cooperating with each other, they generated a greater flow of energy than they could produce by working on their own account as individuals. This process led to the development of empathy for others. It defined the moral sensibilities, characteristics that conformed to the iron law of morality: *rights claimed against* others balanced by *responsibilities to* others. This was the mechanism for sustainable, and what scientists now call superlinear, growth.

The net resources: Rent

Darwin's theory does provide one starting point for interpreting the reality of how hominins, over the last 300,000 years, left traces of evidence for us to excavate. They created the legacy assets bequeathed to us. By trial and error, they developed an evolutionary blueprint. This enabled them to produce and invest the supplementary flow of resources which economists call "economic rent" (hereafter: Rent). Without Rent, humans would not exist.

Proto-humans embarked on the most complex challenge ever undertaken in the universe; a complexity not since equalled by anything that modern humans have created with the tools of science and technology. The evolutionary pattern reveals

- Muscle power
- Moral discipline
- Motivation

These combined to deliver the organising mechanism that balanced outcomes between the component parts of the evolutionary dynamic.

- ***Proportionality***, to ensure efficient use of resources
- ***Momentum***, to ensure sustained growth
- ***Direction***, to achieve shared aspirations

Biologically, humans did have to behave like other species. They had to satisfy their metabolic needs. Economic historian Robert Allen defines that irreducible minimum as "least-cost" way of staying alive".[2] But while other species thrived within the limits imposed by bare-bones subsistence (BBS), our ancestors worked to produce more than their biological needs.

Allen (along with many others) errs in labelling that additional flow of energy as a "surplus", as if those resources were produced without purpose or proprietorship, available for anyone to appropriate on the first-come-first-served principle. His account reveals the error in this perspective. The surplus, he states, is "extracted by the state, the aristocracy, and the rich merchants".

Events prior to the way the elites appropriated the net income is the story of the human project that remains to be told (Box 1.3).

From the beginning of human time, people who laboured to produce more than their metabolic needs did so with intent. This was rational behaviour, a disposition to work with a purpose. To achieve this outcome, they had to develop the force of "agency" – the will to postpone, if not override, the laws of physics and genetics. Evidence of this confluence of forces around the concept of Rent was uncovered at an archaeological site at Kalambo Falls, Zambia, dating to at least 476,000 years ago. Interlocking logs, intentionally

Box 1.3 **Existential net resources**

The historical literature is muddled on how to represent the net resources people produced in antiquity.* Historians and anthropologists are locked in a "chicken and egg" conundrum.

If net resources were the only way to emerge out of the primate family, they were produced with intent. In that case, they were not a surplus. Treating net resources as a surplus creates a circular argument. Which came first in the creation of civilisations: the net resources, or the elites that extracted Rents out of the farmers? If net resources did not exist before the onset of civilisation, then the elites had to force the peasants to produce more than their subsistence. But in that case, how did the elites evolve their power and institutions, without the aid of Rents?

Some scholars avoid the circular conundrum by assuming that "the task of the emerging elite would be easier if they could appropriate an existing surplus, rather than having to stimulate its creation". That, however, leaves unanswered the question of how and why people produced a "surplus" in the first place!

*Paul Halstead (1989), "The economy has a normal surplus: economic stability and social change among early farming communities of Thessaly, Greece", in P. Halstead and J. O'Shira, *Bad Year Economics: Cultural Responses to Risk and Uncertainty*, Cambridge: University Press, pp.69.

Figure 1.1 **Roaming the Laws**

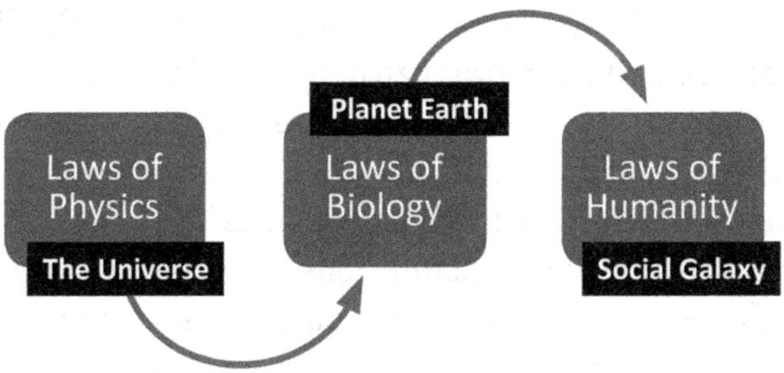

shaped to serve as a platform, confirms the ability to transform nature's resources into capital equipment. The offcuts from a tree were designed "to make life easier, even if it was only by making a platform to sit on by the river to do their daily chores. They used their intelligence, imagination, and skills, to create something they'd never seen before".[3]

This was the expedition out of the forests of Africa. A journey of creation. The net resources manifested themselves in three dimensions: material resources; metrics; and motivation. Combined, these fuelled and gave direction to the Social Galaxy. From intimately personal beginnings emerged the logic of the system, achieved by dialectically roaming through the three sets of laws (Fig. 1.1). First, the laws of physics that define the universe. Second, the laws of biology that regulate life on Earth. Third, the laws of humanity, which enabled proto-humans to exercise sufficient control over the impact of the other two sets of laws to enable them to create their unique way of life. In learning how to combine these three layers of laws, they postponed, to a critical extent, the impact of the 2nd Law of Thermodynamics.

Scientists are still seeking clues to the origins of life that flourishes on Earth.[4] Geneticists can unpack the information encoded in DNA, yielding insights into the formation of biological life. Nobel laureate Erwin Schrödinger elegantly explained how life was the result of the metabolism that replaced the physics of chaos with the order delivered by the forces of biology. Life, in its animal and vegetable forms, emerged by postponing the impact of the 2nd Law of Thermodynamics. Entropy is the de-composition of order into disorder (as with, from hot to cold). Biological life, wrote Schrödinger, originated by "sucking orderliness from its environment". For higher animals, it was "the extremely well-ordered state of matter in more or less complicated organic compounds, which serve them as foodstuffs".[5]

Foodstuffs, provided by nature, consumed in the raw by emerging species. To become human, however, hominins went one giant step further. They learnt to work longer, or more efficiently, to produce an extra layer of energy; some of it in the form of food, but also to evolve the technology of tools to aid their labours. They were not the only hominins to discover the role of tools. The *Paranthropus*, located in present-day Kenya, made extensive use of stone tools.[6] Nevertheless, they became extinct. It was not enough to use tools to gather food for subsistence. Our branch of the hominins used tools to fund the construction of codes of conduct, which fostered the cooperative spirit.

Fire, for example, enhanced the nutritional value of raw food. The earliest evidence for that activity comes from Israel, where archaeologists analysed the charred teeth of carp dated to about 780,000 years ago.[7] Inhabitants of a site near the Jordan River supplemented their diet with carp they cooked in their hearths. "The skill to cook marks an evolutionary advance, as it provided an additional means for making optimal use of available food resources," notes one of the archaeologists.[8] Stephen Pyne, author of *The Pyrocene*, explains: "We developed more compact guts and big heads because we learned to cook food".[9] Enhancing the value of the net flow of resources was the mechanism missing from Darwin's theory of adaptation (Box 1.4).

George Homans (1910–1989), a Harvard sociologist who analysed kinship groups, noted that foragers "have tended to produce a *surplus* of the goods that make organisation successful".[10] Had he dug deeper, and armed with the concept of Rent, he might have understood how the net product became the existential formula for the emergence and development of *Homo sapiens*.

> **Box 1.4 The exceptional species**
>
> Scientists, sceptical of Darwin's theory based on random variation and adaptation, point to the rich diversity of species on Earth and argue that nature innovates change. Andreas Wagner,* an external professor at the Santa Fe Institute, the New Mexico home for a multi-disciplinary group of scholars seeking answers to fundamental questions, argues that the answers are located in the complex networks that organise biological assets.
>
> Innovative evolutionary science, however, remains limited to insights afforded by the flow of just enough energy to sustain the biological system. In the four billion years of evolution, we know of no case of a species whose evolution was contingent on the ability to produce resources net of immediate metabolic needs; let alone the agency to produce those resources to facilitate the direction of travel into the future. Our ancestors were the exception.
>
> *Andreas Wagner (2011), *The Origins of Evolutionary Innovations*, Oxford: University Press.

The fingerprints of our earliest ancestors are all over our bodies, our souls and our communities. Intuitively, they decoded the impact of the law that traces the decay of matter into the state of entropy, and they laboured to replace it with the 1st Law of Social Dynamics.[11] This Law guided them all the way through to historical times. It formed the basis of, and distinguished between, personal and social power.

The metaphysics of Rent

The net flow of energy was invested in what we now call "the common good". By that, we mean the formation of assets that cannot be produced by the labours of people working by themselves. Those assets were needed to meet the needs of everyone in the population.

To succeed in this mission, there had to be an intent that reached beyond any one generation. Otherwise, what was the point of working once the stomach was full? The process was sustained through the generations. They did not know about the transmission of genetic information, but they did love their offspring, and that was good enough to animate the aspirations that revealed glimmers of the future.

The primary logic of the acts of creation was to deliver the flow of energy that could be stored and reused, to sustain the three layers of existence.

- *Current welfare*: investing in the incremental growth of body, mind and soul.
- *Creativity*: nurturing aspirations to improve life for future generations.
- *Conservation*: respecting nature, to continue satisfying metabolic needs.

In scoping out the contours of this evolutionary process, I do not idealise the lives of the foragers. It was hard work, under harsh conditions, with hazards to overcome.[12] Nevertheless, it worked.

One way to trace that evolutionary process is through the emergence of the binary personality. First (out of biological priority) came the social personality. Kinship groups grew into clans and tribes. As the social personality grew richer, so the opportunities arose for experiments in idiosyncratic behaviour. From this emerged individual personalities. That composite relationship drove the evolving humans to aspire to new ways of living; to co-operating in ever more fruitful ways to realise shared, and personal, dreams; to migrating across the planet, conforming to a single evolutionary blueprint (Box 1.5).

Classical economists of the 18th century conceptualised the dynamics of Rent formation in terms portrayed on a graph (Fig. 1.2). The vertical axis measures productivity within a catchment area. Distance from the economic centre (location of the campfire or financial district) is measured on the horizontal axis. Everything below the sloping line (within the boundaries

ABCD) adds up to total income. The slope evokes economic reality: higher productivity towards the centre of the social system, where locations are richer in fertile fields and the aggregation of people and their resources in urban locations. This is where people tend to congregate, yielding the synergy known as the "agglomeration" of productive opportunities.

Box 1.5 **A eureka moment**

Scientists speculate that stone shards originally thought to be the tools of hominids may be the accidental chippings from stones used by macaques to crack nuts.* The *intentional* flaking of stones to create sharp tools was a eureka moment that helped the transition to *Homo sapiens*. Sharpened shards were the first forms of capital. By adding handles to the shards, our ancestors could keep the instruments for later use. This improved productivity and reduced the effort invested in food gathering. From such initiatives, tiny groups could invest more time in non-foraging activities.

Robin Dunbar, Professor of Evolutionary Psychology at Oxford, records that monkeys and apes were limited to communities of 50, constrained in their range of social contacts by the time and effort they could devote to grooming each other. Early humans evolved into more extended relationships (numbering about 150), by feeding the energy-intensive endorphin system in the brain. This enabled them to relate to multiple numbers of people simultaneously, through culture: the combination of skills such as singing, storytelling, feasting and religion, which Dunbar calls "grooming-at-a-distance".**

*Tomos Proffitt *et al* (2023), "Wild macaques challenge the origin of intentional tool production", Science Advances, 10 March, 9(10). https://www.science.org/doi/10.1126/sciadv.ade8159.

** Robin Dunbar (2022), *How Religion Evolved: And Why it Endures*, London: Pelican, pp. 101-102.

Figure 1.2 **Distribution of Income**

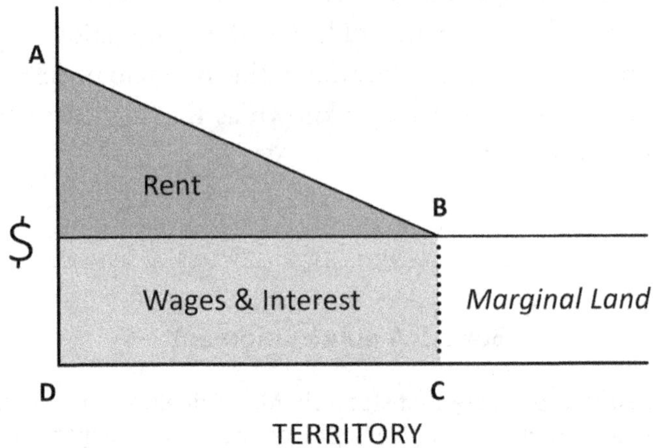

David Ricardo (1772–1823) elaborated on the spatial division of income in *Principles of Political Economy and Taxation* (1817). Rent is highest at the centre and lowest towards the margin (BC in Fig. 1.2). There is an evolutionary reason why people chose not to live beyond the margin. While they may have been able to generate enough to cover metabolic needs, marginal locations would not yield a net income; the income that made life worth living.

Rent is maximised through co-operation. Complementing this social context is the competitive spirit that delivers both personal fulfilment and a balanced relationship between the private and social spheres of life. One outcome is the optimum allocation of productive resources – labour time, tools and the resources of nature – to fulfil social needs. Economists classify the three elements as labour, capital and land.

Fig. 1.2 illustrates the breakdown of the product of people's labour. The primary division is between Rent and the rest. To fulfil metabolic requirements, including aesthetic and recreational needs, people retained as their personal property everything below the horizontal line. This is represented as wages and the rewards for creating the tools needed in the value-creating process. Everything above the line is net income, which was invested in the human project.

Why is the line that divides Rent from the rest shown as flat? Over time, under the pressure of seeking to achieve the best results (through competition), wages and interest are equalised across the territory. This ensured two outcomes: (1) everyone fulfilled metabolic needs; and (2) pooling the difference, the Rents, into the public purse, ensured that no-one could reap an unfair advantage by retaining resources which they did not exclusively produce (Box 1.6).

Box 1.6 **Social metabolism**

In its social form, Rent equalises, and elevates, life-chances. People living in favourably endowed locations share the net benefits with people living in less well-endowed regions, by pooling higher Rents into the public purse. As a result, take-home pay is equalised (but taking into account varying skills) through the synthesis of a free market, assuming that governance is based on evolutionary principles.

UK data illustrates this outcome. In 2022, the median income in London (located at the spatial centre in Ricardo's graph) was much higher than in the other regions. However, it was equalised with other regions after deducting the Rent that people paid for their homes in London.*

*Laura Noonan and Chris Giles (2023), "Londoners more likely to struggle with mortgages", *Financial Times*, March 10. For regional wage differences, see https://www.statista.com/statistics/800644/full-time-weekly-wage-uk-by-region/

Anatomy of the structure

To fulfil its promise, the act of creation became an operating mechanism that had to conform to certain imperatives.

For goal achievement, directional momentum was needed to stimulate motivation. Productive effort generated synergy between the personal and communal parts (to optimise the volume of effort). And, at all times for the earliest human groups, communities conserved the resources in their habitats within the bounds set by nature (to secure their future). The organising mechanism at the heart of this structure was composed of two elements.

First, the dynamic power that drove the evolutionary process. That power was the product of the relationships between individuals, taking into account the productivity-enhancing tools, and the resources harnessed from nature. Power designed to achieve goals. Interactions between the three elements of production were regulated by what economists call "elasticities". This denotes the relative power exercised by nature, by labour and by tools (capital) in production, the existential significance of which is elaborated in Ch. 2.

The power nexus rested on consensus, not conscription. *Onwards and upwards* (Fig. 1.3)!

Figure 1.3 **The thrust of Evolution**

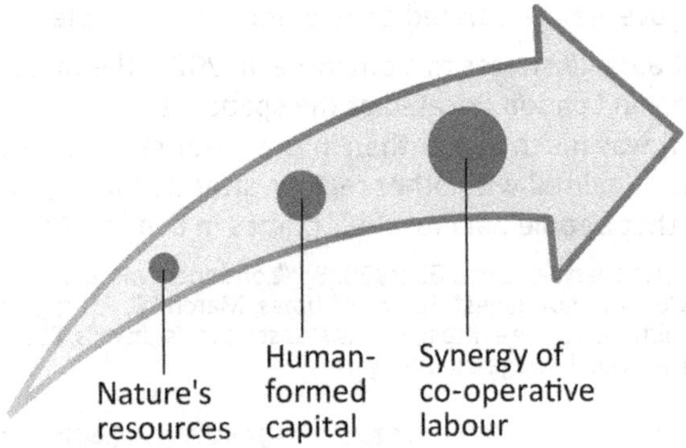

An authority structure constituted the second pillar of the organising mechanism. Initially, in foraging communities, authority was exercised at an intimate, personal level, with people working in harmony with each other. They made the decisions on how to deploy the net income for their mutual benefit. Thus emerged the cooperative spirit.

This combination – consenting to work together to produce the net income, and funding the shared services out of those Rents

– was the nexus that powered the human project. But to secure success, that behaviour had to be disciplined by a code of conduct that prevented individuals from going rogue. The nexus between the production and pooling of the net income was steered to achieve the common good.

This blueprint originated intuitively, with each individual in the kinship group conforming to behaviour that gave meaning to their lives. Through the painful process of trial and error, behaviour solidified into a culture transmitted through the generations. The emerging collective consciousness, as manifested in spiritual and moral sensibilities, made individuals aware of why they consented to this pattern of behaviour.

Much of human behaviour puzzles social scientists, because they remain wedded to the Darwinian theory of adaptation. The confusion begins to evaporate once we recognise why humans are an aberration on Earth. To achieve that understanding, we need to penetrate the processes by which they developed the unique capacity for communication.

In seeking to design a new way of life, the predecessors of *H. sapiens* – from *australopithecines* to *Homo erectus*, *Homo heidelbergensis* to *Neanderthals* – had to reshape the capacity of their minds. Progress would be limited without the ability to think in abstract terms. Beginning with primitive glimpses of the external world, the challenges included the capacity to respond immediately to threatening circumstances; fine-tuning the emitted sounds that related to the objects that became tools; and framing concepts that established the codes of behaviour. This required the evolution of self-consciousness; so that, for example, individuals could be held to account for deviant behaviour that prejudiced the prospects of group survival and progress. The evolutionary need was to ensure social solidarity. The propulsion was creativity, one manifestation of which was the ability to communicate with the aid of metaphors. The outcome was an architecture of the mind that took a million years to achieve (Box 1.7).

To escape the natural world, the primates who would be human had to shed nature's version of sociality. One illustration compares the qualitative differences in food consumption between chimpanzees and humans. Steven Mithen, a British archaeologist and Professor of Early Prehistory, records how food sharing among chimps is "tolerated theft". This behaviour, and its psychological state, compares with the human approach, "the provisioning of individuals to build up social obligations".[13]

Box 1.7 **Two theories of evolution**

Asian colobine monkeys illustrate evolution by adaptation. One branch lives in tropical rain forests; others inhabit snow-covered mountains. The monkeys in cold locations are better at producing bonding hormones that increase the time mothers spend breast-feeding and caring for their offspring. This strengthens relationships and increases the tolerance between males, enabling the evolution from small groups to larger hierarchical communities.* That evolutionary adaptation, however, did not equip them to produce net resources for investment in minds and souls.

Now consider the insights from a study of foragers and farmers in Tanzania. Parents work to feed an extraordinary amount of energy into the bodies of children from birth to the age of five. That food made possible the extended nurturing of offspring who grew up to live longer, more productive lives than the Great Apes.** Back in the mists of time, humans had "stumbled onto a new way of making a living, something unprecedented in the history of life. Instead of pursuing a career as a plant eater, carnivore or generalist, they tried a strange, dual strategy: some would hunt, others would gather, and they'd share whatever they acquired. This co-operative approach placed a premium on intelligence, and over millennia brain size began to increase".***

* Qi Xiao-Guang *et al* (2023), "Adaptations to a cold climate promoted social evolution in Asian colobine primates", *Science* 380(6648). DOI: 10.1126/science.abl8621

** Herman Pontzer *et al* (2015), "Expenditure and Activity Among Hadza Hunter-Gatherers", *American Journal of Human Biology*, 27.

*** Herman Pontzer (2023), "The Human Engine", *Scientific American*, January, p.24.

Mithen specialises in the study of the formation of the human mind. He argues that the prior capacity to express emotions through singing led to the formation of language.

> **Language effectively delivered the capacity for metaphor to the human mind that underlies art, science and religion. Cognitive fluidity also enabled the construction of complex artefacts and the extension of the mind and body into material culture.**[14]

It was no accident; nor was it submission to the laws of physics. It was the existential struggle to formulate a new geometry of life. Early humans located laws in the realm of material symbols, language and aesthetics. Spiritual sensibilities, as Albert Einstein noted, were central to that existence. "What is the meaning of human life, or of organic life altogether? To answer this question at all implies a religion."[15] The sacred life was conditional on the implicit contract: keep producing and investing Rent for the common good. Break that contract, and everything human reverts to nature.

Yuval Noah Harari, author of *Sapiens* (2020), offers a different view. He claims that storytelling is the "the operating system" that matters.[16] This, however, does not explain how one branch of the primates came to be such good campfire storytellers. The evolutionary blueprint holds the answer: the force multiplier that made it possible to emerge out of nature.[17] That force derives from three principles.

- *Co-existence*: sharing territory as a commons.
- *Co-operation*: pooling the means to grow out of nature.
- *Consensus*: on the dreams to be realised.

This combination created energy that was greater than the sum of its parts, according to scholars at the Santa Fe Institute. In their quest for a "science of cities", taking current conditions as their benchmark, they assembled data on multiple aspects of human behaviour and social outcomes in urban settlements across the world. They found that the outputs from all the assets in cities included a bonus. Growth was on a superlinear trend.

Growth was not linear: that is, if you double the scale (whether population, capital investments, size of transport systems, or whatever), you double the output. Rather, the complex interactions of those assets yielded an additional reward, which averaged 15%. There was, however, a problem. Luís Bettencourt, a physicist, Professor of Ecology and Evolution at the University of Chicago and External Professor at the Santa Fe Institute, reports that "the origin of these observed scaling relations and an explanation for the interdependences between spatial, infrastructural, and social facets of the city have remained a mystery".[18] Nature would not reveal the answers to the mystery, for "Our analysis suggests uniquely human social dynamics that transcend biology".[19]

We solve that mystery. To do so, we must continue with the story of our creation, the beginnings of an experiment forever in the making.

References Chapter 1

1 Robert Sapolsky (2023), *Determined: Life Without Free Will*, London: Bodley Head, p.23.

2 Robert C. Allen (2011), *Global Economic History*, Oxford: Oxford University Press, p.9.

3 L. Barham *et al* (2023), "Evidence for the earliest structural use of wood at least 476,000 years ago", *Nature*, Sept. 20. https://doi.org/10.1038/s41586-023-06557-9

4 The most promising field of research is now into the formation of chemicals emanating out of vents of limestone chimneys discovered on the floor of the Atlantic Ocean. Nick Lane (2022), *Transformer: The Deep Chemistry of Life and Death*, London: W.W. Norton.

5 Erwin Schrödinger (1967), *What is Life? and Mind and Matter*, Cambridge: CUP, p.73.

6 Thomas W. Plummer *et al* (2023), "Expanded geographic distribution and dietary strategies of the earliest Oldowan hominins and Paranthropus", *Science*, 379. https://www.science.org/doi/10.1126/science.abo7452

7 Irit Zohar *et al* (2022), "Evidence for the cooking of fish 780,000 years ago at Gesher Benot Ya'aqov, Israel", *Nature Ecology & Evolution*, 6.

8 Joe Pinkstone (2022), "Fish supper may have been humans' first cooked meal", *Daily Telegraph*, Nov. 15.

9 Stephen Pyne (2024), "Life in the Pyrocene", *Scientific American*, May, p.24.

10 George C. Homans (1950), *The Human Group*, New York: Harcourt, Brace. Emphasis added.

11 Fred Harrison (2012), *The Traumatised Society*, London: Shepheard-Walwyn, Ch. 2.

12 Robert L. Kelly (1995), *The Foraging Spectrum: Diversity in Hunter-Gatherer Lifeways*, Washington, DC: Smithsonian Institution Press.

13 Steven Mithen (1996), *The Prehistory of the Mind*, London: Thames and Hudson, p.91.

14 Steven Mithen (2006), "The Singing Neanderthals: the Origins of Music, Language, Mind and Body", *Cambridge Archaeological Journal*, 16(1), p.100.

15 Albert Einstein (n.d.), *The World As I See It*, Dead Authors Society, p.5.

16 Yuval Noah Harari (2023), "By Invitation: Artificial Intelligence", *The Economist*, April 28.

17 Military strategists use the force multiplier concept to secure victory on the battlefield. They formulate plans and deploy weapons that mobilise sufficient force to overwhelm the enemy.

18 Luís M.A. Bettencourt (2013), "The Origins of Scaling in Cities", *Science*, 340, p.1438.

19 Luís M.A. Bettencourt *et al* (2007), "Growth, innovation, scaling, and the pace of life in cities", PNAS,104(17), p.7306.

CHAPTER TWO

The Geometry of Life

Energy in the universe can be converted from one form to another, but cannot be increased, according to the 1st Law of Thermodynamics.

In the Social Galaxy, energy is expanded within a self-sustaining system, transmitting its riches through each generation. From the inception of this unique experiment, Rent was the life force. A blueprint emerged that spanned three overlapping dimensions.

- *Time*: psychology – Rent assuaged people's aspirations.
- *Space*: sociology – Rent sustained kinship communities.
- *Depth*: biology – Rent enriched the human anatomy.

To sustain this project, archaic humans needed to combine property rights with personal practices to secure a balanced relationship between themselves and nature's resources. They also had to neutralise the parasitic virus which they brought with them out of nature. This was a complex challenge which they could not anticipate or articulate. They needed a new doctrine we call property rights.

Property rights would provide the glue that secured a coherent plan of action. Those rights defined

- the individual and social claims on the resources they produced;
- the price that would have to be paid for asserting those claims; and
- the inter-personal relationships that would achieve their aspirations.

This arrangement secured personal freedom and enhanced the vitality of communities. This required people to marry personal rights with social responsibilities, to optimise the extraction of nature's resources and facilitate the exchange of products between themselves. Thus, property rights

- acknowledged people's dependence on the resources of nature;
- respected the assets inherited from earlier generations; and
- ensured the funding to create new assets shared in common.

Property rights framed the strategies that guaranteed an open-ended project, the limits solely confined by the willingness to work to produce the net resources that would fund investment in the shared legacy assets. Thus, property rights defined

- the scope of cooperation: fusing individualism with socialism;
- the capacity for achieving consensus: to solve problems; and
- the direction of travel for the long journey out of nature.

At each stage, property rights were further refined to meet immediate needs: in kinship groups, to feed energy into hungry minds; in clan groups, invest in social rituals; in tribal groups, expand spiritual lives, to enable aspirations that reached into a world unbounded by the laws of physics.

The progressive accumulation of assets had to be protected and sustained. That was the function of the living space – the Social Galaxy – which located Rent at its heart. The pillars of the structure were the rights and responsibilities, without which the correct allocation of net resources would not have occurred. The dynamics were provided by the functional processes that were regulated by the elastic properties, which reflected people's preferences, as evidenced by the push and pull of resource production, allocation and consumption. And at the interface of this system were the customs and practices that facilitated the common good.

Figure 2.1 **The Social Galaxy as a system**

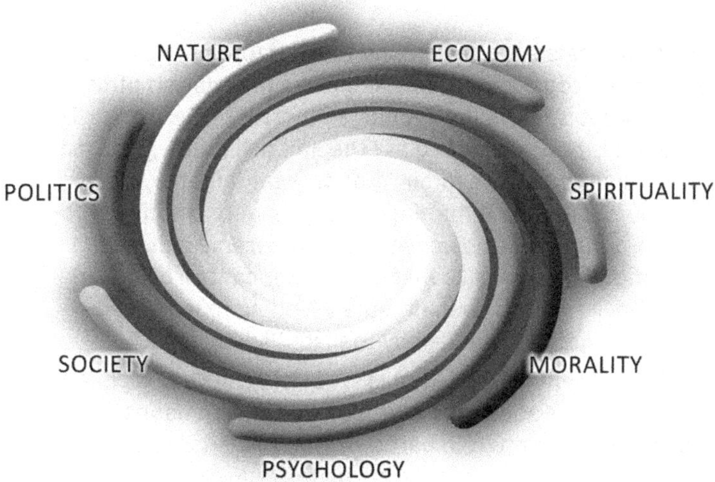

The cumulative effect was the life-force of humanity. The blueprint (Fig.2.1) emerged naturally, in the sense that it was not the product of statesmen huddled around a table to negotiate the principles of a universal declaration. It was the incremental product of trial and error, by fusing the behaviour that manifested itself as the human project.

Phase 1 of the project concluded when foragers innovated ways to grow their food. This breakthrough in the power of human fusion resulted from the will to work together in a state of harmony. Innovations accelerated the rate of growth, laying bare the contours of the geometry of life. The onset of farming required further refinements to the social system. Kinship communities mutated into civil settlements, to cater for larger numbers of people. Spatially extensive areas meant that relationships were extended to the impersonal. New forces had to come into play to accelerate increases in the production of Rent. Refinements to the language, laws and logic of the evolutionary blueprint accelerated the pace of change. Now, the superlinear growth rate, barely visible in the routines of foraging, were laid bare by the infrastructure required by farming (Box 2.1).

Box 2.1 **Communal drives**

Anthropologists are registering the extraordinary gains that stem from cooperation. An example is the analysis of the hunting tools found in Schöningen (northern Germany). This location is now rebranded as "the ambush hunting ground at which entire horse family groups were targeted, killed, and butchered". The hunting strategies were "motivated by a communal set of objectives [which] became a powerful evolutionary force...allowing for greater control over their environments and ultimately leading to increased impacts on the ecosystem by the late Pleistocene".*

The "communal drive hunts" (CDHs) achieved "higher return rates or lower odds of failure" compared with happenstance "encounter hunting". In particular, these CDHs increased the rate of success for hunting large ungulates (mammals with hooves) which have high "escape velocities" to avoid predators.**

*Jarod M. Hutson *et al.* (2025), "Revised age for Schoningen hunting spears indicates intensification of Neanderthal cooperative behaviour around 200,000 years ago", *Science Advances*, 11, p.7.

** Eugène Morin *et al.* (2024), "Why do humans hunt cooperatively? Ethnohistoric data reveal contexts, advantages, and evolutionary importance of communal hunting", *Current Anthropology*, 65(5).

This was people power at work. Personal power exercised by individuals attuned to social needs, which determined the quantum of effort required to produce the net resources. People power determined the elasticities of all the ingredients involved in the production process – the push and pull of the individual inputs that optimised the outcomes to meet today's bare-bones subsistence (BBS) needs with tomorrow's enhanced lifestyles.

People power. It delivered the creativity on which the rate of superlinear growth depended. A schematic representation illustrates that growth as a vertical climb (Fig. 2.2). Realistically, the trend is interrupted by pauses caused by barriers which, from time to time, had to be overcome. This results in the step profile, elongated over long timescales. Nonetheless, the trend continued through time in response to the creative spirit: upwards and outwards, at a rate determined by the consent to work and invest.

Figure 2.2 **Superlinear growth**

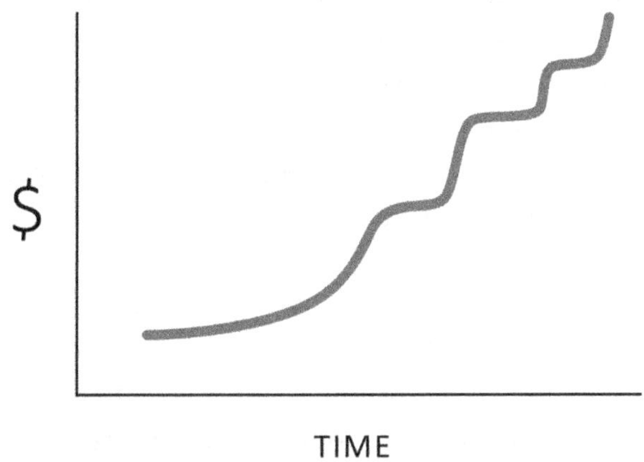

In its social form, Rent benefited everyone in the community. Rent invested in common assets – in their psychological, social or material forms – delivered new flows of Rent. Highways, whether traversed by foot, horse-drawn buggies or high-speed metro trains, illustrated how Rent was created by investments in the infrastructure of transportation.[1] By this means, the private sector – the labour of individuals – aligned with the public sector, to amplify the rate of growth at the cusp of each new era in the human project. That was how the earliest scattered settlements progressively harnessed geometric growth to mutate into complex civilisations.

Human agency

The will to grow out of nature was displayed in the strivings that created the push and pull power that conjoined human labour with the resources of nature. Victory came with agreement over satisfying the BBS needs of the body, with the aspirational needs stimulated by the expanding consciousness. This achievement was the manifestation of free will, which consolidated the power of producers to determine their future.

The power to create was at the core of the construction process that resulted in the Social Galaxy. That power rested on the wisdom to formalise the allocation of resources between what was needed to meet basic daily needs (which included the development of tools like sharpened knives, spears and bows and arrows, through to ploughs and combine harvesters), and to fund the social assets enshrined in minds and souls. This was People Power. The power to gravitate out of nature.

Pre-modern humans did not begin by consciously orchestrating the elasticities that co-ordinated their productive efforts. By trial and error, they resolved the tension between finite natural resources with their escalating aspirations. This was achieved through the formation of the moral consciousness (in relation to property rights), and awareness of the difference between partnership and parasitic behaviour. Apportioning the assembled resources that satisfied everyone, at all levels of sensibility, led to the awareness of right and wrong; and responsibilities to others, to complement claims of rights against others. Slowly but surely, the cumulative effect was the knowledge that enabled them to switch from foraging to farming.

The transition to agriculture was a quantum leap. People, now growing their food, had to fine-tune the social *milieu*. Under the impersonal conditions that prevailed in the urban-based, spatially extensive way of life, new techniques were required, to co-ordinate the production and pooling of Rent for investment in civil society. Without the new tools, the first civilisations could not have sprung to life.

Herodotus of Halicarnassus (484–425 BCE), described the practicalities in terms of geometry. For the Greeks, the word meant "measurement of Earth/land". Personal possession of tracts of land had to replace the commons, so that farmers could invest capital and their labour to raise output. Concurrently, the authority structure had to be adapted, to collect resources for investment in the infrastructure of the emerging urban communities.

> **This king [Sesostris] also (they said) divided the country among all the Egyptians by giving each an equal parcel of land, and made this his source of revenue, assessing the payment of a yearly tax. And any man who was robbed by the river of part of his land could come to Sesostris and declare what had**

> **happened; then the king would send men to look into it and calculate the part by which the land was diminished, so that thereafter it should pay in proportion to the tax originally imposed. From this, in my opinion, the Greeks learned the art of measuring land.**[2]

Statecraft originated in Egypt and Mesopotamia. The geometry of life, however, was formulated during the preceding era of foraging for life. We tend to view the lives of our pre-historic forebears as primitive, but the complex challenges of civilisation bear no comparison with the ferocious obstacles in the evolutionary era funded by foraging. To break free from the grip of the iron laws of physics, the foragers had to compile the most sophisticated formula, with interactions in three dimensions.

- *Bodies*: restructured to produce the power that created a world of possibilities.
- *Minds*: synchronised, to solidify partnerships that made new futures possible.
- *Souls*: generating sentiments to discipline behaviour and suppress deviancy.

The beauty of the relationships, the harmony of the actions, the purpose of the structure – a geometry that expressed a unique sphere of existence, complementing, not constrained by, the wonders of nature.

Evolution was achieved by designing the empirical processes that enabled adaptation to the possibilities they created. The body fed so that the mind could dream, so that they could reach for the stars while creating the sounds and sentiments encoded in their souls. A project intended for the distant future, unseen but confident of its existence, all contingent on one condition: future generations continued to produce the net income – the energy – to sustain the Social Galaxy. That energy, Rent, was the bedrock on which humanity was constructed.

Birds migrate across the skies; tigers roam savannah grasslands, whales coarse through the oceans, guided by their instincts. They have no need to understand the significance of their innate direction finders, or their location in the universe. They are driven by the information embedded in their genes. Proto-humans, to loosen the grip of nature, had to develop a shared consciousness that equipped them to understand what they were doing; which required them to develop a self-conscious awareness of the nature of their existence, and their spatial location in the universe. They did not have an economic theorem to guide behaviour. They relied on moral sensibilities to grope their way forward, as they created the assets that emerged through a dialectical process grounded in three freedoms.

- *Freedom to work*: creating the net income that funded the common good.
- *Freedom to love*: nurturing relationships to procreate future generations.
- *Freedom to shelter*: havens for families to dream and achieve aspirations.

These freedoms organically orchestrated the functions of three dimensions.

- *Nature and humanity*: meshing the laws of physics with human empathies.
- *Personal and public spheres*: optimising benefits from the two sectors.
- *Morality and spirituality*: synchronising behaviour with the aid of rules.

These elements coalesced into the evolutionary blueprint, the architecture that made it possible to exit nature's full control.

Thus emerged the social metabolism. The three freedoms were organically synthesised by the moral code that regulated conduct and expanded the synergy between the working parts (Fig. 2.3). The more people worked to pool net resources, the more fulfilling was the social realm. The moral code was the body of rules that framed the self-balancing metabolism. An inclusive process, everyone playing a part by cooperating with others.

Individuals were the particles rotating in the galaxy, their function to ensure that the net resources were continuously produced and pooled. Rent, the quantum of energy transmitted

Figure 2.3 **The Evolutionary Blueprint**

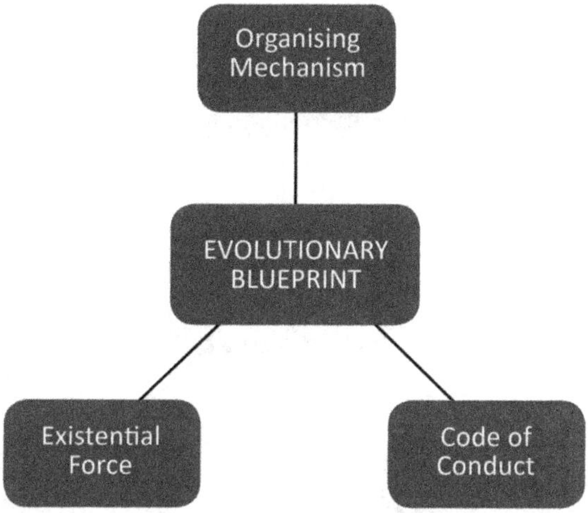

through time, embodied all aspects of what it meant to be human. An ever-growing commons, kept alive by personal aspirations, increasingly self-sustaining as the culture of freedom invented new ways of deepening productivity.

The three ingredients – work, love, shelter – were the compounds of the Social Galaxy's metabolism (Fig. 2.4). They were visible at three levels.

- *Purpose*: conversion of human energy into enriched bodies and moral sentiments, and sustainable living arrangements.
- *Means*: ensuring harmony in the deployment of labour and tools of production to increase fulfilment from net resources.
- *Rules*: codes of authority to ensure equal outcomes for everyone engaged in renewing, and benefiting from, the legacy assets.

The co-operative spirit emanating out of hunting and gathering laid the ground rules for what would one day become the ideal commercial pricing system. Through countless generations, people abided by the core principle: *keep what you work to produce, but pay for the social benefits you receive*. This contract delivered two outcomes.

Figure 2.4 **Pillars of the Social Galaxy**

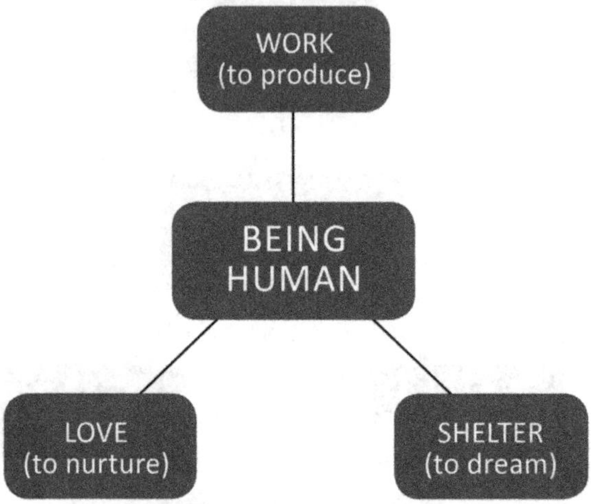

First, individuals balanced personal rights (their *demands on* others), by acknowledging personal responsibilities (*to others*). The primary expression of this doctrine: everyone was required to pool Rent proportionate to the benefits they wanted to derive from their communities.

Second, the model of rights and responsibilities countered the process of entropy. In nature, energy depletes with the passage of time. To sustain the Social Galaxy it was necessary to more than offset entropy. In part, this was achieved by recycling used assets back into the system. Depleted cultural assets were re-vitalised in improved forms for use by future generations (Fig. 2.5).

The metabolic rate was determined by the people themselves, set at the level at which they were willing and able to work. This was *not* a zero-sum arrangement, in which one person's gain was at the expense of others. Everyone contributed, and everyone shared in the benefits. Furthermore, the pie was not limited. It grew. The benefits of the pooled net income accrued at multiple levels, genetically, morally and materially, to enrich the expanding Social Galaxy.

Figure 2.5 **The Social Galaxy's metabolism**

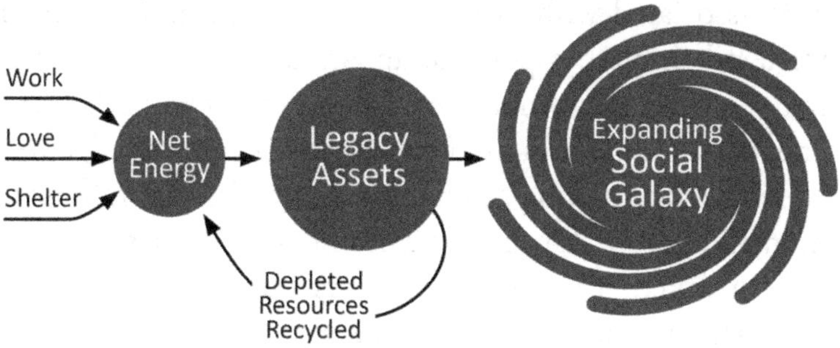

Essential to this process was the creation of monumental spaces.[3] These were imbued with symbolic meanings that awakened and sustained the collective consciousness. People gathered for sensorial experiences, ritualised in both social and spiritual forms. This built memory and created solidarity, the cumulative impact being the extension of identity of the group.

It was not an untroubled growth. Some groups did not make it, others retarded in response to shifts in the climate or variations in the resources available in habitats. The groups that met the challenges remained on the path of evolutionary progress. Some of the cousins of *H. Sapiens* (the Neanderthals) did contribute to the emergence of this world of the imagination, through art and culinary skills. To survive in the cold climes of northern Europe, the Neanderthals departed further from nature by discovering a unique way to keep warm. Some 125,000 years ago, they boiled the bones of animals to render the fat, which they consumed during the lean months of winter.[4] This was an estimated 100,000 years before humans adopted the practice. In the end, however, they disappeared. Our ancestors proved the more resilient. They shaped a self-sustaining system, the repository for the legacy assets transmitted through the generations.

Thus emerged the iron law of politics: *whoever controls Rent exercises ultimate power.*

Political rule

Civilisation, defined as culture and technology in their enriched forms, is associated with urbanisation, in which public affairs are administered through a political apparatus. This social formation required new forms of symbolic communication (Box 2.2). Omitted from the standard definition of civilisation is acknowledgement of the core role of the driving mechanism – Rent in its amplified form. The transition from kinship communities to civil society could not have occurred, if the food producers were unable to fund new authority structures. They pooled the Rents because the benefits would be enhanced personal and social welfare.

The holy men of hunter-gatherer communities became the first specialists in the new field of politics. They were relieved of having to toil in the fields, so that – as High Priests – they could administer the nascent authority structures.[5]

Governance emerged because of the need to organise services that people could not directly provide for themselves. The benefits were intensified spiritual and cultural experiences; and the extension of language in the domain of symbolic configurations. Through this emerged new layers of Rent, formed out of long-distance trading and cultural exchanges.

From the outset, Rent expressed the unifying body of knowledge that captured all aspects of what it took to be human. Evolutionary Rent would enable people to pay for, or renew

- *exclusive occupation* of locations for residential or commercial purposes, to enjoy new personal freedoms;
- *legacy assets*, investment in which secured the vitality and expanded the scale of the Social Galaxy; and
- *access to public goods* such as highways and canals, the infrastructure essential for farming communities.

The commerce that originated in antiquity required the support of a dynamic mechanism to frame both private and communal goals. Rent in its social form was the determining element because, in its space-time components, it is the human equivalent of gravity, as Einstein analysed that force in the world of physics.

Box 2.2 **The formation of identity**

To optimise efficiency, symbolic thinking emerged to communicate information through time and space. The earliest known abstract symbols are cave paintings from the upper Palaeolithic age, the meaning of their dots and dashes still being disputed.*

The striving to communicate tells us that our earliest ancestors wanted future generations to know who they were. There is no written record, prior to the cave drawings, but we can decode their behaviour; their habitats, which contain possibilities; and the trends, extrapolated through to the cave paintings.

* Bennet Bacon *et al* (2023), "An Upper Palaeolithic Proto-writing System and Phenological Calendar", *Cambridge Archaeological Journal*, 33(3).

Increasingly complex relationships entailed wider spatial associations that extended the range of commerce, a process that began far back in the mists of time.[6] These relationships were the outcome of what the American journalist Henry George (1839-1897) described as the human need "to satisfy desires with the least exertion" (Box 2.3). Early humans achieved the least-exertion outcomes through co-operation and consensus, not by working alone, or in a state of adversarialism. By this means, optimum levels of Rent could be produced to fund ever more productive ways of achieving personal aspirations at the least cost.

Elasticities in the new marketplace required the co-operation of governance. This is made clear by the constraint that delivers good governance: ATCOR – all taxes come out of Rent. When revenue is drawn directly out of Rent, the elastic pull-and-push in the marketplace operates at optimum levels, while governance, in turn, fulfils its duty of care to the whole population.[7] The outcome is a self-sustaining system of production and consumption.

The unifying theory

The space-time component of Rent unifies our knowledge about humanity. Analytically, Rent explains relationships at all levels, local, national and global. That is why, in mutating into civilisation, Rent was at the heart of the revision of the evolutionary contract. Amendments to property rights and personal responsibilities facilitated one of the great inflexion points in human progress.

As we saw in Ch. 1 (Fig. 1.1), net income does not emerge at a flat rate across an economic catchment area. Rent is highest at the spatial centre. It drops to zero at the margin, where it is only possible to exist at subsistence level. The spatial centre of the community is more fruitful, but that observation comes with a vital qualification. The centre's productivity is contingent on access to the other regions, into which it sells its goods and services. By their purchase of the goods and services, people across the

Box 2.3 **The metabolic rate**

Henry George viewed the human need to satisfy desires with the least exertion as a law of nature, which shaped political economy.* His reference to nature, as a metaphor, is accurate. Gravity results in movements that follow the course of least resistance (such as water cascading down a mountain). No species goes out of its way to meet its bare bones needs by working for longer than is necessary; including humans. But humanity emerged by working beyond the rate that satisfied physical needs, because consciousness elevated desires beyond what could be funded out of wages.

Failing to distinguish between the two rates (metabolic, and social) led post-classical economists to brand people who accumulated wealth as acting out of greed. In reality, as a social process, the concept of greed should be reserved for those who did not labour for their daily bread.

* Henry George (1898), *The Science of Political Economy*, London: K. Paul, Trench, Trübner, Bk 1, Ch. 12.

Figure 2.6 **Spatial distribution of net income**

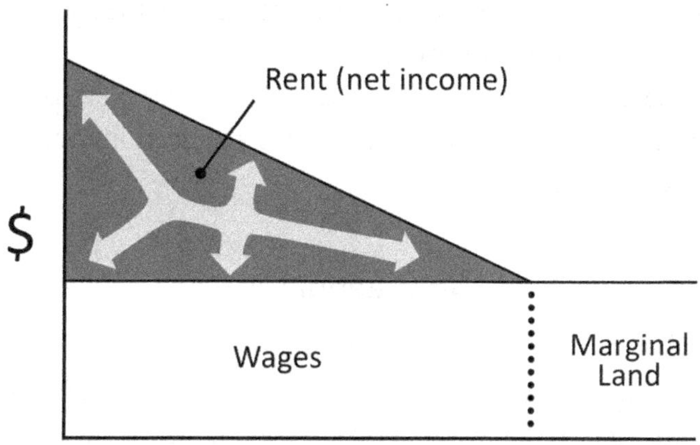

territory contribute to the elevation of Rents in the centre. This means that people at the margin have an equal claim to those Rents. This holistic, mutually beneficial arrangement, derives from symmetry in relationships, dynamism in activity, and democracy in outcomes.

Residents at the margin not only contribute to the formation of Rent through consumption. Over the generations, communities at or near the margin supplied people and creative ideas to the centre, to enable the system to function optimally. Without the inward flow of resources, the centre could not realise its potential, or optimise everyone's prosperity.

The outcome is a 3-way dynamic. As total growth increases, the demand for services from the centre expands, and the equalised flow of Rent supports the communities all the way to the outer boundaries of the social system (Fig 2.6).

In antiquity, tenure rights had to be adapted to accommodate the emerging urban settlements. The logic and spirit of the original evolutionary contract, however, remained the same. People could extract what they needed from nature, by working and paying for it. And, they could share in the benefits of inclusive partnerships by pooling the net income for the common good.

Hellenistic philosophers formulated the geographic reference systems, employing three co-ordinates to calculate locations on the surface of Earth. These conformed to the geometry of life, as formulated by foraging communities.

With the onset of civil society, the former foragers presumed that their blueprint would carry over into civilisation. Something, however, went wrong.

No cheating!

It worked! It took 500,000 years to define and live the new geometry. This happened because the proto-humans did not compromise on the rules for achieving what looked like an impossible mission. By their behaviour they lived what we now call justice. They acquired the freedom to occupy this planet by honouring the rules of good behaviour. The symmetries of their personal obligations, their relationships with others, and their responsibility to nurture nature, left no room for cheating. It was a ruthless compact, which placed the responsibility on everyone to contribute to the resources that made possible the human project. By the way they lived, they evolved the doctrine of property rights and responsibilities which we have now articulated.

That formula was needed when, nearly two millennia after the collapse of civilisations in antiquity, among a group of islands off the coast of Europe, something remarkable happened. People combined the lessons of their ancient ancestors to prepare the superlinear leap out of agriculture. They built vast cauldrons of fire to melt minerals from the earth, to power the construction of the great cities of the future. Britain prepared to lead the way to the industrial mode of production.

The cost of this great leap into the future, however, was great. Geoffrey West, one of the physicists at the Santa Fe Institute, stressed that those cities harboured

> **... a dark side: they are the prime locus of crime, pollution, poverty, disease, and the consumption of energy and resources. Rapid urbanization and accelerating socioeconomic development**

> **have generated multiple global challenges ranging from climate change and its environmental impacts to incipient crises in food, energy, and water availability, public health, finance markets, and the global economy.[8]**

Why did this happen? If Rent is the life force of humanity, everyone would enjoy the benefits of the new phase of growth, living in harmony with each other and with nature. Was my Rent thesis incorrect, or were the prospects of civilisation undermined by an anti-social virus running amok on the British Isles? If the latter, from where did the virus emanate? Did Herodotus offer an insight into its antecedents?

> **The warrior class in Egypt had certain special privileges in which none of the rest of the Egyptians participated, except the priests. In the first place each man had twelve arurae of land assigned him free from tax.[9]**

This description errs in characterising the warrior's possession of land as tax-free. Public servants were granted the use of land, with the Rents as payments for their services to the community. Was that arrangement perverted? If so, how, and why, did it happen?

In the nascent phase of agriculture, arrangements were required to block the cheats who might be tempted to free ride on the backs of their labouring kith and kin. This was imperative, because the full flow of net income was central to the way people controlled their lives. They needed access to all of that flow of energy – which they created – to

- *fulfil daily needs*: access to food and shelter (without which life would not exist);
- *deliver creative decision-making*: without which the system loses its vitality; and
- *propagate organic social relationships*: complying with the evolutionary blueprint.

To repress the production of the net flow of energy, or its diversion to uses other than what inclusively nourished everyone's needs, would be disastrous.

We now know that it did not prove possible to sustain the social status of Rent in the emerging statecraft. Anthropologists have chronicled the way in which hunter-gatherers used the shaming device to maintain good social behaviour. Robert Sapolsky stresses the "considerable evolutionary pressure for detecting cheating" in foraging communities. Those who sought the lazy life – by riding on the backs of others – were subjected to "shaming and mockery, ostracizing and shunning, refusing to share meat, nonlethal physical punishment, expulsion from the group, or, as a last resort, killing the person".[10]

With the onset of civil society, the processes for shaming free riders through personal intervention were obsolete. Statecraft needed to replace personal interventions with new tools, which included the obligation to audit the terms on which priests and princes administered the public's revenue. It did not prove possible to hold the priests and princes accountable for how they curated the revenue they collected. *Missing from the law of the land was the mandate to expose and punish the cheats.*

Herodotus notes that, referring to Pharaoh Sesostris, the resources that were pooled by the peasants were used to advance the interests of his dynasty. Rent was diverted to construct a monumental pyramid to secure his afterlife. As pyramids grew ever higher and more expensive, so the potential for elevating the quality of the lives of peasants was diminished.

Could it have been different? What would it have taken for Neolithic farmers to lay the foundations of urbanisation on terms that did not foment a "dark side"? It was not possible for them to theorise the arrangements appropriate for the emerging civil society. We cannot blame them for what went wrong with statecraft. For the peoples of the British Isles, however, who lived through the Enlightenment, there was no excuse for allowing that virus to spawn itself in the industrial age. They knew what it would take, to lay the foundations of a dynamic industrial economy. So why was the ancestral rule of law negated? That is the story of the culture of cheating. But to understand how this happened, and what we need to do to save the human project, we need a clear appreciation of the process of evolution. In broad terms, this history can be divide into three phases.

The Spiritual Age. In the earliest foraging phase, net resources were largely embedded in the metabolic realm, the body and the brain. This animated the spiritual achievements that provided the codes of conduct. The genius of early humans was to recognise the need for an authority structure that would discipline them, enabling them to distinguish between good and bad, right and wrong.

The Civil Age. Urban civilisation required new systems to regulate the allocation of material products, administer new power structures and organise the needs of growing populations. The emerging market economy also needed investments in material infrastructure, the resources for which could only come from one source: Rent, in its social form.

The Cerebral Age. Today, we are phasing in the third inflection point in the human project. Our legacy assets, translated into data, are being transferred to autonomous humanoids. The fate of humanity hangs on this experiment. Will we reconstruct life to meet the challenges posed by algorithms? Or will we permit humanity to be replaced on Earth by humanoids?

A dangerous interlude emerged at the interface between the first two phases. The Neolithic people were not able to navigate that space on terms that protected personal rights and enforced social obligations. That is why civilisations proved to be unsustainable. Previously, people had exercised direct control over the investment of their net resources. The superlinear growth that transitioned primates into humans was a painfully slow process. There were disappointments galore, but the outcome was an exquisite composition, the Social Galaxy. The rate of growth accelerated towards what turned into the greatest challenge: guiding the transition into civil society, while retaining the people-centred model of decision-making. If successfully executed, the new power structure would shape a benign form of civilisation. Instead, at the outset, the privatisation of net resources resulted in three processes of depletion.

- Deprivation of the lives of those who laboured for their living.

- Destruction at territorial borders to grab the land of neighbours.
- Degradation of nature, to maximise the accumulation of Rent.

The burning question that has still to be addressed is this: Why, and how, did the Neolithic people allow themselves to be taken hostage by the culture of cheating?

References Chapter 2

1 Don Riley *et al* (2025, 2nd edn), *Taken for a Ride*, London: Shepheard-Walwyn.

2 Herodotus, *Histories*, translated by A.D. Godley, 1920, London: Heinemanns, §109, p.397.

3 Juan Carlos Moreno Garcia (2025), *Space and Communal Agency in Pre-Modern Societies*, Oxford: Oxbow Books.

4 Lutz Kindler *et al* (2025), "Large- scale processing of within-bone nutrients by Neanderthals, 125,000 years ago", *Science Advances*. 11, eadv1257.

5 Dunbar, *op cit*, p.201.

6 Emma M. Finestone *et al* (2025), "Selective use of distant stone resources by the earliest Oldowan toolmakers", *Science Advances*, II(33). DOI: 10.1126/sciadv.adu5838

7 For Adam Smith's exhaustive list of examples of ATCOR, see Fred Harrison, Bk 2, *Rent Seeking: the Crime Against Humanity*, Appendix, London: Land Research Trust.

8 Geoffrey West (2017), *Scale: The Universal Laws of Life and Death in Organisms, Cities and Companies*, London: Weidenfeld & Nicolson, p.8.

9 *Op. cit.*, §168, p.169. One arurae was equal to 0.677 acres.

10 Robert Sapolsky (2017), *Behave*, London: Vintage, pp. 324, 325.

CHAPTER THREE

Corruption

It took a million years of creative labour to struggle out of nature. Hard labour, and the suppression of the instinct to cheat, laid the foundations for civilisation, an inflection point like no other in pre-history.

But then, late in the Neolithic age, something happened to cancel the human project. Instead of growth, of the body, the mind and the soul, humanity was tipped into a state of betrayal. Yes, there was growth. Life expectancy was doubled. Huge scientific achievements. Riches galore! All of it driven to serve a single culture: the institutionalised behaviour that our ancient ancestors had suppressed for a million years.

Cheating!

No matter how we twist and turn the achievements, they all amplified the deaths, degradation and dishonour bestowed on what was achieved by those who formulated the template behaviour that became the evolutionary blueprint.

Cheating!

In the fleeting window of opportunity between the end of foraging and the onset of farming, in the late Neolithic age, the would-be cheats succeeded in institutionalising their theft of the resources generated by everyone in society.

Cheating!

On an epic scale. But how was it executed against people who had learnt to censure that bad behaviour? The individuals who aspired to capture the net resources did not have armies at their disposal; or bureaucracies to codify and administer an alien form of behaviour. So how did they manage to ride on other people's backs, without being censured? To create a system that could be transmitted through time? To feed insatiable appetites without working? For the answers, we need to search in the scattered villages of Egypt, each of which was administered by its own authority structure.[1]

For cheating to immerse itself, it would have to be invasive, capturing the whole of what it meant to be human: the bodies (that laboured), the minds (that censured), the souls (that yearned for the good life). The approach would have to be surreptitious; for, if alerted, people would mobilise and resist. And the strategy would have to wield punching power capable of overwhelming the entrenched evolutionary blueprint.

The programme required to satisfy the cheats, would have to encompass three features.

- *Diversion* of net resources that funded people's social needs
- *Hierarchies* that locked in private property inter-generationally
- *Co-option* of labourers into believing that cheating was normal

The threat of direct violence against the working population was not an option. In the beginning, the tools – armies and policemen – were not available. These would emerge after the cheats had accumulated the net resources needed to fund institutionalised forms of coercion.

Nor was it possible to directly invade people's minds, over a short time period. That strategy would require a sophisticated level of education and social administration, to enable would-be cheats to apply psychological conditioning on a mass scale, over an extended period. The knowledge and organisational techniques required to brain-wash the population by direct means, were not initially available.

Was the spiritual life the weak spot? Could power over the spiritual life be used to manipulate the souls of the working population? That was, indeed, how the betrayal of the human project was executed. The cheats anointed themselves as intermediaries between the workers and the all-powerful gods. This had a threefold effect. It

- *elevated* the cheats into a realm beyond the reach of mere mortals;
- *elevated* authority into forms that induced fear and compliance; and
- *elevated* families into practices that authorised private property rights.

Thus was born the dynastic model of politics and lifestyles. The power was personal, and enforced by the authority of the gods. The peasants were overawed, and perverse property rights were transmitted through the generations. This was the only practical strategy for bending the masses to the priorities of those who systematically appropriated their net income. It ensured that the embryonic civilisation emerged within the parameters ordained to deliver systemic cheating.

We cannot, therefore, censure people for dropping their guard. The knowledge required to embed an audit and accountability process into the urban way of life, to protect the social status of Rent, was not available. The status of Rent did need to be redefined, to facilitate the onset of agriculture and urbanised communities, but the information required to design the transition to civilisation on terms that honoured the evolutionary blueprint had not been invented.

The original cheats emerged from the ranks of tribal chiefs and holy men. They became princes and priests, who established the earliest dynastic families. Direct control over the distribution and use of land became the conduit for channelling Rents into their pockets. To facilitate that process, the fusion of two doctrines – on property rights and statecraft – was necessary. This found its practical expression in the revenue system. Tax practices in ancient

Egypt are not only instructive for what happened back then, "but also important in the influence they exerted over the systems of the later civilisations of Greece and Rome, and so indirectly on those of the modern world".[2] Statecraft was designed to privilege cheating.

With the onset of civil society, authentic humanity was systematically eroded. If we are to untangle the existential crises that now confront humanity, we need a complete awareness of how we got to where we are, in the 21st century.

Creating the Culture of Cheating

The kinship model was obsolete. For sound practical reasons, the shift to agriculture needed to incorporate working relationships over great distances. Graduation beyond blood-related associations, to sustain evolutionary growth, was unavoidable. Trading relationships laid the foundations for market economics.

To qualify as an authentically humane civilisation, the evolutionary blueprint had to be enshrined in civilisation's foundations. That would deliver the self-funding process for the required infrastructure. Pastoralism (cattle were an early form of capital), and farming (growing food yielded more Rent to fund intellectual and aesthetic pursuits), extended the quality of life and the scale of economic operations. The new authority and administrative structures, directly funded out of Rent, would expand cultural and technological possibilities, to realise more dreams. Through co-operation, lives would be enriched as people worked together to produce and pool the net resources to fund their urban services. As the harmonic use of these riches contributed to the formation of new layers of net value, so the Social Galaxy would innovate new highways and byways to explore, as the collective consciousness lit up the world of possibilities.

Theoretically, we can derive the dynamics of such a system by focusing on the formation of the power structure. Adjustments would assume a complex form, but with Rent at the heart of the process at all times. The ideal outcome could be achieved by anchoring the system in the ABC formula, as prescribed by the evolutionary blueprint.

A: *Audit and accountability*. Reckoning how much net income was produced, how to invest it, with full disclosure of impacts. Armed with that information, progress could continue along the evolutionary growth path.

B: *Balanced growth*. Mechanisms devised to integrate rights with responsibilities, to outlaw cheating. Dialectically, aligning new rules to optimise the quality of life while devising techniques to steward nature.

C: *Consultative processes*. Fulfilment of people's needs through arbitration of competing visions about the direction of development; achieved through conversations that yielded consensus rather than conflict.

Combined, the ABC principles would constitute the framework of power that remained in the hands of the labouring population. They could appoint Representative Citizens to carry out their will, secure in the knowledge that they could check any attempt to abuse power.

The Egyptians did evolve the geometry that measured the spatial relationships between people; and between people and the natural environment. The scribes equipped themselves to co-ordinate the collection and investment of Rent. They invented arithmetic. But to deter free riding, the ancients also needed a mechanism that replicated the role previously performed by their moral sensibilities. Accountability needed to complement accounting techniques. This was just not possible, under the conditions prevailing in antiquity. Instead, the odds were rigged in favour of the cheats. Their victory sponsored three primary outcomes:

- *state-sponsored violence*. Instead of freedom, people were coerced into compliance by those who had grabbed the community's Rents;
- *involuntary poverty*. The working population endured material deprivation. This initiated a widening gap between rich and poor; and
- *unsustainable systems*. Civilisations collapsed as their structures were deprived of the resources needed to sustain assets in working order.

This outcome was the result of the transition that began some 10,000 years ago (8000 BCE). Farmers began to cultivate the land, but they could not cultivate laws that combined personal property rights with social responsibilities. At the outset, the farmers had no choice but to trust their leaders. That rendered them vulnerable to would-be cheats in the temples and palaces. Some chiefs and holy men realised that, if they stopped rendering their services, they could still reap the Rents. Thus was born the system anchored in conflict and exploitation, with power over the people. The shameless society was born, the sensibilities of human beings overwhelmed by the priorities accorded to materialism. Success amounted to the execution of the most evil of crimes imaginable – the redefinition of what it meant to be human. Rent, and the creative power it represented, was depersonalised and dehumanised into a form that served the exclusive desires of free riders. Civilisation became the site of a continuous civil war, from then until now, the contest focussed on the possession and use of Rent.

In Egypt, the ripple effects can be traced through three social phases: the formation of the Dynastic Age (beginning around 5000 BCE), that overlapped into the Pharaonic Age (beginning 3,000 BCE), and mutated into the Imperial Age, which began with the pharaohs who ruled the New Kingdom from about 1570. The end came with the Hellenic conquest in 332 BCE, followed by the Roman conquest in 30 BCE.

The land grabs sent shock waves that were sustained by the model of governance incubated along the Nile. Enclosure of people's Rents rippled through to modern times (Fig. 3.1). The first order effects displaced foraging communities from ancient habitats (and as occurred during the colonial era and now continues for some pastoral communities[3]). The life-and-death reactions triggered shifts in the nature of property and power, which originated in three stages. First, in the Dynastic age: personal rights and responsibilities were eroded, making it possible to appropriate the community's net resources. People power was converted into privileged power. With the onset of the pharaonic era, power mutated to its impersonal political form, to facilitate the unification of all communities

Figure 3.1 **Tracking Ripples: from Antiquity to Modernity**

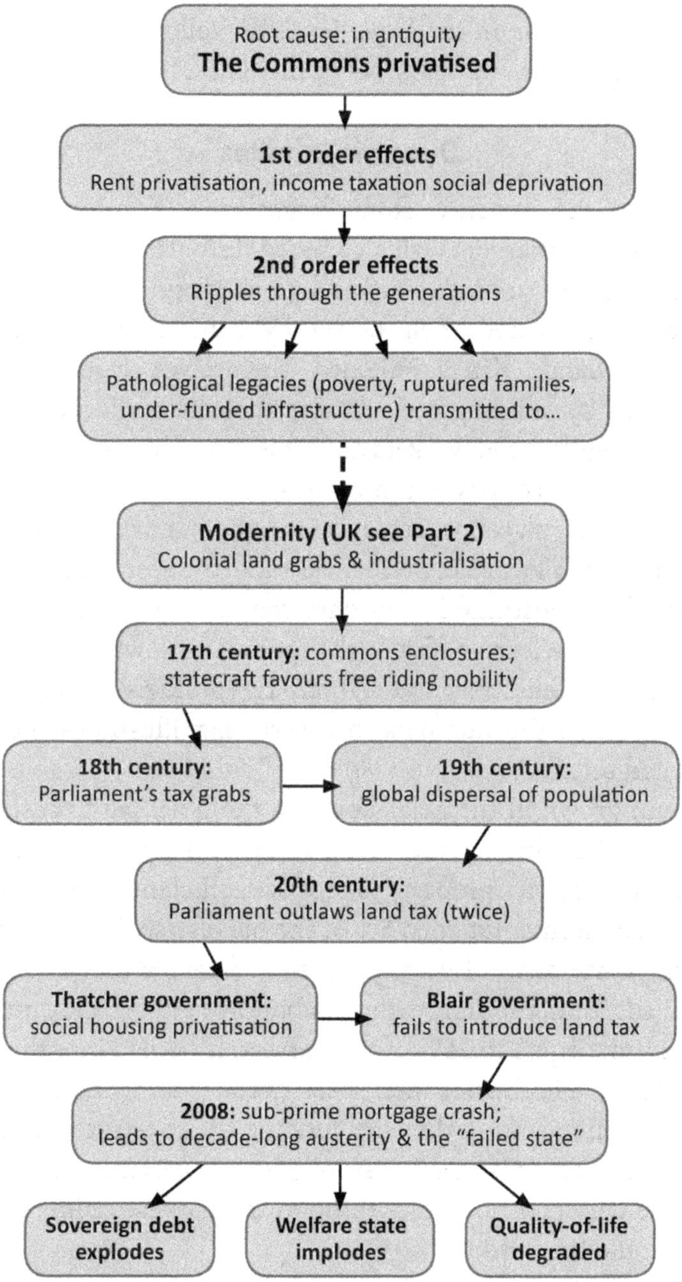

located along the Nile. Finally came the imperial state, the ultimate expression of the insatiable appetites fostered by cheating.

Our historical review begins with "the emergence of the world's first territorial state in the Egyptian Nile Valley [covering] a time span of only about 700 years, between 3800-3100 BCE".[4]

Dynastic Families

To derive the synergy from larger-scale farming practices, pre-dynastic settlements amalgamated into towns. During this transition, chiefs anointed themselves as kings, creating dynastic families that secured their power by controlling the revenue-generating land. Kings shielded themselves from the local populations by building walls around their habitations, appointed scribes to regulate the workers and viziers to administer justice.

The evolution of power centres was made possible by "donations of land [which] placed valuable tools in the hands of the king with which to break local kin solidarities and transfer wealth to loyal subjects".[5] The arithmetic lays bare the pathology of that power. The intent is clear: defraud the population while pretending to serve the common good. Dutch Egyptologist Koenraad van Heel crunched the numbers in a case that illustrates the state-sponsored scam.

Grain grown in the fields abutting the Nile had to sustain the farmers while funding the social infrastructure. In one case, 15 farmers worked on a property to produce sufficient to meet personal needs. Each farmer retained 5% of the harvest, so 75% of the year's growth, in the form of wages, met their families' metabolic needs. But, in addition, through their collaborative efforts, they produced a net income equal to 25% of the harvest. If pooled into the public purse, they could finance their social needs – defraying the costs of controlling floods from the Nile, funding the construction of roads, covering the administrative costs of governance, and so on. Instead, someone who contributed nothing to the harvest claimed the net product: the landlord.[6]

Colonisation of the spiritual life, which in turn infected the mind, overawed people into complicity with the system that exploited them. The dynasts needed vast resources to assuage their appetites, and they acquired these without mercy. The outcome was documented by archaeologist Toby Wilkinson, who reviewed one case in these terms.

> **Although cattle seem to have been reared in large numbers at the site, the local population did not enjoy the fruits of their labours. Their diet was unusually low in beef and cattle products, suggesting that most of the livestock was sent straight to the royal palace and cult centers near Memphis, leaving the cattle keepers themselves to survive on more meagre fare. Even the cereals grown at Imu seem to have been fed preferentially to the cattle rather than to their human attendants. Once again, we see the essentially self-interested nature of the ancient Egyptian monarch. This was not so much enlightened despotism as despotism, pure and simple.**[7]

Cheating made possible the emergence of extensive landed estates. The intermediaries with the gods shared the earthly gains with their extended families, to secure their possessions over generational timescales.

Cheating is a lawless activity. That is why people had to be prevented from appealing to alternative sources of authority for protection of their human rights. Morality, and the authentic spiritual life, were suppressed.

The Territorial State

The dynastic phase was time-limited by the insatiable appetite for Rents. The dynastic model mutated into a statecraft capable of gathering Rents from further afield. The Nile was unified into a territorial state in 3100 BCE (the transition traditionally attributed to King Narmer).

Power was expanded into a statecraft fit for an extensive scale, with laws enforced by courtiers and impersonal institutions. Monumental pyramids served a vital role.

> **[I]t was relatively easy to produce a surplus; easy, too, for the state to siphon off a significant percentage of agricultural production by way of taxation to fund its own projects. The end product of all this economic activity is illustrated in reliefs from**

the Dahshur temple...The king was letting it be known that his pyramid was a national enterprise, involving the whole country – whether the populace liked it or not.[8]

The Step Pyramid, the oldest in Egypt, built about 2,600 BCE, illustrates the nature of the superlinear power of Rent-yielding assets. Whereas the earliest royal tombs were constructed of mud-brick, the Step Pyramid reached 205ft into the sky and was clad in polished white limestone. This was made possible by hydraulic power which, when combined with water, raises productivity on an exponential scale. Within 150 years, the average weight of typical stones multiplied, leaping to 300 kg, eventually achieving over 2.5 tons for the tallest of the three pyramids of Giza.[9] This history provides some sense of the growth of net income and the "clout" exercised by the rulers of Egypt. They accrued sufficient power to control labour and wealth to meet their aspirations, not those of the people who worked in the fields.

The Great Pyramid of Giza, the tomb of Pharaoh Khufu, took 27 years to build, to a height of 146 metres (481 feet). It remained the world's tallest human-made structure for more than 3,800 years.[10] This was achieved, according to Herodotus, because Khufu "brought the country into all sorts of misery. He closed all the temples, then, not content with excluding his subjects from the practice of their religion, compelled them without exception to labour as slaves for his own advantage".

Three generations of huge investments – human, material and administrative – in pyramid-building transformed Egypt but proved an unsustainable drain on its resources.[11]

The earliest confirmed use of the concept of "pharaoh" was contained in a letter to Akhenaten (1353-1336 BCE). He launched his reign as the supreme ruler of the ancient world by pronouncing himself and his wife, Nefertiti, gods on Earth. To remove all competition, he outlawed all the other deities bar Aten, the Sun Disc, which he nominated as the creator, the giver of life which nurtured the spirit of the world. He then pronounced himself as the mediator between Aten and the mortal beings who tilled the soil. By this means, he was able to synthesise the physics of the universe with the metaphysics of the Social Galaxy. He fused the solar god with the human power that produced net energy. The sublime jackpot! The ultimate force multiplier. Unfortunately, for the people of the Nile, he monopolised that power for himself.

As part of his deification, Akhenaten diverted people's Rents into the construction of a monumental city that celebrated his ego. The priests who enriched themselves at the expense of the peasants relocated themselves to that city. The labouring population, deprived of the other gods, could not appeal to competing authorities for justice.

Akhenaten ruled for 17 years. Following his death, his legacy was erased, his city demolished, and the power of the other deities restored on the rock walls of the pyramids. For Egypt, however, it was too late. The culture of cheating had embedded itself. Free riding was a way of life, symbolised by the ever-larger pyramids built to guarantee eternal life for pharaohs. Materially, the ancient civilisation appeared prosperous. Socially, the resilience was ebbing away.

Monumental structures became emblematic features of the culture of cheating as it gravitated through classical times – palatial estates, grandiose public buildings like the Roman Coliseum, all the way through to today's buildings that scrape the sky to combine awe with Rent extraction.

The Imperial Age

There are no boundaries to the egos of cheats. In statecraft, this is reflected in the construction of empires. Trade continued in the eastern Mediterranean, but the age was dominated by military activities. Egypt's rulers applied force in the quest for additional Rental resources from territories like Palestine and Syria. That trend was already established by Pharaoh Sesostris, who reigned during the 12th Dynasty (from approximately 1878 to 1839 BCE), and conquered territories in Asia Minor. Back home, with his spoils, he maintained the pharaonic tradition by diverting resources to construct a monumental pyramid to secure his afterlife. As the pyramids went ever higher and more expensive, so the vitality of society was degraded.

Rent privatisation segregated people into wealth-based classes. Those who could get in on the act did so. Specialists who serviced burial rituals, for example, were not content with the fees they received. The papyrus excavated from cemeteries reveal how funerary overseers "appear to have embarked on lucrative real estate deals"; in which, in Late Period Egypt, "the authorities were corrupt to the core"; with, in one case, the "plunder, murder, corruption, arson, and intimidation" by Egyptian officials and priests in the town of al-Hiba.[12]

Colonisation of minds accompanied the control over social space.[13] Evolution of the earliest empires demonstrated the kinetic power of words. Royal power centres acquired control over the trade in precious metals (bronze, copper, iron), and ensured the acquiescence of their populations by immersing earthly resources in sacred words. Iron became the "precious metal of the sky". This "fenced it firmly within the province of theocratic rulers and elites who were thus more able to claim a monopoly on its use and circulation".[14] Blue glass (lapis lazuli) was designated as "royal". Thus was reinforced the class hierarchy, with the Rent-producing population embedded in the lowest ranks.

Comparing theories

There is little disagreement about the profile of political power that emerged in the Near East. It rested on the trilogy of god/king/land. Statecraft asserted eminent domain over land, the conduit for channelling social Rents into private pockets. Disagreement is over the origins of this form of exploitation. My explanation, which rests on the empirical evidence from the evolutionary blueprint, upsets prevailing social paradigms. To test the plausibility of that thesis, we must contrast it with accounts such as the one advanced by Giorgio Buccellati, a specialist in Near Eastern history. He directs the Mesopotamian Lab at the University of California,

Los Angeles. Civilisation, in his telling, evolved as a natural entity, following the eruption of a new layer of consciousness. His "para-perceptual" thesis leads him to "plausible conjectures".

According to Buccellati, the emerging institutional arrangements in cities abutting the Tiber and Euphrates "must" have resulted from his interpretation of the new consciousness. There are problems with this methodology

First, plausible conjectures. In philosophy, speculations based on hypotheses are legitimate. In archaeology, however, we are dealing with empirical issues whose effects reverberated through millennia. For example, Buccellati claims that we are "the heirs of Mesopotamian perception and political experience".[15] As hosts to ancient knowledge, we need a high level of empirical proof, not speculative hypotheses, to be sure we understand the impact of that history on us.

Second, Buccellati asserts that people accepted as "popular" the imposition of "inequality of social and political stratification". If this is a correct rendition of life along the Tiber and Euphrates, one wonders why kings applied extraordinary measures to coerce their working populations. Closer to reality is Buccellati's acknowledgement that politics was designed to "control", by which he means "domination".[16]

Third, Buccellati claims that a "surplus" first appeared with the onset of agriculture. If correct, that falsifies my thesis. What is the basis of his view? Guesswork. Food cultivation "must" have been inspired by the technical revolution that became the agriculture age, which was the product of para-perceptual consciousness. One consequence, "that could not have been part of the initial intentions", was "the production of a surplus".[17] The odd feature of this assessment: if foraging communities were not already producing net resources, which some might covet, what was the point of their evolving (according to anthropologists) the precautionary device of shaming would-be cheats?

There are other troubling features of the perception that excludes Rent as the evolutionary element in the formation of humanity. On taxation, for example, Buccellati notes that tariffs were imposed on foreign trade. He does not consider the impact of tariffs on the labouring population. Likewise, "the performance of forced labor (corvée) might have been one of the first manifestations of duties".[18] What was natural, and apparently acceptable to the labourers, about that form of coercion?

By contrast, to support my thesis we have the empirical evidence of our bodies. Our minds. Our souls. We can measure what it took to elevate these out of nature. We can assess how the relationships between individuals operated. We can weigh the outcomes. *Humanity originated on the basis of a system patterned into what became a blueprint that would have shaped a different kind of urban civilisation than the one that originated in the Fertile Crescent.*

If, however, we accept Buccellati's account as more reliable than mine, then we must also accept that humanity's fate today was pre-determined in, sealed by, antiquity. His theory is consistent with prevailing narratives (such as Darwin's version of human evolution: see Ch.6 for my assessment of how the cheats warped Darwin's work). And so, to complete our test, we need to compare the history that evolved in the Near East with a case drawn from the same time, and based on the same material foundations; to assess whether an alternative to the outcomes in the Fertile Crescent were possible in both principle and practice. For one revealing case, we need to travel 1,500 miles north of Cairo, to the basin that abuts the Carpathian Mountains. There, people also developed agriculture, including the use of the plough and draft animals. For 5,000 years, between 6,000 and 1,000 BCE, they enjoyed life while successfully resisting the onset of inequality and exploitation. In the territory that now includes Hungary, Croatia and Serbia, they managed to negate the culture of cheating.

Studies of life in the Carpathian basin revealed that "Although farming did increase the potentials for both relational and material inequalities, the potential was rarely reached and then only for short durations. We identify a series of levelling mechanism varying over time". These communities did build monumental structures, but they were designed to foster cooperation. The archaeological evidence points to "the ability of even small-scale societies with ephemeral leadership structures to undertake monumental constructions requiring hundreds of thousands of person hours". Equality was maintained, and "Communal property or land-use rights...probably played important roles in all periods, as social cohesion scores demonstrate". Communities were regulated by "collective, decentralised leadership without coercive power".

> **In sum, it is not that inequalities were never present in our sample but rather that inequalities were never great and did not continue to grow in multiple domains as they did in the Near East.[19]**

The people of the Carpathian basin achieved their feats, and lived as equals, by rejecting the operational techniques of free riding.

Mirror Images

With the shift to farming, humanity had the opportunity to create a new world in the image of the evolutionary blueprint. A world of work, yes; but with the prospect of inventions that would accelerate increases in net income. That would open up new ways to fulfil aesthetic and spiritual sensibilities. With the increase in Rent, the human project would be holding a blank sheet waiting for the inscriptions. What might have been written, if cheating had not mutated into a culture? We will never know. Instead, looking back to the origins of civilisation, we see a mirror image of society as it began to develop into modernity, some 500 years ago.

Extensive urban settlements did require the pooling of labour power to fulfil the needs common to all farmers along the Nile, such as controlling the floods. The first stage of civilisation pre-dated the conversion of net income into money form, which is why people had to devote part of their week to maintaining the social infrastructure.

> **This form of work tax is usually known as corvée labour. Naturally, the brunt of the conscription fell on the peasants, who formed the bulk of the population, while others evaded their duty by producing substitutes or payment to the appropriate authorities.[20]**

But because the net resources – in the form of the products from the fields, which were collected in the granaries under the control of the temples and palaces – were subject to private appropriation, the corruption of power filtered into the social system. Egyptologists have documented cases of how bribery tempted the civil servants.[21] Slavery was an obvious device for state-sponsored cheating. That institution also laid the foundations for the gender problem that remains with us to this day.

> **The workmen were also allocated the services of female slaves who belonged to the central government. These women were attached to the sides of the gang and their task was to grind into flour the grain supplied to the community by the authorities.**[22]

There is, however, one major qualitative difference between then and now. Back then, if there was a dispute over property, the pharaonic system required the intervention of the gods.

> **The Egyptian gods were not aloof and distant but played a direct part in the life of the community. On important matters a god could be consulted by oracle...These consultations were concerned with claims to property and not offices.**[23]

Today, cheating is so well entrenched that we can arbitrate property disputes through secular laws. This is a marker of the triumph of the culture that entrenched cheating into the model of civilisation. And that is why, today, our intellectual communities turn blind eyes on the flaw in the foundations of the model that originated in the Near East. A man-made flaw responsible for the collapses that blight history. Exceptions do not disprove the rule (Box 3.1).

Today, the Organisation for Economic Co-operation and Development (OECD) does acknowledge that our world is at risk from "tipping points". Its warning, however, rests on a myopic focus on the environment. This understates the scale of the looming catastrophe, by ignoring the threats from ideological paralysis; from the statecraft constructed to sponsor territorial conflicts; and from the economic and demographic breakdowns that trigger mass migration.

Box 3.1 Adapting to climate change

Societies were vulnerable to climate change, even when cheating was absent. Even so, because their cultural vitality had not been eroded, they managed to mutate into new ways of living. The civilisation located along the Indus River in present-day Pakistan is illustrative. It lasted for 2,000 years, growing into "well-planned cities, advanced water management systems, and a sophisticated writing system". Then, around 1,300 BCE, it disappeared.

The disappearance is not attributed to inequalities stemming from an exploitative statecraft, but rather to "climate change, seawater retreat, droughts, floods, and shifting river dynamics", along with adaptations in economic behaviour, including trade with Mesopotamia, which encouraged demographic relocation. The social system was resilient, so the decline "was not a sudden collapse but a complex process of fragmentation and cultural transformation, indicating a societal adaptation rather than a complete disappearance".*

* Hiren Solanki *et al* (2025), "River drought forcing of the Harappan metamorphosis", *communications earth & environment.* https://doi.org/10.1038/s43247-025-02901-1

We *can* navigate our way through the catastrophe. The single condition for doing so is the restoration of the social status of Rent. This perspective challenges the authorised version of the state of our world, which is summarised by Adam Tooze, a Colombia University historian. He postulates a "polycrisis" threatening humanity. He is, however, a victim of the "no silver bullet" syndrome. He states: "[I]t no longer seems plausible to point to a single cause and, by implication, a single fix".[24] The OECD would concur. Its attempt to alert the world to the cascading tipping points excludes the existential effects of the culture that corrupts people's lives, liberties and property rights.[25] That cannibalistic form of behaviour now suffuses our modern civilisation.

References Chapter 3

1 Juan Carlos Moreno Garcia (2025), "Leadership in rural pharaonic Egypt: village chiefs, small potentates and informal networks of power in the provincial world", Melina Tamiolaki (ed.), *Leadership in the Ancient World: Concepts, Models, Theories*, Cambridge: University Press.

2 Gwyneth McGregor (1956), "Taxation in the Ancient World", *Canadian Tax Journal*, 4(4), p.271.

3 https://waronwant.org/profiting-hunger/4-financial-sector-land-grabs

4 E. Christiana Köhler (2017), "The Development of Social Complexity in Early Egypt. A view from the perspective of the settlements and material culture of the Nile Valley", *Egypt and the Levant*, 27, p.335

5 Juan Carlos Moreno Garcia (2022), "Houses, regions and state(s): Multiple political experiences in ancient Egypt", in J.C.M. Garcia (Ed), *From House Societies to States*, Vol. 3, Oxford: Oxbow, p.109. Emphasis added.

6 K. D. van Heel (2012), *Djekhy & Son: Doing Business in Ancient Egypt*, Cairo: American University of Cairo Press, p.78. Some landlords took 45% of the yield from "their" land: p.109.

7 Toby Wilkinson (2010), *The Rise and Fall of Ancient Egypt*, London: Bloomsbury, p.77.

8 *Ibid*., p.77-78.

9 Xavier Landreau *et al* (2024), "On the possible use of hydraulic force to assist with building the step pyramid of Saqqara", *PLoS One*, 19(8).

10 Today, the tallest building in the world is Burj Khalifa. At over 820 meters (2,716 feet), and more than 160 stories, it was funded out of the oil Rents of Dubai.

11 Wilkinson, *op. cit*. pp. 87, 91.

12 *Ibid*, pp. 27, 79-80.

13 J.K. Noyes (1992), *Colonial Space: Spatiality in the Discourse of German South West Africa 1884-1914*, Chur, Switzerland: Harwood Academic Publishers.

14 Susan Sherratt (2016), "From 'institutional' to 'private': traders, routes and commerce from the Late Bronze Age to the Iron Age", in J.C. Moreno Garcia (ed.), *Dynamics of Production in the Ancient Near East, 1300-500 BC*, Oxford: Oxbow Books, p.291.

15 Giorgio Buccellati (2025), *At the Origins of Politics: Formation and Growth of the State in Syro-Mesopotamia*, London: Routledge, pp.32, 248.

16 *Ibid*, p.11.

17 *Ibid*., pp.20-21.

18 *Ibid*., p.53.

19 Paul R. Duffy *et al* (2025), "Five thousand years of inequality in the Carpathian Basin", *Science Advances*, 11(32). DOI: 10.1126/sciadv.adu0323

20 Morris Bierbrier (2016), *The Tomb Builders of the Pharaohs*, Cairo: The American University in Cairo Press, pp. 10-11.

21 *Ibid*., pp. 29, 33.

22 *Ibid*., p.39.

23 *Ibid*., p.98.

24 Adam Tooze (2022), "Welcome to the world of the polycrisis", *Financial Times*, October 29.

25 The OECD does acknowledge "the scale and magnitude of tipping point impacts necessitate a transformational, beyond incremental, approach to adaptation" (OECD [2022], *Climate Tipping Points: Insights for Effective Policy Action*, Paris, p.67). It offers no effective strategy for such a transformation.

CHAPTER FOUR

Cannibalism

The struggle out of the forests of Africa led to the creation of that unique space on Earth, the Social Galaxy. The making of that self-sustaining realm can be divided into three processes.

- ***Survival***: to enable biological development of their physical form, proto-humans formulated a behavioural blueprint. Genetic inter-dependence meant that everyone had to be treated as equals, a reality that was enshrined in the rules of conduct.
- ***Synergy***: creation of the cleanest power in the Social Galaxy – fusion of human energy through space and time, facilitated through trade and cultural exchange. That is how humans overcame nature's boundaries, to occupy the whole of Earth.
- ***Sharing***: realisation of aspirations was facilitated with strategies that reinforced cooperation. Rent was invested to grow relationships beyond kinship communities, with the enforcement of codes of behaviour delegated to trusted individuals.

With the emergence of civilisation, Rent was diverted to non-social uses, corrupting the authority structure. The human project was cannibalised. Rent became as toxic for society as bacteria that pollutes blood in the body. Contamination of the blood stream leads to mortality. And so does the pollution of the public's finances. The implication is horrifying.

It means that, unless the error in antiquity is corrected, we are all contributing to the process that will eventually terminate the human project. Did the corruption of the evolutionary blueprint initiate a process of cannibalisation? Was the full creative vitality of humanity diminished to accommodate the needs of free riders?

Ideally, we ought to be able to compare the rate of progress since antiquity against what *might* have been achieved, without the culture of cheating. We cannot make such a calculation. But we can be certain that, unburdened by taxes on wages and on the profits from value-adding production, societies across the five millennia would have been far more creative and contented, materially and spiritually. That this did not happen was the mission of the "cuckoo in the nest". To understand the full impact of that cuckoo, we need to unravel two phenomena. First, we need a full appreciation of the extent to which the power of labour was compromised under the model ordained by the culture of cheating. Second, how statecraft operated in relation to fulfilling peoples social needs.

If the cumulative evidence does verify my hypothesis, the conclusion is clear. We live in times that are more dangerous than (say) the era of two world wars.

The power nexus

Marxists attribute the vulnerable condition of industrial labour to the behaviour of capitalists. Wicked employers exploited workers to boost profits. That theory is untenable, when viewed in the *longue durée*. The vulnerability of working people originated five millennia ago, in the Near East. The dynasts claimed the land, which is how people lost their evolutionary rights of access to the commons. From then on, they were hostages. Outer forms of their status varied, in time and place, but that did not alter the reality: the people who worked to create the wealth were dependent on the people who, through their control over land – not capital – could siphon off the net income for private use. So, understanding the labour market must begin with the power relationships ordained by those who treated land as their exclusive asset.

The balance of power between people, and the distribution of income, did not follow a simple arithmetical rule. It hung on the psychology of the free riders. Their appetites were insatiable. That became a practical problem for them. If they did not leave sufficient net income to fund public services, they would lose their grip on the structure that discriminated in their favour. So they extracted as much Rent as they dared; leaving sufficient to fund social infrastructure at their desired level of efficiency. Insatiable appetites, then, became a critical part of the forces that working people had to navigate, if they were to put food on their tables.

The overriding mission of the lords of the land – the Rentlords – was to cut costs of production. The greater the productivity, the larger the share of output that remained as net income. One strategy was to intensify the squeeze on labour. By controlling the land, the lords exercised ultimate power over labour and the tools employed in production. That is how the mechanism called elasticity comes into play.

Under the evolutionary process, the power dynamics linking labour, land and capital were controlled by the people who worked for their living. They established a harmonic relationship between the three factors of production. That was based on the willingness of people to work, which determined how much labour power was devoted, how the tools were accumulated and applied to production, and the availability of the resources of nature. This synchronous relationship was contingent on the consent of people to work together to achieve mutual goals. They wanted to achieve more than their metabolic daily needs. That required an extra layer of resources that could only materialise by working in unison, to meet their aspirations for biological, intellectual and moral progress.

If that model had been applied in the transition to civilisation, the cooperation and consensus model would have prevailed; with no exploitative power in the hands of anyone. Cheating would be disallowed. Institutions would have emerged to ensure transparency and accountability in the public sector, where the common good was administered. But, by privatising Rent, the relationships between labour, capital and land were ruptured; power was enhanced in favour of those who controlled the land. Labour was subordinated into the state of dependency. The power nexus was transformed; perverted.

- ***Land*** became the tool of dominant power. Its fixed supply enabled owners to command a premium from production.

Owners controlled the pull-and-push between the productive agents. Their property rights enabled them to withdraw from use the natural resources that people needed to remain alive. Now, nature became hostile; not because it was fixed or limited in supply, but because of the barbarity of its owners; who were able to force others to yield their net resources.

- ***Capital***, originally a passive agent, was transformed in the markets to a role that enabled owners to capture a slice of the Rents.

Because free riders diverted much of the net income away from funding social needs, governments were left with budget deficits. They had to borrow funds to cover necessary costs. People who owned capital realised that, by transforming capital into liquid form (a process now called "financialisation"), they could lend to government; and extract a share of the nation's Rents.

- ***Labour*** was left with no choice. To remain alive, people had to accept their state of dependency, or migrate to foreign lands.

Bereft of land, people became hostages. Formerly, under the evolutionary process, they were at the centre of wealth creation. Now, they were pushed to the margins, forced to act as supplicants if they wished to remain alive.

The one constraint on the power of the free riders was from the risk of pushing too hard, to the point where too many people might migrate; in which case, Rents would not be produced. So, the working population had a measure of influence at the bargaining table. The degree of power they could exercise varied according to circumstances.

- If people lived under the conditions prevailing along the Nile, where irrigated land was limited, shading off into desert, they had few alternatives. Labour lacked bargaining power. Free riding pharaohs held all the cards.
- If people lived in the fertile Carpathian basin, they could up-stakes and move to land elsewhere; the would-be cheats could only secure a short-lived toehold before withering away. The producers held all of the cards.

The Rent grab model devised in antiquity provided the template for exploitation that was sustained across five millennia. Variations in the mode of governance (whether Athenian democracy, Roman autocracy or the universal suffrage of modern times) made little qualitative difference. Predatory statecraft changed its guises to suit circumstances, but it continued to ripple through the ages to the 21st century.

The state of inhumanity

Slavery was one method for harnessing people's labour power. It remained a practice from antiquity through classical times (both in Greece and Rome) into the modern era. The colonisation of North America and the Caribbean islands illustrates the process. The British monarchy, in allocating land grants to its feudal aristocrats, laid the foundations for free riding on a new continent. Three features of that history illuminate the embedding of the culture of cheating.

First, beginning in the 17th century, land grants were for territory appropriated from indigenous tribes. The noble owners of the plantations did not intend to work the land themselves: many of them remained in England, using their Rents to transform medieval manor houses into county palaces. Slavery was a necessary feature of the early plantations because "free labour" was not available to grow tobacco and cotton. Therefore, slaves had to be imported from Africa.

Second, insatiable appetites. In the 18th century, not content with controlling the eastern territories of America, the United States created by the Founding Fathers embarked on grabbing yet more land to the west. The aspiration was made visible on the dollar bill. This displayed an incomplete image of an Egyptian pyramid. The concept was crafted in 1782. Each of the 13 member states was registered by a step up the pyramid. The top half of the pyramid was detached, the space to be filled in with future acquisitions of territories. The US territorial land grabs included the victory over Mexico in the war of 1846. Mexico ceded 55% of its land, including Nevada, Utah, and portions of California, Arizona, and New Mexico. The predator state's appetite knows no bounds.

Third, during the 19th century, it became clear that slavery was not necessarily the best way to maximise Rental returns. The slaves took no more than their wages to meet their BBS levels, but they had no reason to help their masters to expand productivity. To harness the opportunities of the new industrial era, which had dawned in the British Isles, it was more efficient – from the perspective of the Rentlords – to employ "free labour". The abolition of slavery came at great cost, in the form of the civil war.

And so, the push-and-pull between land and labour continued to favour the lords. For the granular evidence, we have to turn to the documentation bequeathed by the surveyors of land in the British colonies. Their texts are called cadastral surveys, not contracts for the commodification of human beings. But their maps register how Rent was extracted from the "free" tenants who migrated from England, or from the slaves extracted from Africa.

When British merchants shipped African slaves to colonies in the Caribbean, or the Carolinas, what did they trade in the marketplace? The price paid in the slave markets took account of the cost of feeding and sheltering the slaves. That cost ("wages") was covered by the sale of the cotton or tobacco crops. Slave traders and landowners shared the net revenue. The price of slaves was the trader's portion of the Rent, in its capitalised form.

Edmond Smith, the Professor in Economic Cultures at the University of Manchester, provides a dispassionate account of the costs. The increased competition among British traders drove up the prices. African traders increased their price for an enslaved person from £3 to £10. That, consequently, drove up prices in the Caribbean from £14, to £23. There were, of course, bonanzas. In one case, a transaction in Barbados in January 1796 netted the investors £24,453 for the 421 people who survived the voyage – an average of £58 for each slave.[1]

Bid prices varied. A young and strong man was worth more than an older and weaker man, or a woman. There was no single price because, although wage costs were similar for all slaves, the net produce generated over a working lifetime varied by age and muscle power. That variation influenced the price of each transaction in the slave markets. The price of young and strong slaves was at maximum levels, with the price sliding according to age and gender. Such windfalls were nothing, however, compared to what Rome's slave-owners achieved; they raised the price of some slaves by educating them (Box 4.1).

Box 4.1 **Cashing in on slaves**

In classical Rome, a slave born into the household of the master could be educated to administer the paperwork of the landed estate. He could also then be resold for a premium price. One such slave was sold for 700,000 sesterces. This was "a huge sum that could have bought someone a country estate or a grand house in town", reports Harriet Flower, a professor of classics at Princeton University and author of *Intellectual Property: Learned Slaves and Educated Freedmen in Republican Rome* (2025).*

Some Rentlords turned the education of slaves into a business. Using children born to slaves within their household (so there was no cost price for acquiring them), the slaves were given one year's tuition in reading and writing, then sold to other estate owners.

* Harriet Flower (2025), "The Wealth of Knowledge", *History Today*, Nov., p.80.

According to the Trans-Atlantic Slave Trade Database, 12.5 million Africans were shipped to the New World between 1525 and 1866; 10.7m survived the passage. That trade served a twin purpose for the beneficiaries of the culture of cheating. First, within the UK, it provided jobs as tradesmen for the people whose ancestors had been ejected from the commons. Second, as labour, Africans were preferred above the indigenous peoples living on the Caribbean islands; especially since the "merciless Indians" might resist displacement from their ancestral lands. So, for example, on the island of Antigua, the British merchants, planters and traders "brooked no compromise: they thought that annihilation was the only way to ensure their assets were safe. More violence was ordered, and yet more land was secured for Britain's capitalists to exploit".[2]

Prosperity during the early phase of Britain's industrialisation came at a great price. Of the 2.85m slaves trafficked on British ships during the 18th century, 500,000 died during the voyage. When they arrived at their destination, they were exposed to merciless working conditions on the plantations. **Result:** slaves were expected to live for just seven years; with a quarter of them dying within the first three years.

The trade in slaves was outlawed by Britain in 1807. It would be another three decades before slavery was abolished in the British dominions. By then, however, abolition did not matter. The working population was *in situ*. The law did not forbid the private ownership of land or extraction of Rent. In terms of the distribution of income, therefore, nothing changed. Because, as owners of the land, the lords continued to annex the Rents produced by "emancipated" workers.

The cannibalisation of human beings is further illustrated by the history of Clean Slates.

Ritual fresh starts

Effective governance is signified by the measures employed to remediate socially significant problems. In ancient times, governments introduced Royal Proclamations that purported to offer a fresh start for people who had lapsed into debt, and who had forfeited their land. Those initiatives, however, failed to cure the systemic problems, which led to the need for new rounds of fresh starts.

The ritual of fresh starts began in Sumer in 2,400 BCE. Debts were cancelled and land restored to the peasants. Some farmers no doubt fell into debt, and lost their land holdings, through either personal failures or interventions of events over which they had no control (such as shifts in climate). But the peculiar feature of the proclamations is their cyclicality, which suggests a structural flaw remained embedded in economic relations. A flaw that automatically restarted the process that led back to debt, servitude and landlessness.

The terms of Clean Slates reveal the systemic flaw. The proclamations did not reform the property rights that enabled owners of land to collect the net income. Debt forgiveness edicts stretched from the one issued by Hammurabi (1792–1750 BCE) of the 1st dynasty of Babylon, to the Rosetta Stone record of the decree issued by Ptolemy V of Egypt in 196 BC; through to the interventions of Solon and Cleisthenes and land reforms in ancient Greece. None of these changed statecraft; Rent extraction remained rooted in the social systems.

Clean slates found their expression in the Hebrew Bible, renamed as the Jubilee initiative, as ordained by God. Leviticus (Ch. 25) describes how, every 49 years, land should be returned to the families that lost it; and debts should be cancelled. Alas, the systemic problem was not solved.[3] People kept losing their land when they could not redeem their mortgages. Restoring rights of access to land, without also restoring people's social rights to the Rents of the land they farmed, meant that slates were not wiped clean. The proclamations were mere pauses in the exploitation that ruptured people's capacity to meet their needs. Restoring land did, however, serve the purpose of the Rent-takers. People pushed off the land could not work to generate Rents for the lords, or for the financiers who took a slice of the Rents through the mortgage system.[4]

What began in antiquity, continued apace in modernity. It need not have been so. The first rigorous analysis of clean slate economics emerged in the salons of Paris. The school of philosophers known as Physiocrats located the concept of the net product (*produit net*) at the centre of their theorising.[5] Adam Smith travelled to France to study the principles for good governance. The result was *The Wealth of Nations* (1776). This scoped out the equity and efficiency arrangements for the peoples of the British Isles. It was all there, in Vol. 2, Bk. 4, Ch. 2: collect Rent as government revenue, and people would be free to go about their business within the framework that Smith metaphorically called the "invisible hand".

Today, post-classical economists sneer at Smith's economic model, that people could enhance the welfare of society even as they focused on fulfilling their own needs. What they choose to ignore is the nature of the statecraft that Smith defined for his model. There was no ambiguity about his recommendation. In Bk 5, Ch. 2, he stated that

> **ground rents are altogether owing to the good government of the sovereign, which, by protecting the industry either of the whole people, or of the inhabitants of some particular place, enables them to pay so much more than its real value for the ground which they build their houses upon... Nothing can be more reasonable than that a fund, which owes its existence to the good government of the state should be taxed peculiarly, or should contribute something more than the greater part of other funds, towards the support of that government.**

In France, a finance minister, Anne Robert Jacques Turgot (1727–1781), advocated that fiscal reform to the king, with the warning that this was necessary to address the disquiet he detected among the populace. Turgot was quickly dismissed.[6] The revolution came in 1789, the king's head was removed by guillotine, and

France has since progressed through five republics and at least 12 constitutions, without a clean break from its cheating past.

In 19th century Britain, Smith's advocacy of Rent-as-public-revenue was brushed aside. The sharpest hatchet was wielded by the Rev. Thomas Malthus, who attributed problems like poverty to the behaviour of poverty-stricken people.[7] In economics as an intellectual discipline, a turning point might have occurred in 1890. Alfred Marshall revived the concept of elasticity. But shorn of its existential life force – the process for controlling personal and social destinies – elasticity appeared in a sanitised version in Marshall's influential text. He accommodated the ideology that served the culture of cheating.[8]

The outcome, in the 20th century, was a flurry of fantasy theorising, as characterised by Alfred Malabre, the then economics editor of the *Wall Street Journal*. Economics was not a science.

> **A more accurate description, I submit, would be that it constitutes, at best, a pseudoscience and, at worst, a guessing game, often wildly inaccurate, frequently carried on by clever bamboozlers whose academic credentials may far exceed any possible contributions they make to the betterment of mankind.**[9]

And so, we are left with the legacy from antiquity: a perverse statecraft that licenses the cannibalisation of human vitality by creating indebtedness and landlessness.

The lost heritage

If the evolutionary blueprint had been honoured, cultural innovations would have far exceeded the intellectual, artistic and technological achievements of the past five millennia. The order of magnitude of that decline is beyond what we can imagine. Instead, the values of free riders dominated the earliest civilisations. The decline from achievable levels began slowly, as communities shifted away from the evolutionary growth path. Downward episodes over the past five millennia caused the implosion of communities. In each case, the trend accelerated as the people who privatised Rent-yielding assets consolidated their power until, finally, society

Figure 4.1 **The Division of Rent**

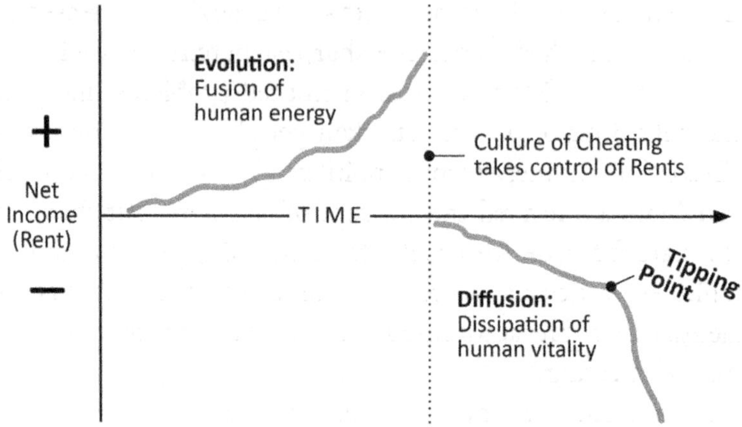

reached a precipice. The cheats, having exhausted populations of their vitality, inaugurated the collapse.

Fig. 4.1 offers a schematic representation of that process. The downward line tracks the decrease in people's ability to achieve personal and social aspirations of the material, moral and spiritual kinds. Over time, as the gap between privatised and social Rents widened, aspirations slipped further away from what could have been achieved if authentic freedom had prevailed.

The foragers who turned farmers did not intend this outcome. They constructed new social spaces that enabled them to survive in new climes, like the Arctic regions of the northern hemisphere. As they spread across the planet, they preserved the delicate balance between the forces that enabled hominins to emerge as humans. The outward manifestation was the spiritual life, the contemplative powers of which channelled moral sensibilities to guide behaviour.[10] Their experiments in new ways of living stress-tested the evolutionary model they brought out of Africa. They confirmed that the human project depended on personal responsibility for producing and disposing of the net resources for their shared benefit. *Direct control over Rent was the fulcrum point of the evolutionary process.*

What happened at the eastern end of the Mediterranean polluted democracy in classical Greece. Solon's land reforms in

594 BCE preceded that political system, which helped to preserve household kinship structures; but which also accommodated slavery. Slaves working on the land enabled the private accumulation of Rent so that citizens could pontificate in the squares of Athens. Slaves toiling down the silver mines were central to Athenian power. Slave owners received a 30% return on their investments.[11]

That the land-owning aristocracy's culture shaped the fate of Greece is not contested. During the 8th century BCE, the economy flourished, delivering prosperity "especially for the aristocracy, whose political control over their own polis was based on their tenure of the best and the largest amount of land". This also saw "the rise of serious social problems in Greece, which were linked directly or indirectly with the land". One solution was to drive the imperial project: conquest of land enabled the off-loading of poverty-stricken people.[12]

Hesiod, a Greek poet (thought to have been active between 750 and 650 BCE), was one victim. His brother, Perseus, bribed judges so that he could take possession of the land Hesiod had inherited. Hesiod then wrote *Works and Days* to address the issues of farming and morality. He warned against free riding, declaring that

> **Both gods and men are angry with a man who lives idle, for in nature he is like the stingless drones who waste the labour of the bees, eating without working; but let it be your care to order your work properly, that in the right season your barns may be full of victual.**[13]

Idleness was a way of life for those who owned Rent-yielding assets. Rome employed the Athenian model. The Empire's "root purpose…was to funnel wealth to be spent in Rome…a racket based on rampant exploitation". Captive humans were "a vital pillar of Roman life", gouging the Balkans and North Africa "to take vast plunder, including human bounty". The Rents extracted out of those regions funded monumental buildings, with slaves "a commodity for better-off Romans to buy for their own leisure and convenience, to staff their sprawling urban villas or rural super-farms".[14]

Marcus Licinius Crassus (115–53 BCE), the General-statesman who featured prominently in transforming the republic into an empire, was "the richest man in Rome". His fortune came from land speculation. One of his tricks was to wait while neighbourhoods burnt down before buying up the properties at cheap prices. He then rented homes to the displaced peasants who had suffered from the clearances, who crammed into the city to survive on "bread and circus" morsels.

Lifestyles of the aristocracy depleted the social institutions, including the armies that were supposed to control the far reaches of the empire. Rents were extracted from as far afield as the wall built in England to keep out the marauding Scots. Territorial expansion was driven by the logic of the economic system developed on home soil. Peasants displaced from their farms within the Italian peninsular became refugees in Rome. This encouraged the further expansion of the empire, to resettle the landless. Archaeologist Tesse Stek notes that

> **Whereas the ruling elites were unwilling to distribute the land they controlled to landless Romans, newly conquered areas posed no such problem; colonists could be sent out from Rome to farm those lands instead.**[15]

There would come a point, however, where the bread and circus subsidies for the landless would weaken Rome beyond salvation. Enter the barbarians, the men on horseback who emerged from the north. First, they flooded into the peripheral regions. They sacked the cities and, in 439, the vandals captured Carthage, from which Rome received much of its grain. Rome was sacked in 410 AD, with the *coup de grace* in 546. The western end of the civilisation disappeared into dust.

Globalisation

One of the legacies of the refusal to institute authentic clean slates was the globalisation of slavery in a corporate form. Amsterdam was first off the financial grid. Its history is analysed by Franklin

Obeng-Odoom, the Professor of Global Development Studies at the University of Helsinki.

First, in the East Indies, Rent and slave economics emerged at the beginning of the 17th century and rippled through to the 21st century, to shape people's lives in the oil-rich city of Balikpapan, on the Indonesian island of Borneo. Over those four centuries, Holland grew rich out of the Rents of slaves and the fossil fuel Rents that were transported back to Amsterdam.

The corporation established by the States General of the Netherlands in 1602 provides the spatiotemporal thread. It originated as the United East India Company, mutating into the Royal Dutch Company for the Working Petroleum Wells in the Netherlands Indies, then replaced by the Royal Dutch Petroleum Company. This corporate structure enslaved an estimated million people in the 17th and 18th centuries.

Obeng-Odoom insists that "privately appropriating property in persons and property in land drives persistent social stratification around rent theft regardless of [the] policy regime, economic system, or developmentalist paradigm". Today, the Dutch slave legacy is visible in the economics of the property tax administered in Balikpapan.

> **[T]he city authorities do not tax land values nor tax rent. The incidence of tax is property value (made up of both land and building value), not land values *per se*. In any case, Indonesia has one of the lowest property tax rates (0.5%) in the world... [T]he effective tax rate remains around 0.2%. So, speculation is encouraged. Not only do they privately appropriate what has been publicly and socially created value, speculators also siphon this money out of Balikpapan. As rents rise, both social and spatial mobility for local residents become even more difficult.**[16]

Obeng-Odoom does not pull his punches. Economic researchers tend to apply theory "mainly to states and markets, capital and labour, not to transnational oil corporations, their rent theft, and the social identities they (re)produce". As the Dutch grew richer, funding infrastructure like the dykes that kept out the North Sea – creating more useable land from which to extract Rent – the people of the East Indies grew poorer, their Rents "historically drained to the Netherlands, the quintessential 'rentier nation'".

The geopolitical dramas were, at all times, accompanied by the suppression of people's creative possibilities. Regulations were enacted to deter rather than empower people's spirit. Divide, rather than unite, to rule over, rather than for, the human project. The outcome is neatly captured by British historian Mark Galeotti.[17]

> **We have to recognise that our banks are full of dirty money, our foreign policy depends on deals with kleptocrats, our supply chains are packed with counterfeit, our glittering cities are built on foundations of stolen sand and speculative fraud, and our consumer goods and raw materials alike are produced by trafficked labour.**

That summarises the infrastructure of the culture of cheating. It cannot be sustained. But it gets worse. In its social form, Rent provides the scaffolding that channels information between all the working parts in people's lives. Moral sensibilities reinforce biological processes, ensuring the unimpeded flow of information and resources. Moral sensibilities enable individuals to remain alert, so that they can deter acts of attempted cheating. What happens when obstructions are introduced? As an analogy, consider the physics of the human body, and the central nervous system that conveys information and energy from the brain and through the spinal cord to all parts of the anatomy. Integral to this operation is the immune system, the network of cells, tissues, organs, and substances that help the body fight infections and other diseases. Damage the immune system, and the operational systems of the body break down.

When cheating completes its cannibalisation of society, the pathological outcomes are deadly. Societies, inevitably, collapse. If net income haemorrhages out of the system, the Social Galaxy begins to implode. The human commons loses its vitality. This initiates an anti-evolutionary drama, which manifests itself in obvious ways. Free riding results in

- ▸ *under-funding* of investments in bodies, minds and souls; thereby diverting people from evolutionary progress;

- ► *forces* the labouring population to work harder, carrying others on their backs, which reduces time for aspirational pursuits; and
- ► *imposes* a debt burden on unborn generations, which defeats the parental desire to bequeath legacy assets in a better state than those they inherited.

The withdrawal of Rent from its Social functions is the root cause of the persistent collapse of civilisations. A singular cause is denied by historians. We must, therefore, subject it to granular examination; not least because the experts do not articulate a convincing alternative route to the re-humanisation of society.

References Chapter 4

1 Edmond Smith (2025), *Ruthless: A New History of Britain's Rise to Wealth and Power*, New Haven: Yale University Press, pp. 299, 301, 313.

2 *Ibid.*, p.125.

3 Michael Hudson (1993), "The Lost Tradition of Biblical Debt Cancellations", New York: Henry George School of Social Science. https://michael-hudson.com/1992/03/the-lost-tradition-of-biblical-debt-cancellations/

4 Michael Hudson (2018), *...and Forgive Them Their Debts: Lending, Foreclosure and Redemption from Bronze Age Finance to the Jubilee Year*, ISLET. ISLET- Verlag Dresden.

5 V.R. Mirabeau (1764), *Philosophie rurale, ou economie générale et politique de l'agriculture.* Amsterdam: Libraries Associées. Reprinted, Aalen: Scientia Verlag, 1972. F. Quesnay (1766). *Premier problème économique.* In INED, François Quesnay et la physiocratie, Vol. I. Paris, 1958.

6 A.R.J. Turgot (1999), *Formation and Distribution of Wealth: Turgot's Reflections on Capitalism*, Kenneth Jupp (Editor), London: Othila Press.

7 James P. Huzel (1969), "Malthus, the Poor Law, and Population in Early 19th England", *Economic History Review*, 22(3).

8 Alfred Marshall (1890), *Principles of Economics*, Bk III, Ch. IV. He does acknowledge the ATCOR thesis, in a discussion confined to effects at the local property tax level (Appendix G). The macro-economic impact of statecraft (good or bad) was ignored.

9 Alfred L. Malabre, Jr. (1994), *Lost Prophets: An Insider's History of the Modern Economists*, Boston, Mass: Harvard Business School Press, p.7.

10 Ken Wilber (1999), *The Marriage of Sense and South: Integrating Science and Religion*, New York: Broadway Books, p.205.

11 https://www.moneymuseum.com/en/archive/exploiting-the-mines-by-renting-slaves-88?&slbox=true

12 Terry Buckley (1996), *Aspects of Greek History 750-323 BC*, London: Routledge, pp. 35-36.

13 Hesiod, *Homeric Hymns, Epic Cycle, Homerica*. Translated by Hugh G. Evelyn-White (1914), London: William Heinemann, versus 225, 293.

14 Dan Jones (2021), *Powers and Thrones*, London: Apollo, pp. 24, 28, 65-66.

15 Tesse D. Stek (2018), "Early Roman Colonisation Beyond the Romanising Agrotown, Village Patterns of Settlement and Highland Exploitation in the Abruzzi Mountains, Central Italy", in Bleda S. Düring and Tesse D. Stek (eds), *The Transformation of Rural Societies and Landscapes*, Cambridge: Cambridge University Press, p.148.

16 Franklin Obeng-Odoom (2024), "Balikpapan as a Developmental Environmentalist City: A Stratification Economics Approach", *The J of Environment and Development*, pp 6, 16. https://journals.sagepub.com/doi/full/10.1177/10704965241300206 See also Franklin Obeng-Odoom (2019), Review, *Journal of Economics, Race, and Policy*, p.205.

17 Mark Galeotti (2025), *Homo Criminalis: How Crime Organises the World*, London: Ebury Press.

CHAPTER FIVE

Collapse

Spiritual narratives include scary forecasts about End Times. Corrections to personal behaviour were needed if communities were to survive. Prophetic voices emerge to alert people to fundamental problems in their societies. Themes common to the apocalyptic narratives include a final judgement; the message conveyed by a messianic saviour; the prospect of salvation through enlightenment. The detail is provided by historical and cultural contexts.

Now, we can translate those eschatological stories into language that combines the natural and social sciences. Horrifyingly, secular knowledge leads us to the same conclusion: the End is nigh. But, forensic science also reveals the mechanism that threatens extinction. That, in turn, reveals the tools needed to navigate the apocalypse, so that survivors may build a better future.

Natural scientists analyse our proximity to the moment when the Doomsday Clock strikes midnight. They combine data that references the environment with trends in the political world (such as autocrats threatening to use nuclear weapons in disputes over land). If they are correct, humanity really is on the precipice of extinction; pivoting, apparently, at just 89 seconds to midnight.[1]

Social scientists have a more difficult struggle to pin down the reasons for the alarm bells. They do point fingers at the damage inflicted on the environment, but without identifying the root cause(s). In the words of American historian Jared Diamond, threats of collapse are deeds of "unintended ecological suicide".[2] Rare is the warning in the form presented by Singapore's Prime Minister in 2024. He noted that the middle class was suffering from high house prices, and "when the broad middle falls behind… [t]he centre does not hold. Societies begin to fracture and collapse. Do not assume this cannot happen here. It can – and it will – unless we take decisive actions to prevent it".[3]

Colin Renfrew, a British paleolinguist, was influential in the formation of the theory of collapse of civilisations. As Professor of Archaeology at the University of Cambridge, his seminal studies traced the process by which civilisations, starting from small beginnings, gradually imploded. He concluded that there was no single, obvious cause of those collapses.[4]

I do attribute collapse to a single cause.

In the past, technologically sophisticated societies were corroded from within, over an extended period of time. The vitality of populations was systematically eroded. There comes a time when the social structure cannot sustain itself. The inflection point is defined by the rate at which the quantum of Rent produced by the labouring population falls below the amount being extracted and devoted to non-social purposes. A slight push is all that is needed to topple the system.

The difference, today, is that the threat is not confined to the collapse of civilisations in spatially confined regions. The whole of humanity is at stake, because each of four existential threats are global in their reach. Those threats matured over the past five millennia, manifested in property rights, the associated pricing system, and a statecraft that privileges irresponsible behaviour.

The slow motion

Cheating as an inter-generational pandemic became the slow motion earthquake that complemented nature's fault lines, the fractures in the Earth's crust on which many of the earliest cities were constructed. In the late Bronze Age, earthquakes helped to raze some of those cities to the ground. Far more serious, in its lasting effects, was the cultural fault line. A resilient population can rebuild cities demolished by nature. Cities demolished by the culture of cheating remain flattened, because the population had lost its social compass points.

The Near Eastern model of civilisation emerged as a system designed to fail. Decision-making was shifted away from the working population, and onto privileged Rent-takers. Violence in its various guises replaced the consensus and cooperation that stabilised communities up to the Neolithic phase of the human project. The rate at which the vitality of the population was eroded was amplified, over time, leading to eventual collapse.

We have inherited that statecraft. Governance deploys tax-funded policies that are self-defeating. Law-makers may be sincere in wanting to solve problems, but when they fund their policies with taxes they automatically amplify the population's traumas. Palliative policies transmit ripple effects, which pile yet more pressures on governments for yet more interventions with strategies that create positive feedback loops; which, consequently, intensify the need for yet more interventions funded out of burdensome taxes.

To sustain that social system, the beneficiaries had to suppress the prospect of being shamed by their victims. Owners of Rent-yielding assets had to ameliorate their feelings of guilt, for the suffering they caused, and they had to deter those who might speak truth to power. One strategy was to cultivate prejudices that would soften the sense of shame. The clues to this formula for shaping and preserving misbehaviour were buried in the tombs of antiquity, but the archaeologists who began to excavate the evidence did not decipher their significance. They were hostages to the prejudices that licensed the culture of cheating (Box 5.1).

The earliest civilisations were creative. The benefits of the innovations, however, were more than offset by deeds of deprivation and destruction. For the farmers along the banks of the Nile, the Tigris and Euphrates, the tools for surveying the landscape, and the arithmetic needed to quantify the grain grown in the fields, proved

Box 5.1 **Colour's hidden meaning**

Timothy Kendall, a Northeastern University anthropologist, summarised the prejudices shared by the European excavators of Egyptian sites in these terms:

> *The racist/colonialist view that Africa and African peoples were incapable of high cultural attainment naturally resulted in the view that Egypt was a non-African country, more closely connected to the Near Eastern and Mediterranean worlds and populated by peoples more akin to "civilized" Europeans. To these scholars, inner Africa was perceived only as a source of raw materials and slaves. Such interpretations of ancient history were important in order to maintain European authority and power within Africa.**

This assessment of the global north/south division offends the authorised doctrines of 21st century liberal philosophy. To preserve economic privileges, however, statecraft continues to operate within its sentiments.

*Timothy Kendall (2005), Review, *African Studies Review*, 48(1), p.189.

to be more useful for malign than beneficial purposes. However, we need to stress that it need not have been like this. There was nothing normal, inevitable, about the injustices that emerged in Near Eastern antiquity. People who migrated out of Africa had mastered the art of preserving harmony to sustain their missions in life. Deterrents against the temptations of idleness did work. Creativity driven by aspirations need not have ended up rupturing the co-operative spirit.

Unequal outcomes were possible, even in the most egalitarian of communities. There was no law against individuals working harder, or better, to improve their personal condition. But evidence from around the world emphasises how those who settled in urban communities could, and did, remain egalitarian. One example is the Cucuteni–Trypillia culture (c. 5050 to 2950 BCE).

The farmers located in towns across a vast territory spanning present-day Moldova, Romania and Ukraine did not need elites to organise their lives. The beautiful pottery they produced appeared in ordinary homes, not privileged centres of power (which were conspicuous by their absence). After 2,000 years, the shift in weather patterns caused the demise of the towns, some of which contained as many as 3,000 dwellings. People moved on. Researchers have wondered whether inequality caused the disappearance of this culture, but concluded that the construction of "mega-sites successfully avoided wealth inequalities between individual households".[5]

In the settlements of Egypt and the Fertile Crescent, cheating did curb the humane kind of creativity. The achievements that did occur were of the monumental kind that reinforced civil conflicts and territorial warfare. These stunted the innovations that would have furthered human evolution.

Rome illustrates the egregious effects of such irresponsible behaviour. The Roman Empire deployed a large part of its net resources to secure and sustain its dominance. At home, the culture of cheating required monumental structures (like the Colosseum), in which to amuse the people dispossessed of their farms. Abroad, viaducts and roads were built, to facilitate military might. These operational requirements increased the need for building materials like concrete, and the silver to pay for the infrastructure. That, in turn, required intense mining and smelting of silver and lead ores, the costs of which were not born out of the Rents accumulated by the nobility, but by others. Researchers have now deciphered the Arctic ice core records that measure lead pollution levels from 500 BCE to 600 CE. Europe's non-elite, rural majority paid a heavy price. Air pollution contaminated the blood of children with lead, which in turn reduced intelligence levels.[6] One ripple effect was the reduction of aspirational levels and innovative capacities.

The traces of that empire are visible across Europe today. In England, grass covered mounds mark the site of one Roman-era lead mine in the Mendip hills.[7] There are no traces, waiting to be excavated, of the innovations that might have been. Rome's culture of cheating channelled creativity away from the benign possibilities, those that would have reinforced harmony between people and the stewardship of nature.

Today, social scientists wrestle with the veneer rather than the root cause of the collapse of civilisations. Current wisdom is summarised by Eric H. Cline, professor of classics and anthropology at George Washington University. He reviewed the evidence in *1177 BC: The Year Civilisation Collapsed*. Do events in the late Bronze Age bear any resemblance to those that prevail today? Could collapse happen again? "I have long believed that the answer is yes; it's a matter of not *if* but *when*."[8] Cline does not include the formative role of Rent in his analysis. His catalogue of the crises that preceded the synchronised collapse of eight states in the eastern Mediterranean is otherwise exhaustive. Those states were related through commerce and cultural exchange. They spanned territories from Egypt, through Mesopotamia to the Aegean. Cline concludes:

> **[N]o unequivocal proof has been offered as to who or what caused...the collapse of these civilisations and the end of the Late Bronze Age.**[9]

What was beyond doubt, apparently, was the "perfect storm" of "multiple interconnected failures". Cumulatively, these led to the demise of empires and city civilisations. The one fresh insight Cline offered: the collapse was not due solely to the influx of the mysterious Sea Peoples, the migrants who sailed from the western end of the Mediterranean, who fought to occupy land in the Fertile Crescent.

Nature did contribute, with its earthquakes. Nevertheless, Cline noted, humans added to the tragedy through the synchronisation of multiple events and processes. These can be summarised under four headings. First, economics: the fragility of extended trade links. Second, the environment: droughts and famines, which prevented farmers from growing the food they needed. Third, diplomacy: the rupture of personal connections between rulers, which nullified international agreements. Fourth, politics: rebellious lower-class people storming palaces and raiding storerooms.

Other scholars focus explanations on "the concentration of power and control in the palaces", or economies skewed to favour the acquisition of bronze and other prestige goods (known today as conspicuous consumption). But no unifying theory is offered to account for the loss of vitality that foredoomed those civilisations. Cline reviews the synchronised chaos in terms of a theory of complexity. Multiple objects interact to the point where social systems were not able to sustain themselves. This theorising, however, is no more than a description of the prevailing times and of empirical events "on the ground". Something was missing from the scientific method.

An ontological enquiry

A comprehensive search for the template human personality, and behaviour, must combine archaeological and genetic evidence derived from the whole of human existence. This includes evidence from 500,000 years ago, in the Middle Pleistocene, and the discovery of *Homo bodoensis*, one of our earliest ancestors in Africa. Paleoanthropologists contest the pre-historical evidence.[10] That is why we need to crosscheck the evolutionary Rent thesis with empirical evidence excavated from civilisations buried within the last 5,000 years.

Genetics brings us closer to objective analysis when we test the evolutionary blueprint with this question: would Rent in its social form restore humanity's evolutionary mechanism for the benefit of everyone in the community? If the answer is "Yes!", then the obverse must be true: Rent in its privatised form causes disintegration, the pathological symptoms radiating out from the original crime of land enclosures.

Culture, by itself, does not exercise agency. People are the agents, with culture at their service. But what if a population has been schooled into accepting certain practices as normal, such that they confine their behaviour to attitudes that are anti-social in character? That is what the Athenians did, as elegantly summarised by Edward Gibbon (Box 5.2).

Box 5.2 **The origins of Entitlement**

In his History of the Decline & Fall of the Roman Empire, Edward Gibbon (1737-1794) – Enlightenment historian and Member of Parliament – did not employ Rent as a diagnostic tool. He did, however, describe with precision the malaise that grips society, once a sufficient number of citizens feel entitled not to work for their living. Referring to the Athenians, he concluded:

> *In the end, more than freedom, they wanted security. They wanted a comfortable life, and they lost it all – security, comfort, and freedom. When the Athenians finally wanted not to give to society but for society to give to them, when the freedom they wished for most was freedom from responsibility, then Athens ceased to be free and was never free again.*

There is one route only to that social pathology: living off the net income that others labour to produce.

Free riding, in its institutionalised form, collapses the immune system of societies. In its place, it substitutes a cultural organism which combines three elements.

- The social apparatus (statecraft, institutions, values) which prioritise the needs of the cheats.
- Compliant populations: people sustain the arrangement in the belief that it was "natural".
- Aspirations of the cheats, who do not pay for benefits received, or pay for the damage they inflict.

Collapse is inevitable, once the authentic immune system is replaced by the alien system. And so, we return to the four existential threats faced by humanity today.

Four Horsemen

The Book of Revelation was a late addition (about 95 CE) to the Christian New Testament. Its apocalyptic warnings accurately reflected the history of antiquity. Pithily, Verse 15 in Ch. 6 drew attention to "kings of the earth, and the great men, and the rich men, and the chief captains, and the mighty men, and every bondman, and every free man". The metaphors of the four horsemen reminded people of the horrors of conquest, the sword symbolising war and bloodshed; the scales representing unequal outcomes in the distribution of resources. Nothing was left to the imagination about the fourth horseman on the pale horse – Death. It brought mortality and destruction.

Figure 5.1 **The Black Hole awaits**

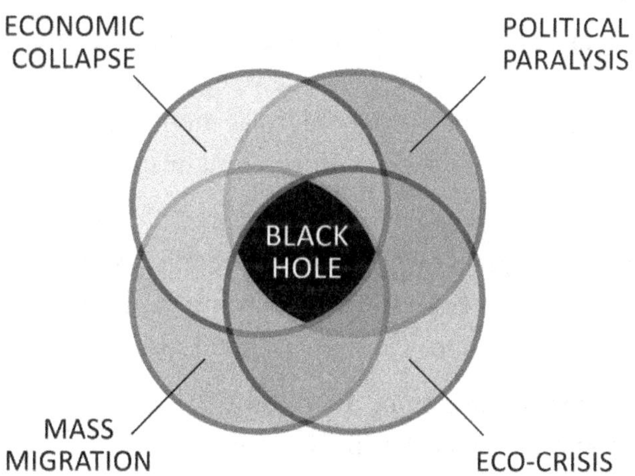

The message was clear: by confronting bad behaviour, people would be saved. They had that on the authority of God. Failure to act, on the other hand, leads to the collapse summarised in the Venn diagram (Fig. 5.1). Today, we are faced by four existential threats. If we fail to apply the one organic remedy, our species will collapse into the lurking black hole, which is waiting to claw us back into the folds of physics.

Driving blind is a fair metaphor for the state of our world in the 21st century. We remove the blinkers by acknowledging Rent as the existential flow of energy. With that insight, everything changes. Hope replaces the despair that now grips the global community of nations. The need for speed is self-evident. Autocratic politicians are willing to threaten the use of nuclear weapons, heralding what US President Joe Biden called "the prospect of Armageddon".[11]

Treating Rent as private property shapes the production and consumption behaviour of 8bn people. The globalised market pricing system pollutes every economic transaction, from local food markets to international supply chains. What are the consequences?

- *In relation to nature*: Rents originating in the use of nature's service are not devoted to protecting the environment. Outcomes include extinction of species, depletion of soil, and pollution of the air we breathe.

The costs are enormous. According to one estimate, the global economy is losing up to $25tn a year, because sectors such as agriculture, energy and fishing fail to account for how their actions fuel interconnected crises in nature, climate and human health.[12]

- *In relation to people's welfare*: dispossessed of their traditional access rights to land, people are traumatised and displaced from home communities. This triggers mass migration to Europe and the USA.

Time and again, the excuse offered for the inadequacy of support from public services is the insufficiency of funds. People work to produce sufficient funds, but a large part of that net income does not end up in the public purse at their service.

- *In relation to power*: when trust is lost in political leaders, the impulse is to transfer allegiance to Strong Men. Autocrats offer to dismantle laws and deploy violence (including wars) to solve problems.

In Europe, increasing numbers of countries have begun to succumb to the lure of Far Right populists.[13] France's National

Rally leader, Marine Le Pen, celebrated these electoral advances as "the triumph of the peoples" in favour of defence of national interests, safeguarding of identities and resurrection of sovereignties.[14]

- *In relation to statecraft*: ideology induces law-makers into persisting with policies that consistently fail to erase the problems that blight people's lives. In doing so, they prioritise the culture of cheating.

Consider what would happen if, in 2028, the four crises were forced to converge at the end of the 18-year business cycle. In 2008, when real estate markets crashed across the globe, the banks were "too big to fail". They were bailed out by governments. Today, governments are saddled with unrepayable sovereign debts. This time, they are locked in the "too big to fail" trap. Private investors will not want to bail them out. Central banks know that printing money merely makes things worse, through hyperinflation. What then?

Rent as Unifying Theory

In physics, a theory of everything remains elusive. For the Social Galaxy, the theory of Rent provides the unifying paradigm.

The prophetic voices of old were not able to spell out their warnings in mathematical equations; or elaborate remedial proposals framed in financial calculations. We can now do so, to unify our understanding of the human project in terms of a few evolutionary principles. That approach, however, stumbles on a problem. Lawmakers and their intellectual communities are marooned in false philosophies. They devise experiments in academic laboratories rather than the laboratory of life. We need to stress this barrier to survival, if there is to be hope of a global conversation taking place on an informed basis.

Once upon a time, people acted as stewards of their habitats because personal wellbeing depended on responsible behaviour. They did so with the principles of co-operation and consensus, rather than corruption and collapse. But as we have noted, with the onset of urban cities, responsible behaviour was debilitated by the diversion of Rent. Those with power fragmented the rights-with-responsibilities equation. One result was encouragement of over-consumption of natural resources. This over-consumption was not due to demographic pressures (many scholars continue to believe that "over-population" is a driving force), but the result of the willingness to cheat future generations for short-term gain. Africa is now one of the victims. Although all of the continent's countries emit just 4% of global pollution, their economies are losing on average 5% of GDP because of climate change, increasing up to 15% in some countries.[15] Humanicide is viewed as a serious prospect.[16]

To avoid repeating the mistakes of history, we need to transform the conditions that cause collapse with reforms that promote cooperation and consensus. That cannot happen, however, while scholars continue to align their theoretical work with baseless doctrines. Martin Nowak, a Harvard Professor of Biology and Mathematics, illustrates the doctrinal barriers to informed conversation. In stressing the need for altruism and cooperation, he elaborates the results of his laboratory experiments with narratives that create a false impression of the practical problems in the way of people who wish to lead fulsome lives. Despite the wealth of textual evidence, Nowak recycles the false doctrines that colour the minds of students. Two false doctrines illustrate this tragedy.

One recounts a story about the "tragedy of the commons", which Nowak says is "more relevant today than ever before". The original essay was published in 1968, but "has recently been reprinted dozens of times".[17] The problem is this. The author, Garrett Hardin (1915–2003), attributed the over-exploitation of nature in its common forms to people who behaved selfishly, without consideration of others with whom they shared those resources. The thesis made a huge impression on academia and among activists working to address the eco-crisis.

Twenty years later, Hardin was approached by Robert Andelson (1931–2003). The professor of philosophy at Auburn University,

Alabama, explained that the damage to nature was not as described in Hardin's Science article, but due to the irresponsible behaviour caused by the pricing system. Hardin revised his treatment of the tragedy, with the clear understanding that the fiscal system was at the heart of the problem. This is how he summarised the issue.

> **To serve the needs of society, responsibility needs to be defined in the following way: *An agent is fully responsible when he pays all the costs of the benefits he receives*...Irresponsibility opens the door to malfunction and uncontrollable costs...For instance, the theory extends to the capture, by speculators, of gains in the value of real estate as a result of community development.**[18]

Hardin's revision located the fiscal system at the heart of the problem of the eco-crisis. And yet, that elaboration continues to be ignored by scholars, who promote the thesis in its original form. Which is why they also then go on to recycle the false doctrine attributed to Adam Smith.[19]

Smith famously wrote that people going about their business, served their personal interests, without thinking about the common good. Smith's metaphor was the "invisible hand". Scholars are sceptical that anyone who "intends only his own gain" could be led by an invisible hand to "promote…the public interest". This was Hardin's original interpretation: self-interest could not be combined with also serving the common interest. Except that it *could*, if people working to serve personal needs also pooled the net income for investment in the common good. The symmetry of that arrangement, both moral and financial, ensures holistic outcomes. A worker churning out pin-heads on his factory's conveyor belt does not need to philosophise about fulfilling social responsibilities: all he needs to do is earn his wages and pay the location value of his home into the public purse. But scholars recycle the "invisible hand" model without including the fiscal context. Consequently, Smith's worker is characterised as a selfish individual in a selfish marketplace that renders society vulnerable to all kinds of traumas, including the environmental crisis.

By locating social problems within the Rent paradigm, the realities that surface on the ground are clarified. That makes it possible to avoid the errors of the past, if the will to do so exists. The material means to do so are available in superlinear abundance.

Superlinearity

Ants, when they co-operate, generate a pulling power 80 times their own body weight, on average. In extreme cases they can even reach over 200 times their body weight.[20] And so with humans, with one qualitative difference. Ants do not have a choice. They operate on the basis of genetic endowments that serve their queen well, but there is no debate about alternative forms of behaviour. With humans, there is a choice.

Growing food, and developing the urban lifestyle, amplified the human project by an extraordinary magnitude. But that, it turned out (as noted in Ch. 2), came at a terrible price, according to Santa Fe Institute's former president, Geoffrey West: the "dark side" characterised as greed.[21] Was this a choice on the part of the late Neolithic people who invented agriculture? The knowledge to establish institutional guardrails against "greed" was not available. That knowledge was formalised in scientific terms, beginning in the 18th century, with philosophers like Adam Smith. Why, then, do our intellectual communities continue to treat humans as no different from other species, for purpose of comparative analysis?

Fig. 5.2 illustrates the "generic laws" to which science conforms. In terms of their metabolic needs – the amount of calories required each day to remain alive – men and women are treated on a par with ants and elephants. The figure plots humans and other species by relating body mass to the metabolic rate. The straight line is interpreted as confirming that humans behave according to the same laws as guinea pigs and horses. Calorie intake scales with body weight.

For other species, the metabolic rate is defined by biology. For humans, however, bare bones subsistence is dwarfed by the need for resources that fuel the energy-hungry intellectual, aesthetic and spiritual dispositions. The fact that some species, like ants, can punch above their weight, tells us nothing about the qualitative

Figure 5.2 **The Metabolic rate of animals**

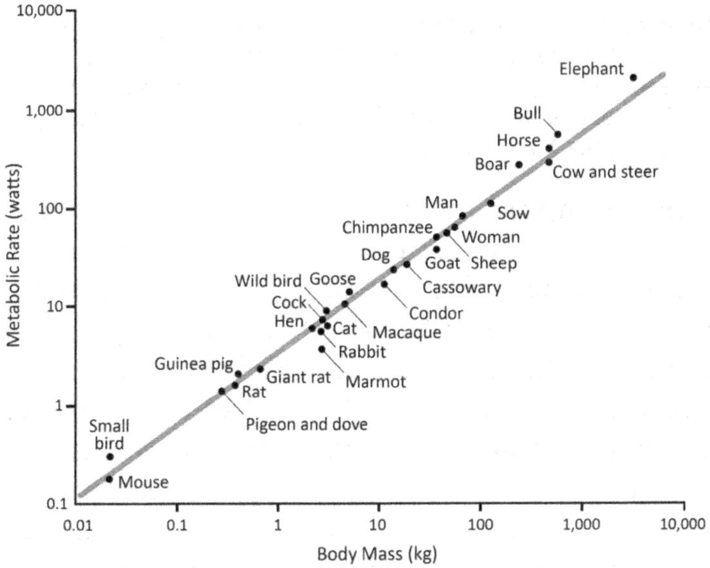

Source: Geoffrey West (2017), *op. cit*, p.3

differences. This is emphasised by West's reference to civilisation's "dark side". But the problems to which he draws attention were not a structurally intrinsic feature of the human project. Using house sizes as a proxy for location values, archaeologists have demonstrated that – at the outset of civilisation – there was nothing inevitable about greed, inequality and the rest of the sad litany to which West draws attention.[22] But in that case, why do some societies display poverty and its associated pathologies through intergenerational timescales?

On the social scale, people are pressured to conform to the culture that frames their communities. If the structure is composed of customs and practices that prioritise irresponsible behaviour; which intentionally suppresses compassion; and is animated by acquisitive greed, there will be winners and losers. That disposition, which originated in antiquity, remains with us to this day. Therefore, it is not surprising that scholars at the Santa Fe Institute, who chronicle the performance of urban life, find it daunting to make science-based predictions. They are, however, correct to register the need for a unified theory that addresses all issues, for

> **The difference between 'policy as usual' and policy led by a new quantitative understanding of cities may well be the choice between creating a "planet of slums" or finally achieving a sustainable, creative, prosperous, urbanized world expressing the best of the human spirit.**[23]

There is no mystery about the root cause of slums. Researchers continuously scrutinise the relevant clues. They pinpoint three characteristics: space (which shrinks, thanks to denser settlement and more intense use of infrastructure); increased productivity (which raises net incomes); and, through diversification, increased specialisation (which amplifies the production of net income). When combined, these characteristics increase the Rents on a scale that is proportionate to a population's social needs. But because the minds of scholars are closed to the evolutionary significance of Rent, the superlinear bonus – 15% – is celebrated without serious attention to what people *could* and *would* deliver, if liberated from the culture of cheating.

Wilful blindness

Diagnoses based on the two-factor model of economics – labour and capital – turn blind eyes on Rent. Santa Fe Institute researchers, for example, specialise in understanding the mechanisms that unify the complex worlds of physics, biology and society. They omit the role of Rent from their diagnoses, however, which necessarily circumscribes the significance of their research. That, in turn, contributes to the failures of governance, such as the inability to deliver affordable housing for everyone, or to control temperatures at levels set by human needs. The existential significance of that reality is revealed by a study of 166 countries, which found that weather patterns were intimately related to activity in all sectors of wealth creation.[24] On current trends in rising temperatures, over the next 25 years several hundreds of millions of people are consequently at risk of displacement.[25] Without effective development policies in their countries, many of them will traverse the borders of Europe and North America.

In antiquity, the people who transitioned from foraging to farming were not able to choose the evolutionary paths that best served their interests. If the knowledge had been available, it would be fair to assume that they would have established their civilisations on the co-operation-and-consensus paradigm. This did not happen, because the net resources essential for funding the earliest cities were misappropriated. Then, over the ages, the owners of Rent-yielding assets exercised veto power over the funding policies of governance.

Today, law-makers are wilfully blind. In Britain, for example, the government budgets of 1910 and 1931 provide a record of attempts to eliminate the deadly influence of cheating. With the documents available in the House of Commons Library, Britain's parliamentarians have no excuse for failing their constituents. Remedial action is urgently needed; but it can only arise when the decision-makers are correctly informed as to the structural roots of the threats facing their nations.

References Chapter 5

1 2025 Doomsday Clock Statement – Bulletin of the Atomic Scientists https://thebulletin.org/doomsday-clock/2025-statement/

2 Jared Diamond (2005), *Collapse: How Societies Choose to Fail or Survive*, London: Allen Lane, p.6.

3 Chris Wright (2024), "Singapore prime minister tries to shore up disillusioned middle class before election", *Financial Times*, Sept. 2.

4 Colin Renfrew (1978), "Trajectory Discontinuity and Morphogenesis: The Implications of Catastrophe Theory for Archaeology", *American Antiquity*, 43(2). Colin Renfrew (1979), "Systems Collapse as Social Transformation", in C. Renfrew and K.L. Cook (eds), *Transformations: Mathematical approaches to Culture Change*, New York: Academic Press.

5 Robert Hofmann *et al* (2024), "Trypillia mega-sites: a social levelling concept?", *Antiquity* 98, p.395.

6 Joseph R. McConnell *et al* (2025), "Pan-European atmospheric lead pollution, enhanced blood lead levels, and cognitive decline from Roman-era mining and smelting", *Proceedings of the National Academy of Science*, 122(3).

7 Roman-Era Lead Pollution Linked to IQ Drop Across Europe https://scitechdaily.com/roman-era-lead-pollution-linked-to-iq-drop-across-europe/

8 Erick H. Cline (2021), *1177 BC: The Year Civilization Collapsed*, Princeton: University Press, p.xv. Emphases in original.

9 *Ibid*., p.173.

10 Mirjana Roksandic, Predrag Radović *et al* (2022), "Homo bodoensis and why it matters", *Evolutionary Anthropology*, 31(5). https://doi.org/10.1002/evan.21954

11 https://www.reuters.com/world/biden-cites-cuban-missile-crisis-describing-putins-nuclear-threat-2022-10-07/

12 IPBES (2019), Global assessment report on biodiversity and ecosystem services of the Intergovernmental Science-Policy Platform on Biodiversity and Ecosystem Services. Bonn: IPBES secretariat. https://doi.org/10.5281/zenodo.3831673

13 Sam Jones (2024), "Far right set for comeback in Austria with a nod to Nazi past", *Financial Times*, Sept. 28.

14 James Crisp and James Rothwell (2024), "Le Pen hails rise of far Right across Europe after Austrian election", *Daily Telegraph*, Oct. 1.

15 https://www.uneca.org/stories/experts-call-for-more-support-as-africa-loses-significant-gdp-to-climate-change

16 Chris C. Stewart (2005), "Humanicide: From Myth to Risk", *Journal of Futures Studies*, 9(4), p.24.

17 Martin Nowak with Roger Highfield (2011), *Super Cooperators*, Edinburgh: Canongate, p.201.

18 Garrett Hardin (1991), "The Tragedy of the Unmanaged Commons", in R.V. Andelson (Ed), *Commons without Tragedy*, London: Shepheard-Walwyn, pp. 176-177.

19 Nowak, *op. cit*., p.204.

20 Madelyne Stewardson *et al* (2025), "Superefficient teamwork in weaver ants", *Current Biology*, Aug. 12.

21 West, *op. cit*, pp. 8, 286.

22 Timothy A. Kohler *et al* (2017), "Greater post-Neolithic wealth disparities in Eurasia than in North America and Mesoamerica", *Nature*, 551, 30 November.

23 Luís Bettencourt and Geoffrey West (2010), "A unified theory of urban living", *Nature*, 467, p.912.

24 M. Burke *et al* (2015), "Global non-linear effect of temperature on economic production", *Nature*, 527.

25 Chi Xu *et al* (2020), "Future of the human climate niche", *PNAS*, 117(21). https://doi.org/10.1073/pnas.1910114117

CHAPTER SIX

Genocide

Genocide is deployed by the culture of cheating as an instrumental strategy. It emerges in two forms. The primary case is the violence that displaces people from their homeland. The secondary variant arises as an incidental consequence of cheating, in which people are trapped by the culture's statecraft, and results in genocide. Gaza became such a case. What occurred was provoked by the terrorist group Hamas on October 7, 2023. By the summer of 2025, children were being starved to death on that strip of Mediterranean land. Bullets killed fathers who went in search of food. Mothers wailed as the concrete of their apartments collapsed on them. Meanwhile, ample food was parked nearby, beyond the reach of two million hungry people.

Ultimately, though unwittingly, most of us enable this inhumanity, by engaging in the market for real estate. This is a horrendous proposition: how does buying a home, to raise a family, render us complicit in genocide?

The general hypothesis asserts that the culture of cheating channels the pathologies that define our world. Instead of consensus and co-operation, the direction of travel favours deception and destruction to fund the insatiable appetites of free riding. The evidence to validate my genocide thesis, however, must demonstrate two issues beyond doubt.

- The culture of cheating was not inevitable. An alternative civil society could have emerged in antiquity, but was blocked by free riders.

- History confirms that genocidal behaviour was enshrined in statecraft, and is retained as an enabling strategy into modern times.

By delving into the evidence, we will be confronted with horrifying insights into how our behaviour is manipulated in the pursuit of unearned wealth. Central to this process is the statecraft that eviscerates the authentic human behaviour that could have emerged during the transition into agrarian civilisation. Instead, for 5,000 years, destruction and suppression punctured the aspirations of people who laboured for a better life. That history crafted genocide as a strategy intended to serve the culture of cheating. The lawyer who coined the concept of genocide provided the historical proof we need.

Raphael Lemkin (1900-1959), a Polish Jew, worked tirelessly to enshrine the crime against humanity in a declaration adopted by the embryonic United Nations, after World War 2.

> **Generally speaking, genocide does not necessarily mean the immediate destruction of a nation, except when accomplished by mass killings of all members of a nation. It is intended rather to signify a co-ordinated plan of different actions aiming at the destruction of essential foundations of the life of national groups, with the aim of annihilating the groups themselves. The objective of such a plan would be disintegration of the political and social institutions, of culture, language, national feelings, religion, and the economic existence of national groups, and the destruction of the personal security, liberty, health, dignity, and even the lives of the individuals belonging to such groups.**[1]

What was the incentive for such behaviour, if not the resources in and on the land occupied by the victim population?

Lemkin presented his account to the UN as the most important feature of genocide. Despite his efforts, it was excluded from the Convention on Genocide.

> **I defended it (cultural genocide) successfully through two drafts. It means the destruction of the cultural pattern of a group, such as the language, the traditions, the monuments, archives, libraries, churches. In brief: the shrines of the soul of a nation. But there was not enough support for the idea in the Committee...So with a heavy heart I decided not to press for it.**

If the UN had accepted his definition of genocide, might the second half of the 20th century have taken a different course? It was not to be. There was a logic in the refusal to accept Lemkin's definition. *It implicitly outlawed the root motive for genocide – the appropriation of a population's Rent-yielding resources.*[2]

After the world war, Lemkin began to write a book that chronicled the history of genocide. He wrote the Introduction, and listed the cases that he would document. These included episodes from antiquity, the Middle Ages and modern times. He died before completing his manuscript. Fortunately, he did complete some chapters. These document the way the crime spanned civilisations from ancient times.[3] His cases relate to the primary reason for genocides – the land grabs, which entailed the erasure of the occupants on those territories.

We need to supplement Lemkin's account with one vital additional insight. If genocide is intrinsic to the culture of cheating, specific cases cannot be treated as idiosyncratic deviations from a historical sequence. They must feature as part of an intentional process designed to enrich the conquerors who grab other people's territories.

Gaza falls within the second variant of genocide. The history that culminated in Gaza, verifies genocide as one policy instrument at the disposal of the culture of cheating. This history begins in ancient Egypt and the victimisation of the Jews.

Ostracism

Around 1,600 BCE, Jacob and his family, numbering seventy persons, migrated to Egypt. They settled down and proved to be good citizens. Why, then, were they eventually viewed as a threat to the power of the pharaohs? Their crime was to defend the integrity of their religion, a spiritual life that encouraged adherents to create their heaven on Earth, without waiting until they were dead. That belief system nurtured an independent consciousness. It required the Jews to arbitrate between good and bad behaviour; to distinguish right from wrong. That meant they retained the capacity to judge the actions of earthly powers. *The spiritual life provided guidance from an alternative authority, which posed a practical problem for those who needed to manipulate people's minds.*

For the roots of the animosity against the Hebrew people, we have to go back to about 1,300 BCE and the reign of Rameses III. They lived in a fertile area called Goshen, which they farmed for three centuries with royal permission. That happy history came to an end when Rameses decided to build a capital in the Nile Delta. He needed cheap labour, so he fabricated a false narrative: the farmers of Goshen were foreigners who (one day) might become a threat to the security of his state. The solution: turn the farmers into serfs. According to Exodus 1: 13-14, "And the Egyptians made the children of Israel to serve with rigor: And they made their lives bitter with hard bondage in mortar and in brick, and in all manner of service in the field." Not content with turning them into bricklayers, the Pharaoh issued a genocidal edict.

> **When ye do the office of midwife to the Hebrew women...if it be a son, then ye shall kill him; but if it be a daughter, then she shall live (Exodus 1:16).**

The Jews decided to exit Egypt. Moses told them about a Promised Land, in Palestine, that was rich in milk and honey. The rest is tragic history. As pharaonic power grew, so the vitality of their civilisation dissipated down the Nile. When the mysterious migrants called the Boat People sailed in from the west, they were able to overrun the first extensive civilisation on Earth, and contribute to the collapse of the Bronze Age. King Merneptah (1236–23 BCE) put up a good fight, but the migrants could not be stopped. Egypt was hostage to an energy-sapping culture.

As for the Jews, anti-Semitic sentiments were disseminated by "the Greek retelling of Ancient Egyptian prejudices".[4] After Manetho, an Egyptian priest, "The picture usually painted is one of universal and virulent anti-Judaism". Examples of anti-Jewish sentiment are recorded in Alexandria, on the western edge of the Nile River delta, in the 3rd century BCE.[5] From the origins in antiquity, through to modern times, the Hebrew people were hounded by those who needed scapegoats to sustain the culture of cheating. It was that culture that led to the genocide perpetrated by Nazi Germany and, in turn, drove the surviving Jews to secure their survival by returning to the Promised Land. There, operating with the prevailing tools of statecraft, they supplanted Palestinians from their homes to create the state of Israel. And so, nearly 80 years later, we end up in Gaza and the latest episode in genocide, as verified by a United Nations commission,[6] and Omer Barto,[7] who had served in the Israeli Army before migrating to America, where he is Professor of Holocaust and Genocide Studies at Brown University.[8]

The proximate cause of the genocide was the atrocity in which Hamas killed 1,195 Israelis and took 250 hostages back to Gaza. Why did these Palestinians commit this crime against humanity? The answer is rooted in the reason why the Jews fled to Palestine after the holocaust. They supplanted the Palestinians to create a Jewish state. That deed was the result of Hitler's plan to cleanse the German folk; and to grab other people's territories east of Germany. But Hitler, in turn, might not have achieved the power to commit his crime, but for the intervention of Prussia's landowning nobility.

Anti-Semitism was not a socially significant force until the Reich came into being in 1871.[9] With the creation of a centralised state, the political power's need for "the Other" kicked in, which is how we arrive at Hitler. He was not able to secure a majority in the election of 1933. Nevertheless, he was appointed Chancellor by the Junkers, the landowners of Prussia.

The Prussian nobility supported Hitler because they feared the onset of socialism. They believed the Nazis could curtail that threat, and that they, the Junkers, could control Hitler. Germany's President, Paul von Hindenburg, and the Chancellor, Otto von Bismarck, were Junkers. Harrison Brown, an English journalist with a front seat in the events of 1933, noted how "The Nazis were hauled into office by the Junkers and the industrialists after they had passed the zenith of their influence and had begun to disintegrate".[10] One result was the immolation of six million Jews in gas ovens.

One of Raphael Lemkin's chapters deals with how the Prussian aristocracy executed the genocide of the Herero in South-West Africa in the late 19th century.[11] By incremental steps back through such episodes in history, we end up with the anti-Semitism that originated in ancient Egypt. Louis H. Feldman (1926 –2017), an American Professor of Classics and Literature at Yeshiva University, noted that "one of the great puzzles that has confronted the students of anti-Semitism is the alleged shift from pro-Jewish statements found in the first pagan writers who mention the Jews... to the vicious anti-Jewish statements thereafter, beginning with Manetho about 270 BCE". There was no puzzle about the origins of anti-Semitism. The Semitic mind-set preserved the capacity for independent thinking that was perceived as being at odds with the needs of the culture of cheating.

The Gaza genocide was the logical outcome of the culture of cheating, whose statecraft obstructed attempts to enable Jews and Palestinians to co-exist in Palestine.

Are we *really* free?

Why, in our age of science, and with the freedom we allegedly enjoy to think and communicate, do our intellectual communities remain silent on the causal roots of genocide? To conclusively prove that genocide is a characteristic of the culture of cheating, we need to demonstrate that free riders captured humanity in all the realms of being.

Britain, for example, although it celebrates the notions of freedom and equality, did not escape the traps laid by free riding. Cheating was purposefully embedded in three elements in the shared mind-set: language, and the ideals of the Enlightenment; diagnosis, guided by empirical methodology; and the efficacy of politics, as ordained by the UK's unwritten constitution.

Language

The Enlightenment was a philosophical movement that swept across the UK from the 17th to the early 19th centuries. It stressed reason, liberty, religious tolerance and progress through respect for natural rights. Within that framework, how did the culture of cheating sustain itself?

The landed aristocracy understood the kinetic power of words. Language was manipulated to pay lip service to the spirit of the Enlightenment while discriminating in favour of the privileged minority. Forensic language was relegated to the natural sciences. For public policy, emotive terminology was the name of the game. By this means, it was possible to promise to solve problems without identifying Rent as the problematic issue. So, today, we face existential threats. How are these treated by our intellectual communities?

Thanks to science, we know all we need to know about the existential nature of the threats and their single root cause. That is why our intellectual communities ought to have progressed beyond the resort to emotive language that inspires divisive political doctrines.[12] In reality, we are still stuck with the symbols of the past. An example is offered by Luke Kemp, the author of *Goliath's Curse* and research associate at the Cambridge-based Centre for the Study of Existential Risk. His diagnosis (unintentionally) distracts attention from the one remedial policy that could save humanity.

To draft laws in language that would heal the deep wounds in the body politic, parliamentary draftsmen need precisely defined concepts. Luke's narrative does not contribute to that goal. He says we are "cursed" by problematic nation-states, which he calls "goliaths". Their quest is for "lootable resources", which implies piratical interventions rather than the organised process of statecraft that extracts net incomes from working populations. The earliest farmers generated a "surplus"; as if those Rents were not as intrinsic as wages to the daily needs of the producers themselves.

Individuals driven by the quest for "status" displayed "greed".[13] Each of those concepts sends people down linguistic rabbit holes where they get lost in the dark.

Empiricism

Empiricism was central to the doctrines of the Enlightenment. Knowledge would be accumulated by contesting old ideas. And yet, today, three centuries worth of data fails to ring alarm bells. Cyclical patterns that emerge with eerie regularity are not the product of random events, or exogenously imposed disturbances. So why do academics fail to ask awkward questions? Take the case of differences in life expectancy.

According to Carl Benedikt Frey, an Oxford University scholar, early in the industrial revolution "In major industrial cities like Manchester and Glasgow, life expectancy at birth was some staggering ten years shorter than the national average".[14] According to conventional wisdom, "worsening of mortality in towns would have exacerbated the trade-offs between health and wealth entailed by migration to towns, and depressed the 'biological standard of living'".[15] But how is that trade-off explained?

Frey attributes the 10-year gap, which remains with us to this day, to a "technology trap". Innovations increased productivity, but also caused the obsolescence of skills that reduced people to poverty and lower-wage jobs. But why attribute this "trap" to technology? The ripple effects from economic progress were structurally determined, as prescribed by property rights and fiscal policies. The net gains from innovation could have been channelled into reskilling displaced workers, or smoothing their transition to new occupations under terms that ensured egalitarian outcomes. Increased Rents, however, were not used for that purpose. Instead, they were devoted to conspicuous consumption or the purchase of tax-privileged land.

For 250 years of industrial activity, western societies were, indeed, trapped; but not by technology.

Statecraft

The gruesome saying "There's more than one way to skin a cat" means there is a choice. In relation to net income, it evokes the multiple ways in which Rents were extracted out of a society for private use. The conduits for that extraction became more complex, once the economy reduced its dependence on agriculture. The outcomes, however, were always the same. In the 17th century: the main conduit for extracting Rent was the ownership of farmland. In the 18th century: capital that funded factory-based production enabled entrepreneurs to extract some of the Rents. In the 19th century: corporations intensified Rent extraction on a global scale (as, for example, Britain deploying violence to force China to accept the import of opium for its drug addicts).

Figure 6.1 **Real house price index**

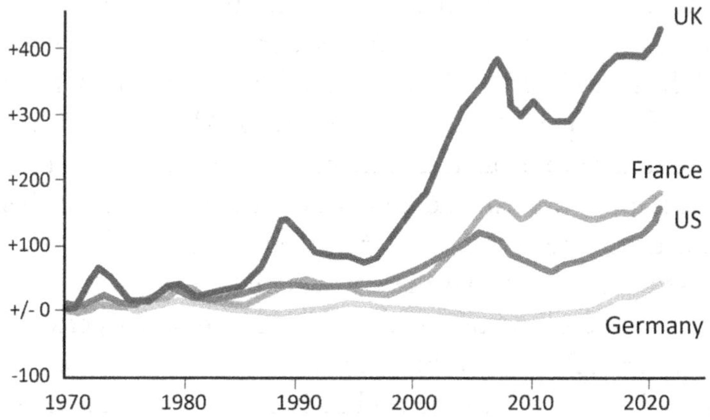

Source: ONS, STATISTICA, HM Treasury

In the 20th century: high finance carved out an increased share of Rents through mortgages for the residential market. This is illustrated in Fig. 6.1. Statecraft caused the cyclical boom/busts in the economy. After World War 2, the increase in real house prices reveals three complete property cycles. Germany was an initial exception. Note that house prices serve as proxies for land prices. They peaked just before the recessions of 1974, 1992 and 2010.

The data for the 2020s promises a re-run of the cycle, with house prices peaking in 2026, and the business cycle ending in 2028. The upward thrust is driven by Rent. The trends in bricks and mortar travel in the opposite direction, as the value of buildings depreciate over time.

But why do governments permit the predictable disruptions associated with property boom/busts? An IMF working paper acknowledges that "unbalanced developments in real estate markets can also be an important factor contributing to vulnerabilities and possibly crises in the financial sector". It notes, however, the "lack of good quality and timely data [from] real estate markets". Most international databases "do not include real estate indicators – such as prices, rents, vacancy rates, construction costs, real estate lending, and stock prices of real estate companies".[16] How can we explain that void in the data? Was it that "the system" did not want to know the facts?

The 18-year periodicities tell us that the cycles are caused by something in the structure of the system. The cycle is not a secret; certainly not to Gordon Brown, one of Britain's former Chancellors of the Exchequer. When he entered HM Treasury in 1997, I wrote to him to explain that he had 10 years in which to reform fiscal policy, to prevent the 2007 peak in house prices. Otherwise, I warned, the peak would be followed by havoc. He repeatedly promised Parliament that there would be no more housing boom/busts, but he took no remedial action. House prices peaked in the last quarter of 2007, and the rest was predictable history.[17]

In 2023, Brown was the lead author of a book that alerted the world to *Permacrisis*. This offered *A Plan to Fix a Fractured World*. The authors included a Nobel Prize winner and the president of a Cambridge University college. Their diagnosis linked the 2008 "housing sector collapse" to the financial sector, with no reference to the irresponsible behaviour licensed by statecraft (at the time of the crash, Brown was the UK's Prime Minister). They discuss "the next financial crisis" without offering the timing of that event. They placed their faith in "new models [that] can bring new prosperity, higher productivity…sustainable pathways to development", without proposing effective reforms to property rights and fiscal policies. Instead, they relied on technology to raise productivity; failing to acknowledge that new technology raises net incomes that elevate land prices which are the root cause of the collapse of property markets.[18]

Statecraft, and the intellectual communities that presume to inform law-makers on how to conduct governance, are *in hoc* to the culture of cheating. The individuals to whom I refer are not outliers. They are representative of how the culture of cheating triumphed, in capturing the collective consciousness of even brilliant intellectuals and sincere statesmen.

False consciousness

In the Indictment I lay out in Ch. 7, I trace the culture of cheating back to antiquity to establish how the free riders of old, by capturing culture, deprive us of the freedom to realise authentic human aspirations.

This verdict on property rights will provoke some people to retreat into denial. I acknowledge that it is hard to relate personal circumstances to the cheating that drives the outcomes to which I have alluded. That is why, in acknowledging the harrowing implications for "ordinary" people, we need to burrow deep into the behaviour of cheating. Otherwise, we will fail to create the global conversations we need, if we are to face up to reality. One starting point is the need to acknowledge the state of false consciousness.

The concept of a collective consciousness that has been intentionally manipulated will be viewed with suspicion. It is not consistent with the idea that we are free agents who enjoy the benefits of the Enlightenment. Most of us are not aware that our minds are coloured by an alien doctrine. Humanity has been subjected to mental conditioning for five millennia, ever since kings began to embed their images on coins of their realms.

If cheating has captured the collective consciousness, this should be revealed in the way we conduct economics. Branko Milanovic, a distinguished economist at the City University of New York, offers one point of entry into this discussion.[19] He subjected global inequality to forensic study, and concluded that this state of affairs could not be altered "if the losers remain disorganised and subject to false consciousness".[20] The gains from globalisation would remain unevenly distributed, but Milanovic was uncomfortable with his formulation of the problem.

> **I do not like the term 'false consciousness' because it seems to imply that there is an 'authentic consciousness' which I do not believe exists. I use it because I lack a better term. What I mean by it is that middle class and poor people are being diverted, largely by design, from looking after their own economic interests into caring about other concerns, especially social and religious ones that are often divisive.[21]**

In his view, this mental condition did not necessarily arise "from any sort of backroom conspiracy, but rather from a collectively manufactured elite consensus".

In terms of practical outcomes, what is the difference between a backroom conspiracy, and a "collectively manufactured elite consensus" – when the elites control the tools of mass communication? Take the case of the UK's landowners and their power to muzzle the masses through their control of Parliament. For centuries, they kept the landless peasants under control. To facilitate their free riding on the backs of the working poor, they disguised the scale of their ownership of land. That explains their fury when, in the 19th century, the Ordinance Survey started to map Britain to a large scale. The aristocrats attacked the government for allowing this initiative! The maps "exposed the size of their landholdings, and buildings so deep in private estates that they were well shielded from public view".[22]

Based on Milanovic's account, is he a victim of false consciousness? This is implied by his orthodox approach to economics. He prioritises the two-factor model (labour and capital), not the classical three factors (land, labour and capital). This leads him to the conclusion that the "most significant contributor to inequality" is "capital income". Capital, as he acknowledges, is mobile (so it cannot include land, which is immobile). The owners of capital can escape taxation by moving to tax havens (they cannot take land with them). But we are expected to believe that the balance of power lay with capitalists, not the Rentlords.

Based on the two-factor model, Milanovic's mind is diverted from the politically distinctive influence of the owners of Rent-yielding assets. So when he mentions rents, the analysis is confined to the struggle between labour and capital.[23] Missing is the seminal role played by the owners of land. Also absent is the optimum policy for the distribution of equity and the realisation of efficiency in the markets. This is illustrated by his discussion on taxation, and his comparison of Taiwan and Canada.

Taiwan enjoyed lower tax rates and a smaller government than Canada. And yet, both countries achieved similar metrics on the Gini inequality index. For Canada to match Taiwan, it had to engage in a massive tax transfer of income. Taiwan engages in almost no redistribution.[24] How do we account for this contrast? Milanovic's readers are not informed that the difference is attributable to the philosophy of Sun Yat-sen, the first president of the Republic of China. He advocated Rent as public revenue. So, when Dr Sun's party (the Kuomintang) was driven onto Formosa by the Communists in 1948, it instituted a land-and-tax reform that lay the foundations for the thriving free society that became Taiwan (much to the *chagrin* of the Chinese Communist Party).[25]

But we cannot appreciate the extent of the traumatic nature of false consciousness by confining diagnosis to individual behaviour. Its malign influence originates in the cultural milieu. This brings us back to Lemkin's definition of genocide, and the reason why it was rejected by the western powers that steered the formation of the United Nations as a global institution.

Towards an indictment

Mark Mazower, the professor of history and world order studies at Columbia University, explored the influences that shaped the UN and its affiliated institutions. His appraisal of the agreement to enact the Universal Declaration on Human Rights explained why Lemkin's definition of genocide could not be adopted.

The USA could not countenance the prospect of a foreign agency "meddling in domestic affairs, especially in the South".[26] Lemkin's definition of genocide rendered the US vulnerable, because of the treatment of black citizens. And so, in the end, the convention was reduced to a declaration on *individual* human rights. The practical outcome was summarised by Mazower in the following terms.

> **[T]he voting down of the cultural genocide clause revealed the deep misgivings many states had at allowing their own actions to be brought before an international court. Once passed, the convention fell into abeyance, and became little more than a plaything of the Cold War confrontation. No international penal tribunal was set up as it had envisaged and its existence on paper did nothing to deter the numerous examples of state-organized violence that erupted in the 1950s and 1960s across the world.**[27]

Colonialism played its part in narrowing the UN agenda to preclude the cultural approach. Thus, one of the influential voices was Jan Smuts (1870–1950), the South African prime minister who combined military and statesmanship roles, through which he became a prominent voice in the aftermath of the world war. Back home, he was a segregationist, the policy that led to apartheid. Through his influence, the small nations of Africa did not have a voice in the corridors of power, where the terms of the UN declarations were being mooted. Thus,

> **when Smut's preamble called for the United Nations to 're-establish faith in fundamental human rights, in the sanctity and ultimate value of human personality, in the equal rights of men and women, and nations large and small,' he was not committing himself to the dismantling of the segregationist state in South Africa, still less to that of the British Empire as a whole.**[28]

The cultures annihilated by European powers, when they seized vast territories in Africa and the Americas, were not to be represented in any declaration on genocide.

The culture of cheating triumphed! When the Convention on the Prevention and Punishment of the Crime of Genocide was adopted by the UN General Assembly on 9 December, 1948, there was no risk that nations locked into the culture of cheating would be brought to book. The refusal to adopt Lemkin's definition of genocide meant that the community of nations lacked an effective doctrine to guide attempts at preventing the massacres of the post-war decades. These stretched from Rwanda in the Global South, to Bosnia in the European north and Cambodia in the Asian east.

This history of civilisation leaves us with an outlook apparently devoid of hope. How do we overcome that despair? We need an informed conversation that explains how the barriers to the better future can be overcome. I initiate that conversation in Ch. 7, by proposing that we indict the culture of cheating in the court of public opinion.

That conversation needs to be based on an honest understanding of the full facts. That means we cannot proceed on the terms proposed by Maurice Saatchi, who made his fortune as an advertising tycoon in Britain. In a newspaper article, he explored the prospect of indicting the UK Government. Given Parliament's sovereignty and Crown immunity, he acknowledged the practical difficulties of an indictment. Nonetheless, he formulated his charges. In doing so, he reveals the severe limits to the consciousness of the governing class that shapes Britain's destiny.[29]

Saatchi expressed anger with the waste in the public sector. He desired small government, and a reduction in the funds spent on people's welfare. We are invited to believe that this would sponsor economic growth. He overlooked the needs of the population, which would entail an *increase* in public spending on things like health, and the need to remediate the historic damage inflicted under the pricing system authorised by the culture of cheating (which includes damage to the natural environment). He does not point out that, even under the deadweight losses of current fiscal policies, *people produce enough to cover their social needs*. That the funding is not available is due to the fact that a large slice of socially created net revenue is diverted into private pockets. And so, we are treated to the standard linguistic analysis, which reveals the psychological prejudices embedded in the authorised paradigm.

Independence Day, for example, is acclaimed as the point in the year when people stop "working for the government". That was when they became free to work for themselves. Reality check: people do not work for the government. People pay taxes to fund the services that they require. Elected governments act as their agents. For tactical purposes, however, the culture of cheating has to separate taxes from services. Which is why taxation is characterised as "raids" on people's incomes. Raids, of course, are violent, if not unlawful. But from where would governments collect revenue to fund public services, if not from the public?

Taxes are, indeed, arbitrary and discriminatory. To characterise them as "raids", however, is to purposefully colour minds against government. In doing so, attention is diverted from the policy that would be neither arbitrary nor discriminatory.

The Saatchi formulation of an indictment would quickly be discredited in a court of law. But in the court of public opinion, people would be left bewildered. Saatchi does not offer clarity. All he could offer was the hope that someone should "take away the stale pudding now on our plate and bring us a lovely, big, freshly baked cake". Does that enlighten anyone as to the justice-based, efficient source of public finance? I suggest that it merely deepens frustration with the failures of governance, which tempts people to shift their allegiance to autocrats.

My indictment is framed against governance that persists in depriving people of the freedom to enjoy the symmetry forged by our ancient ancestors. That symmetry was based on the triadic elements of the human project: the capacity of individuals to exercise agency; the power of the moral life to enforce codes of behaviour; and, the generosity of nature.

References Chapter 6

1 Rafael Lemkin (1944), *Axis Rule in Occupied Europe*, Washington, DC: Carnegie Endowment for International Peace, p.79.

2 Fred Harrison (2012), *The Traumatised Society*, London: Shepheard-Walwyn, p. IX.

3 Raphael Lemkin (2012), *Lemkin on Genocide*, Edited and Introduction by Steven Leonard Jacobs, Lanham, Maryland: Lexington Books.

4 Louis H. Feldman (1996), *Studies in Hellenistic Judaism*, Berlin: Brill, p.177.

5 Edward H. Flanner (1985), *The Anguish of the Jews: Twenty-Three Centuries of Antisemitism*, Mahwah, NJ: Paulist Press. pp. 11–12.

6 https://www.ohchr.org/en/press-releases/2025/09/israel-has-committed-genocide-gaza-strip-un-commission-finds

7 Omer Barto (2025), "I'm a Genocide Scholar. I Know It When I See It", *New York Times*, July 15.

8 Omer Barto (2023), *Genocide, Holocaust and Israel-Palestine*, London: Bloomsbury.

9 Giles MacDonogh (1994), *Prussia: The Perversion of an Idea*, London: Sinclair-Stevenson, p.346.

10 Harrison Brown (1934), "Junker versus Nazi", *Current History*, 39(6), p.668. Brown had to make a quick exit from Germany because his "bold criticism of the new regime made it dangerous for him to remain there".

11 Lemkin, *op. cit*, pp.267-277.

12 Franklin Obeng-Odoom (2025), "Property and Power", *Journal of Economic Issues*, 59(3). DOI: 10.1080/00213624.2025.2535935

13 Luke Kemp (2025), *Goliath's Curse: The History and Future of Societal Collapse*, London: Penguin.

14 Carl Benedikt Frey (2019), *The Technology Trap*, Princeton: Princeton University Press, p. 8.

15 Romola J. Davenport (2020), "Urbanization and mortality in Britain, c. 1800–50", *Economic History Review*, 73(2), p.481.

16 Paul Hilbers *et al* (2001), Real Estate Market Developments and Financial Sector Soundness, IMF WP/01/129, p.28.

17 Fred Harrison (2010), *2010: The Inquest*, London: DA Horizons, pp. 9, 13, 15-17.

18 Gordon Brown, Mohamed A. El-Erian, Michael Spence with Reid Lidow (2023), *Permacrisis: A Plan to Fix a Fractured World*, London: Simon & Schuster, pp. 131, 282, 286-87.

19 Milanovic formerly served as lead economist in the World Bank's Research Department. He is a visiting professor at the London School of Economics. His publications have been celebrated with prizes.

20 Branko Milanovic (2016), Global Inequality: *A New Approach for the Age of Globalization*, Cambridge, MASS: Belknap Press, p.217.

21 *Ibid.* p. 201-202.

22 Simon Heffer (2025), "The maps that world rulers hoped no one would see", *Daily Telegraph*, Nov. 1.

23 *Op. cit.*, p. 106.

24 *Ibid.*, p.219.

25 Fred Harrison (2008), *The Silver Bullet*, London: IULVT, pp. 95-99.

26 Mark Mazower (2009), *No enchanted Palace: The End of Empire and the Ideological Origins of the United Nations*, Princeton: University Press, p.131.

27 *Ibid.*, p. 132.

28 *Ibid.*, p.64.

29 Maurice Saatchi (2025), "The People v UK Government: British citizens are now slaves of the state", *Sunday Telegraph*, Nov. 9.

Part 2

The Making of a Failed State

PROLOGUE

Life and Death

THE existential role of Rent will be denied, either out of self-interest, or because of the horrific implications. But we cannot ignore the claim that the appropriation of net income for self-serving purposes is a threat to humanity.

How could the deniers falsify the thesis? By demonstrating that proto-humans evolved without producing net resources; that they were not self-creators, and that proprietorial ownership is not determined by evolutionary process. If the deniers prove that *Homo sapiens* evolved without the aid of net resources – without energy that exceeded their daily metabolic needs – they might also be demonstrating that Rent did not precede the onset of civilisation. In that case, the "surplus" originated with agriculture, and was not spoken for before the onset of urban settlements. In which case, those who assumed leadership can make a case for being the legitimate owners of Rent.

I will approach the interrogation of the Rent thesis via an alternative route.

To validate the existential sanctity of net resources, I will seek to prove that the private accumulation of Rent is the killer of our species. That, beyond doubt, Rent privatisation delivers the mortal punch at three levels of human existence.

Chapter 8 investigates the proposition that, at the personal level, privatisation results in deaths via the psychological impact on individuals.

Chapter 9 interrogates the social process: do deaths arise on an inter-generational scale?

Chapter 10 approaches the killing syndrome from the holistic viewpoint. If it is true that free riding is driven by an insatiable appetite, our species is locked into a death loop that ends with extinction.

To focus diagnosis, we need a case study that features the elements that are disputed by the deniers. For reasons explained in Ch. 7, the ideal case is provided by the United Kingdom.

Having accumulated the evidence, what then?

To animate conversation with cathartic effects at both the individual and societal levels, I propose that we address the issues in the form of an indictment. If the privatisation of Rent is the cause of the most heinous crimes against humanity, it must be abolished. We cannot rely on the ancestral strategy – shaming. Laws are needed to amend the pricing system. This will only happen if enough people forge a democratic majority in favour of a financial mechanism that would deliver peace and prosperity for everyone.

We all share a personal responsibility for taking the appropriate action. That responsibility stems from one of the primary evolutionary motives: the wish to deliver, to our children, a better life than the one we enjoyed. That entails the following implication: if the foundations of the social system harbour a fatal flaw, and if we fail to take remedial action, we are culpable for the outcomes.

To aid our deliberations, I have framed the indictment within three propositions.

- The institutions, values and codes of conduct we bestow on our children, cause deaths on a callous basis.
- Language nurtures children into accepting multiple deprivations that are unbecoming of civilised society.
- Humanity is not a lost cause. Humane sentiments, if activated, would empower people to enjoy full lives.

We begin by considering whether there is something fundamentally wrong with the doctrine of the "rule of law". This rule enforces human rights, while remaining silent on reciprocal obligations: our social responsibilities. Is that why the culture of cheating has not been outlawed?

Britain, through colonialism, planted the culture of cheating in much of the rest of the world. That is one reason why the UK serves as the best case for understanding how the cultural virus was immersed across the planet.

Democratic conversation unclutters minds, and achieves consensus on appropriate courses of action. Two articles in the *Financial Times* illuminate the terms of the conversation on which we need to embark.

Eight distinguished economists offered an analysis of how the Starmer Labour Party, which was elected to govern Britain in 2024, would "have a real chance of genuinely fixing the foundations of the UK economy and ushering in the period of national renewal" if it increased investment.[1] That renewal was "so sorely needed". Absent from their diagnosis, however, was any reference to the deadweight effects of taxes on "fixing the foundations". If their diagnosis is correct, that the "root of many of the problems we now face as a country" could be addressed without restructuring the fiscal system, our indictment would serve no purpose.

On the next page of the *Financial Times*, however, was an article by Martin Wolf. He argued: "Economists do not know which key to turn to deliver growth".[2] In his view, effective governance would have to include

- higher spending on investment such as infrastructure

- liberalising the planning system to free the property market
- encouraging innovation and the supply of risk capital
- opening the economy to innovators from abroad

Wolf asked: how could all of this be achieved? His plan included reform of the way Britain was taxed, "and of land in particular".

Could a phased-in removal of taxes on earned incomes, replacing the revenue with a direct charge on Rent, yield the benefits itemised by Wolf? Who better to consult than John Maynard Keynes (1883–1946), the single most influential economist of the 20th century? He was a Fellow of King's College, Cambridge, who, as reward for his services, was elevated to the House of Lords as a baron.

In the 1930s, Keynes developed a theory of how governments ought to operate. He also offered a prediction: 100 years in the future – in 2030 – people would be working a 15-hour week. A wonderful prospect! *Earning our living by working three hours a day.*[3] And yet, today, we not only work more than double those hours; the quality of life of a significant number of people in rich western countries is bedevilled by pathologies such as mental illness and addiction to drugs. Ultimately, I contend, these are manifestations of a single root cause, which did not feature in Keynes' theorising. He simply wished it away.

In 1925, he declared that "land" played no part in his model of society.

In Keynes' view, issues like systemically-induced unemployment did require attention. But in that case, what should attract government remedial action?

> **Some will say — the Land Question. Not I — for I believe that this question...has now become, by reason of a silent change in the facts, of very slight political importance.**[4]

Even as he penned those words, frenetic land speculation was driving up the price of Florida's sand dunes to astronomical levels, triggering the land boom that provoked the stock market Crash of '29.[5] That led, in turn, to the Depression of the '30s.

Following World War 2, Keynesianism was embedded in the minds and models of the intellectuals who advised lawmakers.

The collective consciousness of the masses was marinated into accepting that politicians could manage risks in the markets by other means. Until, that is, the hollowness of the promises turned the masses against their elected representatives; many of whom, in frustration, switched allegiance to would-be autocrats like Donald J. Trump, the President who vowed to be a dictator on Day 1.[6]

I acknowledge that the story I elaborate is dis-spiriting. But if it is true that the social system engineers deaths on a systemic scale; and that the extinction of other species stem from the pricing system that transmits the killer syndrome, then it is incumbent on all of us to face reality, and act honestly.

References Part 2, Prologue

1 Lord Gus O'Donnell *et al* (2024), "UK national renewal requires step change in public investment", *Financial Times*, Sept. 16.

2 Martin Wolf (2024), "Reeves must produce a credible growth plan", *Financial Times*, Sept. 16.

3 J.M. Keynes (1930), Economic Possibilities for our Grandchildren, in *Essays in Persuasion*, New York: W.W.Norton, 1963.

4 J.M. Keynes (1925), "Am I a Liberal?" *The Nation and Athenæum*, Aug. 8 and 15.

5 https://fcit.usf.edu/florida/lessons/ld_boom/ld_boom1.htm

6 https://apnews.com/article/trump-hannity-dictator-authoritarian-presidential-election-f27e7e9d7c13fabbe3ae7dd7f1235c72

CHAPTER SEVEN

Indictment

If we are hostages of the culture of cheating, and therefore denied access to the holistic remedial policies, cheating is the ultimate crime.

Rent is the evolutionary product that combines the resources emanating from nature, and from the Social Galaxy. If this is correct, the blueprint delivers the balanced, dynamic characteristics of the human project. It also proves that shaming the would-be free riders was an existential imperative.

To test this thesis, we will scrutinise the proposition that unscrambling the evolutionary blueprint is perilous for humanity. If the facts support that conclusion, we have no choice but to acknowledge that we must indict and judge the culture of cheating before the court of public opinion.

The indictment is not levelled against individuals who benefit from the culture. We all need to unite behind the cause of justice. Through forgiveness and informed conversations, strategies can be evolved to ensure that everyone gains by complying with the rights-with-responsibilities formula. To achieve that outcome, however, we need to acknowledge that a criminal act was committed and continues to be perpetrated.

The implications could not be more serious. I allege that the European model of democracy was structured to propagate the most egregious of crimes, a direct assault on what it means to be human. People die on an epic scale, every year, without anyone – or anything – being held accountable. To sustain this indictment, therefore, I need to provide evidence of

- motive: the inducements that encourage the crime;
- guilty minds (*mens rea*): as revealed in deeds; and
- the culture's fingerprints all over the crime scenes.

There is one reason, above all, why the UK best serves as our case study. At the outset of modernity, the British Isles nurtured a culture that was as close as we can hope to get to the circumstances that prevailed in pre-dynastic antiquity. Gaelic clans occupied Scotland. Safe behind Hadrian's Wall, which was constructed by the Roman Empire, the Scots were free to evolve their communities according to ancestral principles. Therefore, how they gravitated out of the clan model lays bare the processes and results of modern culture.

This analysis is central to understanding what went wrong in antiquity; how the emerging model of civilisation was deformed at the outset; and the consequences that rippled through the millennia to modern times. When we view Gaza as behaviour sponsored by statecraft, we know that something did go seriously wrong with the human project. Gaza was not an aberration. It was the culmination of a process spanning three millennia. We need a precise analysis of the history and social mechanisms that lead to such tragedies, to determine whether we are, indeed, hostages of the culture of cheating. In this exercise, we are aided by the science of epidemiology.

Epidemiology is a medical discipline that traces symptoms from root causes. Applied to the culture of cheating, we can trace the ripple effects that emanate from first order deeds – the enclosure of nature's commons for selfish ends. The ripples course through the second, third etc. order effects. This diagnostic process lays bare the traumas that rupture people's employment prospects, the lives of their families and the resilience of their communities.

Table 7.1 **Architecture of the culture of cheating, and its inter-generational consequences**

I Laws	II Governance	III Society	IV Psycho-biology
Property rights to favour privatised rent	Taxation ordains sub-optimum economy	Enclosures normalised via indoctrination	Displacement triggers mental traumas
↓	↓	↓	↓
Asset owners relieved of corresponding responsibilities	Govenments deprived of revenue resort to debt	Communities ruptured: spatial apartheid and class conflict	Language exploits the kinetic power of words
↓	↓	↓	↓
Perverse price signals exploit people and habitats	Scramble to "get on the property ladder"	Loss of trust in politicians; people seek alternative leaders	Personality disorders and premature deaths

The evidence can be assembled via four routes (Table 7.1). First, the laws enacted to discriminate in favour of those who own Rent-yielding assets. Second, the accommodating revenue system enforced by government. Third, the social strategies that normalise the pathology of land enclosure. Fourth, the psycho-biological effects embedded in, and transmitted through, each generation. Combined, these reveal the pathological impacts licensed by statecraft. Humanity is corroded from within itself. And, through colonialism, we achieve an understanding of how Rent is extracted on a global scale; as when indigenous peoples are supplanted from their homelands. The outcome is sustained erosion of the consciousness to achieve what people would otherwise have accomplished, in the pursuit of human – that is, humane – aspirations.

The loss of symmetry in society's working parts is induced by the cheating behaviour that becomes *the* crime against humanity. It envelops us along three dimensions: the past, the present and the future.

The past and biology. When people are displaced from their homelands, subsequent generations are deprived of the right to wholesome lives. Outcome: deterioration in the physical condition of the victims below what they would otherwise have achieved.

The present and sociality. By depriving communities of social Rents, institutions that were supposed to enrich personal experience and interpersonal relationships were impoverished. This corrupts the vitality of communities that could have emerged.

The future and the existential threat to our species, as illustrated by the digital technology that is being developed in the 21st century. This remains a contested issue, as yet insufficiently understood, which I fear will deliver the death blow to humanity (Ch. 13).

Before proceeding with this interrogation, we need to confront one really awkward problem. It relates to the scientific tools used to investigate the past and present; on which we rely for assessing the future of humanity. If science is a robust method for revealing reality, how can we explain its failure to alert us to the way in which humanity's collective consciousness has been perverted? The only viable answer is that the social sciences were bent to serve the culture of cheating. Did this *really* happen? If so, how?

The "Survival of the fittest"

To survive in the age of science, by retaining control over people's minds, the cheats *had* to intervene, first and foremost, in the science of evolution.

Charles Darwin and Alfred Russel Wallace co-created the theory of evolution. They explained how species evolved by adapting to their natural habitats. They assumed that humans evolved on similar terms. Might they have modified the theory, as it applied to humans, to incorporate the role played by Rent in the emergence of *Homo sapiens*? They might well have done so.

Wallace, a Welshman, undertook his fieldwork in the Amazon River basin (1848-1852) and the Malay Archipelago (1854-1862). He published his findings in 1858.[1] And as it happened, he came to understand the economics of Rent. Referring to Henry George's *Social Problems* (1883), he explained:

> **[U]nder our present laws and customs inequality would very soon arise, and after a time we should find a certain proportion of rich men who have no need to work and who do not work... Not only do they employ large numbers of personal servants, but they keep a host of men employed in producing luxuries who before produced necessaries and comforts for the whole population...Hence the proportion of unproductive to productive labour increases continually, which means in other words that the productive labourers have to work harder than ever and for longer hours, and this they would certainly do only under stress of necessity – that is, of poverty.[2]**

Given time, and with the aid of the existential role of Rent, might Wallace have fine-tuned his insights into how humans evolved out of nature? He might well have done so, but for the intervention of Herbert Spencer (1820-1903), who co-created sociology, the science of society.

Spencer diverted the science of human evolution in a manner that well served the landed nobility. Why and how did this happen, given that he initially achieved notoriety as a critic of the aristocracy?

Spencer made his mark with 10 essays in the *Nonconformist* in 1842 and 1843. He attacked the Corn Laws and championed free trade, which would cut the cost of food. The landlords in Parliament, however, favoured protectionism, which raised the Rents of their agricultural estates. And that, for Spencer, was a violation of natural law, as he explained in *Social Statics: The Conditions Essential to Human Happiness Specified, and the First of Them developed* (1850). This book became a foundation text for sociology. Inequality, he insisted, yielded "a pathological state of unrest and social crisis".[3]

Spencer subjected Victorian society to forensic scrutiny. He believed that science could deliver remedies to the gross inequalities that divided Europe. His insights appeared as Chapter 9 of *Social Statics*, in which he offered a trenchant critique of the privatisation of socially generated income. The rules of tenure converted property laws into "an infringement of the law of equal freedom".[4] Spencer denied "the rectitude of property in land". No passage of time or number of transactions could legitimise the injustice that stemmed from the original land grabs. Title deeds were a fraud. Land was a bequest from God, and society was the steward of people's right of access to Earth.

> **In our tender regard for the vested interests of the few, let us not forget that the rights of the many are in abeyance, and must remain so, as long as the earth is monopolised by individuals. Let us remember, too, that the injustice thus inflicted on the mass of mankind is an injustice of the gravest nature.**[5]

The political implications were clear, for "if pushed to its ultimate consequences a claim to exclusive possession of the soil involves a landowning despotism".

In Spencer's view, the highest civilisation would result from a tenure in which people were co-heirs of the soil. Owners should pay Rent to society in exchange for the benefits they received from occupying land. By this means, "the earth might be enclosed, occupied, and cultivated in entire subordination to the law of equal freedom".

This analysis held out the prospect that sociology could stand alongside classical economics. Spencer's conclusions harmonised with the policies elucidated by Adam Smith. Together, economics and sociology could project society along an evolutionary path grounded in the principles of fairness and efficiency. At the heart of that model of society was the rectitude of a public finance that socialised the nation's Rents and privatised the earnings of people's individual labours.

Spencer was emphatic: "[T]o deprive others of their rights to the use of the earth is to commit a crime inferior only in wickedness to the crime of taking away their lives or personal liberties".[6] Spencer was not addressing a fossilised practise: enclosure of the English commons continued into the 19th century. His analysis was a direct challenge to the power of the landed class. His chorus on liberty could not be left on the public record. It had to be expunged from the public's consciousness. *The author had to be bought off.*

Sell-out Spencer

In the annals of scientific endeavour, there are few betrayals to compare with Herbert Spencer's heinous rejection of his own work. People are entitled to change their minds if they discover errors in the evidence. In Spencer's case, the facts did not change. He did. He was seduced by the good life.

One approach to preserving the status quo was Spencer's intervention in the theory of evolution. He coined the concept "survival of the fittest", which Darwin adopted.[7] How did this happen, and what purpose did it serve?

As Spencer's fame spread, his celebrity status attracted invitations to the fashionable salons in London and speaking tours in America. He acquired a taste for the sporting life, which he could indulge as weekend guest at the stately homes of the aristocracy. And so, he modified his views about the right of land owners to pocket the nation's Rents. When *Social Statics* was republished in 1892, Chapter 9 was missing. "I had relinquished some of the conclusions drawn from the first principles laid down," he declared in the Preface to the new edition. Gone was all mention of the evils he had originally associated with the nobility's land grabs.

In the intervening 40 years, his veritable library of books on biology, ethics and philosophy reveal how his mind was marinated to accommodate the rejection of his original analysis of land tenure. Hypocrisy now infused his definition of justice, which required that there

> **shall be maintained a due proportion between returns and labours: the natural relation between work and welfare shall be preserved intact. Justice [entailed the] principle of equivalence which meets us when we seek its roots in the laws of individual life.**[8]

According to this formulation, landlords *failed the test of equivalence between returns and labour, between work and welfare.* Landlords *were*, of course, entitled to a return on the capital equipment which they may have provided, but that return was not "rent". Call it profit, or interest, or anything you like; it was distinct from *economic rent.*

Conveniently for Spencer, his version of the theory of evolution ensured that "evil perpetually tends to disappear". People apparently adapt themselves to their environments. Adaptation occurred in "the acclimatization of plants, in the altered habits of domesticated animals, in the varying characteristics of our own race". And yet, the "moral evils" which he had itemised in Ch. 9 continued to haunt humanity, rippling through the ages as the product of a cult-like process which prevented millions of people from achieving happiness.

According to *Social Statics*, there was just one explanation for the inability of people to achieve their potential: they were prevented from working in ways that gratified them into the state of happiness. But sociology was not going to serve as a tool for censuring the culture of cheating, because Spencer disabled the discipline. He abandoned his "law of equal freedom", which he had defined thus:

> **We have seen that the right of property is deducible from the law of equal freedom, that it is presupposed by the human constitution, and that its denial involves absurdities.**

In bringing down the blinkers on people's minds, Spencer exposed himself as a charlatan. To rationalise his betrayal, he redefined his theory of property. If land ownership entailed iniquities, he attributed the guilt to the ancestors "of all existing men".[9] And he admonished the critics who, in lamenting injustice in their home territory, were silent about the land grabbing that was taking place abroad. The critics were hypocrites!

Spencer's clinching argument in favour of the *status quo* relied on a false account of the alternative. Nationalisation of land, he argued, would result in worse evils.

> **Under the existing system of ownership, those who manage the land, experience a direct connection between effort and benefit; while, were it under state ownership, those who managed it would experience no such direct connection. The vices of officialism would inevitably entail immense evils.**[10]

Nationalisation was *not* the only option, and Spencer knew it. Henry George had elaborated the alternative fiscal strategy, which did not entail the state taking anybody's land. All it required was that people should pay for the benefits they received by pooling their share of socially-created net incomes. But that would have reduced the land holders to a status equal to other citizens. That could not be allowed! They were at the top of the hierarchy, Britain's class system. They were entitled to preside at the top because, after all, life was all about the *survival of the fittest*!

Gone global

Does Spencer's treachery prove that the western mind remained hostage to the culture of cheating? Might the perversion of the science of society be an exception based on the fallibility of one individual who could not resist temptation? We need to supplement this theory with a nuanced account based on the impact on the whole population. We shall focus on the granular evidence relating to three issues: the crimes against humanity that surface as deforestation (for free riding's impact on nature); death (for the impact of statecraft on humanity); and debt (for the impact that transcends time and generations).

The Past: Deforestation

During the foraging stage of evolution, people paid for nature's resources with their labour. Labour inputs were proportionate to the value of the extracted resources. Consequently, resources were not subject to reckless over-consumption. Had the civilisations of antiquity emulated that rule, farming communities would have chopped down trees to fire up the smelting of iron ore on a sustainable basis (as happened in communities in the Carpathian basin).

The systematic abuse of nature began with the onset of the Iron Age (about 1,200 BCE). Iron was fashioned into swords that equipped Egypt's third phase of pharaonic development, the territory-grabbing imperial state. Trees were cut to meet the needs of militarisation, so that the pharaohs could conquer other people for their natural resources. Irresponsible deforestation began in earnest. That culture reverberated through classical times to enable the Roman Empire to impose its fist of iron on territories as far afield as England. Time and again, "deforestation and soil erosion often turned once-prosperous civilisations into desolate areas. A Dark Age, which consumed fewer resources, followed the Iron Age".[11] All because those civilisations failed to employ the pricing system that required people to pay for what they extracted out of nature.

Following the feudal interlude, Britain began to gouge nature when coal replaced timber to fire up the cauldrons. This was more efficient at churning out iron shaped as cannons that fired balls from the sailing ships sent to conquer the New World, and to extract slaves from the Old World. Emissions escalated as the furnaces damaged the climate, wildlife habitats, and the Social Galaxy.

To maximise Rent, no price was paid for the disposal of waste. An OECD report enables us to trace the ripples from the first order deeds. One consequence, through the inhalation of particulates, was damage to people's brains. This reduced economic productivity, particularly among high-skilled workers, because of increased absenteeism and reduced cognitive and physical performance at work.[12]

The impact on nature is horrific. Degradation, which includes soil erosion and deforestation, which originated in antiquity and continued into the modern era with toxic emissions from industrialised production. Today, the integrity of 60% of the global land area has been transgressed, with 38% already at high risk of degradation.[13]

The Present: Death

Second and third order ripple effects are responsible for premature deaths of people on a horrendous scale. According to the Preventable Deaths Tracker, the UK's annual preventable deaths exceeds 125,000.[14] Some of those deaths would be due to behaviour for which the individuals concerned must accept personal responsibility. The majority, however, are the systemic outcome of cheating, as manifested through deprivation (leading victims to seek relief, as with the resort to narcotics); and the degradation of the fabric of society (under-funded public services induces suffering with mortal effects). One outcome is the spatial variation in the duration of healthy lives. In 2023, among the regions of England, the highest male healthy life expectancy at birth was observed in prosperous London (63.9 years), where people lived seven years more than those in impoverished communities in the North East (56.9 years).[15]

Premature deaths are inflicted by the laws of the land. Two centuries ago, a 10-year gap in mortality rates existed between London and the regions. That gap remains in place today, despite the 20th century's Welfare State. Over those two centuries, property rights and the enabling statecraft were not amended. Consequently, Britain in 2023 endured "The gap between the local authorities with the highest and lowest life expectancies [that] was just over 10 years for men and just over 8 years for women".[16] In 2024, Sir Keir Starmer's Labour Party won the general election with a "health mission" to "halve the gap in healthy life expectancy between the richest and poorest regions in England". Their 10 Year Health Plan

> **sets out how technology will be used to reduce inequalities in access and outcomes, promising that healthy life expectancy will increase over the period of the plan...we will have begun narrowing the wide and widening health inequalities that unjustly divide our country.**[17]

Technology, far from being the solution, actually amplifies the traumas. Technological innovations increase the net benefits, which are converted into the privatised form of Rent. Starmer's government had no plans to neutralise that effect. Britain remained off the list of the 20 countries with the highest life expectancy; in fact, its ranking was falling.[18]

Across the western world, which prides itself on the democratic form of governance, avoidable deaths of citizens on a horrendous scale are the result of wilful public policies.

The Future: Debt

Across the globe, total indebtedness in 2024 was equivalent to 236% of Global GDP (Fig 7.1). Sovereign debts arise because governments fail to balance their books. This occurs because they enable much of the social revenue to be channelled into private pockets. That, in turn, corrupts one of the primary human aspirations.

A better life for one's children was one of the motivating forces that enabled humans to elevate themselves out of nature. People innovated and invested additional resources to enhance the lives of future generations. But the private appropriation of Rent necessarily meant that state and household budgets were continually in deficit. That is why social needs were not funded. The only way to appear to balance the books was to borrow. This created the indebtedness that became mortgages on the lives of children yet to be born. The evolutionary motive was corrupted, thrown into reverse.

Figure 7.1 **Global Debt as % of Global GDP: 2024**

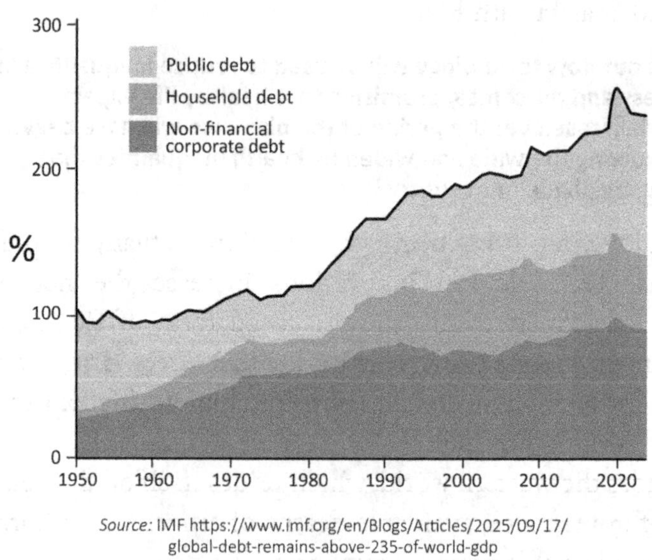

Source: IMF https://www.imf.org/en/Blogs/Articles/2025/09/17/global-debt-remains-above-235-of-world-gdp

This is a despicable form of betrayal of the human project. Future generations are forced to endure diminished lives, because they have to work to produce revenue to pay the interest on sovereign debts incurred by their forebears. The cannibalistic effects are reflected in growing levels of despair and deprivation. Today, fewer young people are securing the jobs they need to fund their futures. Marital and fertility rates are dropping, and mental ill-health rates are rising.

That this process originated in antiquity was documented by Egyptologist Von Heel. A man called Hepy took out a loan and offered collateral that included his own children.

> **They (the capital sum plus interest) will be on my head regarding the securities you will require from me, whichever one, be it house, male servant, female servant, son, daughter, silver, copper, clothing, oil, emmer, or whatever in this world.**[19]

Offering one's child as collateral was brutal, noted von Heel. The *same* outcome arises when governments extend their sovereign debts in perpetuity, rather than fund public services out of the net incomes produced while they are in power. That is why, once they are born, many children are locked into impoverished lives. This is structural poverty, ordained by the social system's cultural DNA. Meanwhile, some owners of Rent-yielding assets splurge their unearned riches on monumental yachts costing half-a-billion dollars each, which are moored, most of the time idle, in basins along the French Riviera.

In plain sight

The culpability of statecraft is beyond question, because none of the traumas caused by cheating is a secret to lawmakers. They countenance discussion on any remedial policy except fiscal reform, despite the valiant efforts of a few scholars, among whom we count John Muellbauer.

In 1990, writing from Nuffield College, Oxford, he informed me that "to influence thinking at the Treasury and the Bank [of England], a good piece of academic research written up in a widely circulated research paper probably has the best chance of succeeding".[20] He spent nearly five decades documenting how public policies transmitted failure through the housing market. From Official Fellow in Applied Economics to Professor of Economics, in scholarly articles in peer-reviewed journals to articles in the mainstream media, he spoke truth to power.

In 1988, directly addressing Prime Minister Margaret Thatcher, he was blunt with an article headed: "Why we need a national tax on imputed rents". He warned that tax reductions and priorities that favoured house owners would lead to "serious jeopardy".

In 1989, in a paper presented in the House of Commons, he made plain the reason for the North/South divide: "[T]he lower supply elasticity of land in the South East accounts for much of the rising differential when aggregate demand for housing in the UK increases".

In 1990, Muellbauer's article in *Economic Policy* caught the attention of *Financial Times* columnist Sam Brittan for its "almost bitter" attitude towards the Treasury, which had ignored his advice to include house prices in their forecasting models.[21]

In a study called *The Great British Housing Disaster and Economic Policy*, he accused developers: "Land speculation plays its part too: as prices rise, some land is held back in the hope of being able to sell at a higher price later".[22] There was a fiscal remedy.

> **[B]y basing the tax on site values rather than total property values and by including residential land not yet built on in the tax base, the disincentives against construction and improvement of property would be avoided.**

He was unrelenting in advocating "The case for a tax on land".[23] Whitehall and Westminster studiously ignored his advice, but that did not deter the professor. For the benefit of the OECD, he used UK evidence to illustrate flaws in the economic and fiscal regimes.[24]

- Credit-fuelled housing booms: price volatility is severe, contributing to poor productivity in the economy.
- House prices inhibit mobility. "We have high taxes on moving and low taxes on homeownership…The whole system is clogged up."

- Compared to other countries, "So much of the money has gone into increasing land values and not into improving infrastructure".
- A broken planning system curtails the provision of social housing and traps money in land instead of capital formation.

In 2022 he explained that a house that cost £100,000 to build would sell for £317,000. Land captured £217,000. That revenue could have been invested in public infrastructure to raise levels of productivity. The *Daily Telegraph* reported Muellbauer's findings.

> **When homes are more unaffordable, low-income households spend a larger share of their income on housing. The OECD found that this in turn leaves them with poorer access to health, education and the internet. Ultimately, this leads to fewer jobs opportunities. Younger people who grow up in poor quality housing face a lifelong impact on their earnings.**[25]

The solution? Replace property taxes with a "green land value tax", to "resolve conflicts between affordability and equity and meeting climate goals and to reduce intergenerational injustice and social exclusion". Still, no response from lawmakers.

How could such an academically well-placed scholar like John Muellbauer be ignored for more than 40 years? What makes it possible for law-makers to persist with policies that are known to fail? How can a nation like the UK, at the forefront of the Enlightenment, continue to believe that politicians can resolve painful, socially-significant traumas? There is one answer only to these questions: wilful blindness, wrapped up in what lawyers call an unwritten constitution.

Over Muellbauer's four decades, governments carefully avoided any proposal that targeted the gains reaped by free riding. Developers, apparently, want to build homes to match supply to demand, but were constrained by "market failure". The market is a scapegoat, as attested by the large number of vacant dwellings. The dysfunctional nature of the property market stems from the incentives licenced by law and fiscal practice. Systemic failure is not the result of oversight, a blind spot, ignorance. It is purposeful, the outcome of a culture designed to deliver failure for the people who work to produce the nation's net income. The evidence is in plain sight, and was in action during the Covid-19 lockdown, which killed millions of people.

Many people began to work from home, using laptops to communicate with colleagues. The savings from reduced travel costs were capitalised into higher prices for spacious residential properties located in rural areas at the end of the commuting line.[26] Governments pumped money into those communities to sustain the lockdown period; money that was captured by homeowners, as revealed by the upward jerk in the trends of rising prices on both sides of the Atlantic. Fig 7.2 illustrates what happened in the UK.

First, notice the upward bump in the trend. The Covid-19 virus was unleashed in 2020. In the second half of that year, government pumped the first tranche of money into the economy, in what eventually totalled upwards of £400bn. Ostensibly, the funds were intended to help families and enterprises survive the pandemic. But, over the following two years, during which over 200,000 people died, the government was busy transferring a vast amount of money to the owners of residential properties, the values of which went sky-high.

Second, notice the trend since 2010. House prices took off after the use of taxpayers' money to bail out the bankrupt banks that were "too big to fail". Governments poured trillions into the western economy to sustain the system. While the people who worked to add value to the wealth of their nations endured a decade-long austerity regime, in the UK the Acts of Parliament sent deadly ripples through the population. Under-funded public services resulted in the deaths of tens of thousands of people every year, even as the price of residential properties continued to reach for the skies.

Third, notice that the graph forecasts growth all the way through to 2029. After the upward blip funded by the pandemic financial shot-in-the-arm, house prices returned to their cyclical trend. The 2029 forecast was provided by the government's independent

Figure 7.2 **UK average house prices: £000s**

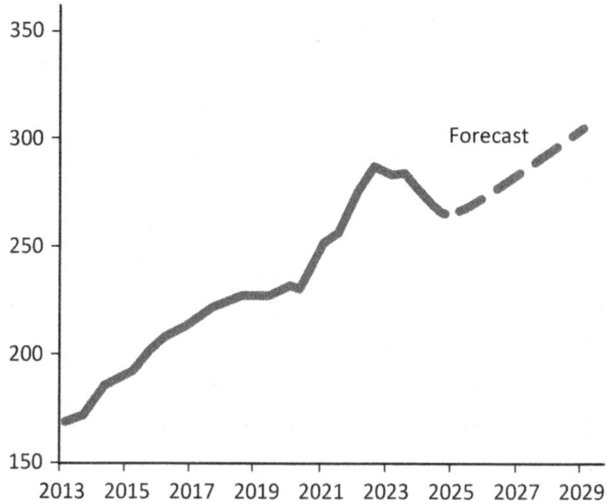

Office for Budget Responsibility (OBR), the agency created to provide "authoritative analysis of the UK's public finances". If I am correct, this forecast not only lacks authority; it is an irresponsible projection that offered false comfort to law-makers who really believe that cutting taxes (and, therefore, under-funding public services) delivers higher economic growth. Despite the historical evidence, according to the OBR, house prices will continue to grow all the way through to 2029.[27]

Whichever way we twist it, in the marketplace the owners of Rent-yielding assets hold all the aces in the pack!

Wilful blindness

The virtue of a constitution that is unwritten is that nobody can be held accountable when a nation's Parliament fails to fulfil the electorate's aspirations. Those who fathered the UK's constitution achieved this, by not disclosing on paper the pillars on which the nation was structured. So if they were driven by ulterior motives, which they wished to shield from public gaze, they could not be challenged. Which is how it came to pass that the UK was formed on principles that were concealed in a constitution that was not written; against which the victims could not appeal, because they would be drowned in the verbiage of dissembling lawyers.

A constitution that honestly reflected reality would be used to reveal the intentions of those who wielded power, exposing the *modus operandi* of those who prevailed over the law. That is why England, and then the British Isles, remained within the orbit of an unwritten constitution. That unwritten document kept everyone guessing, except those who exercised ultimate authority. Jurist William Anson (1843-1914), explained that the British constitution was not written "for the information of those who live under it or for the guidance of those who have to work it... in authoritative documentary form it is not to be found". *Carte blanche* for someone! Anson, who served as Warden of All Souls College, Oxford, drily observed that an English student might be prepared to regard the constitution as "a monument of political sagacity, if he can only find it". This was consequential, for a "constitution which is nowhere set forth in a written form must needs be more liable to change".[28] And changed it was, over the ages, to preserve the unfolding needs of those who held the assets that yielded the nation's Rents. Change, without the scrutiny that was warranted. The victims had no source of authority to which they could appeal. Which is why, *when the land grabbers deprived people of their traditional right to occupy and use the commons, the consent of the commoners was neither sought nor granted.*

The nobility who assumed exclusive rights to the net income of the nation inflicted gross injustices against which there was no possibility of appeal. Legislation, designed to maximise the interests of the owners of Rent-yielding assets, was under the control of the landed peers of the realm, who were cloaked with the veneer of sovereign authority. So, whenever anything went seriously wrong, the fault could be shifted onto anyone, or anything, except where it belonged.

The success of this legalistic ploy is illustrated by the intervention of the Rev. Thomas Malthus (1766 –1834). He went to great lengths to argue that poverty was the fault of low-income people who bred too many children. He was not ignorant of the reality. He had written *An Inquiry into the Nature and Progress of Rent* (1815), and expanded his analysis in *Principles of Political Economy* (1820). He had a platform to explain the realities on the ground, in which people who were dispossessed of their access rights to land were condemned to live in poverty. Instead, he remained silent on the realities; and on the role of the East India Company in expropriating people from their land on a global scale. Was it a coincidence that he taught political economy at the East India Company's college at Haileybury, in Hertfordshire?

The people of Britain did not consent to their unwritten constitution. Based on the indictment supported by the evidence from the next three chapters, people can now pronounce their verdict in the court of public opinion.

Is the culture of cheating a crime against humanity?

References Chapter 7

1 Ulrich Kutschera and Uwe Hossfeld (2013), "Alfred Russel Wallace (1823–1913): the forgotten co-founder of the Neo-Darwinian theory of biological evolution", *Theory in Biosciences*, 132. DOI 10.1007/s12064-013-0187-2

2 http://people.wku.edu/charles.smith/wallace/S369.htm

3 James Fulcher and John Scott (2007), *Sociology*, 3rd edn., Oxford: Oxford University Press, p.27.

4 Herbert Spencer (1850), *Social Statics*; New York: Robert Schalkenbach Foundation, 1995, p. 104.

5 *Ibid*, p.112.

6 *Ibid*, p.113.

7 Charles Darwin (1868), *The Variation of Animals and Plants under Domestication*, London: Murray, p.17.

8 Herbert Spencer (1879), *The Principles of Ethics*; 1978, Indianapolis: Liberty Fund, Vol. 1, p.312.

9 Herbert Spencer (1893), *The Principles of Ethics*; Indianapolis: Liberty Fund, 1978, Vol. 2, p.455.

10 *Ibid*, p.460.

11 James K. Galbraith and Jing Chen (2025), *Entropy Economics*, Chicago: University of Chicago Press, p.123.

12 https://www.oecd.org/en/publications/the-impact-of-air-pollution-on-labour-productivity_318cb85f-en.html

13 Fabian Stenze *et al* (2025), "Breaching planetary boundaries: Over half of global land area suffers critical losses in functional biosphere integrity", *One Earth* 8, p.3. https://www.cell.com/one-earth/fulltext/S2590-3322(25)00219-2

14 https://preventabledeathstracker.net/?utm_source=substack&utm_medium=email

15 Healthy life expectancy in England and Wales – Office for National Statistics https://www.ons.gov.uk/peoplepopulationandcommunity/healthandsocialcare/healthandlifeexpectancies/bulletins/healthstatelifeexpectanciesuk/between2011to2013and2021to2023

16 Sonja Stiebahl and Bukky Balogun (2025), *Inequalities in life expectancy*, London: House of Commons Library Research Briefing, p.19.

17 *Ibid*, p.14.

18 *Ibid*, p.35.

19 Von Heel, *op. cit.*, p.38.

20 Personal communication, 22 May 1990.

21 Samuel Brittan (1990), "Consumer wants it now", *Financial Times*, May 17.

22 John Muellbauer (1990), *The Great British Housing Disaster and Economic Policy*, London: IPPR, p.7.

23 John Muellbauer (1989), "The case for a tax on land", *Financial Times*, March 20.

24 John Muellbauer (2022), "Why we need a green land value tax and how to design it". https://www.oecd.org/tax/federalism/local-housing-equity-workshop-agenda.pdf

25 https://www.telegraph.co.uk/business/2023/02/12/how-britains-broken-housing-market-crushing-growth/

26 https://www.nationalpropertybuyers.co.uk/blog/home-worth/how-coronavirus-covid-19-affected-uk-house-prices/

27 OBR (2023), *Economic and fiscal outlook*, November, p.43.

28 William R. Anson (1922), *The Law and Custom of the Constitution, Vol. 1: Parliament*, 5th edn., Oxford: Clarendon Press, pp. 6-7.

CHAPTER EIGHT

The Rentlords

Britain did more than any other nation to shape the world we have inherited.[1] To highlight the driving force, we begin in the highlands of Scotland.

Right up to the onset of modernity, the Gaelic clans had retained their authentic cultural tradition. Ethnic Scots escaped the traumas inflicted by the conquering Roman army, whose troops built a wall to isolate them in their homelands. Secure beyond Hadrian's Wall, the Scots also escaped the long Dark Age of feudalism that followed the collapse of Rome. So, for a thousand years, they were free to enjoy their traditional culture based on co-operation and consensus as they clustered within their clans.

Was this history a blessing, inoculating them against the cheating virus that infected the rest of Europe? Does their fate illuminate the cultural causeway between the corrupted ancient past and the onset of our globalised civilisation?

Something terrible did happen to the Scots. So traumatic, that it left an indelible mark on their collective psyche. They were vulnerable, because they had spent so much time immunised behind the wall. The impact of the shock is summarised in a single statistic, which marks the Scots as exceptional in Europe. They top the European league for deaths from overdoses of narcotics.[2] Fig. 8.1 evokes an astonishing level of despair that drives the former clansmen to seek refuge in opioids, with a death rate over three and a half times that of England and Wales.

Figure 8.1 **Drug deaths in Scotland**

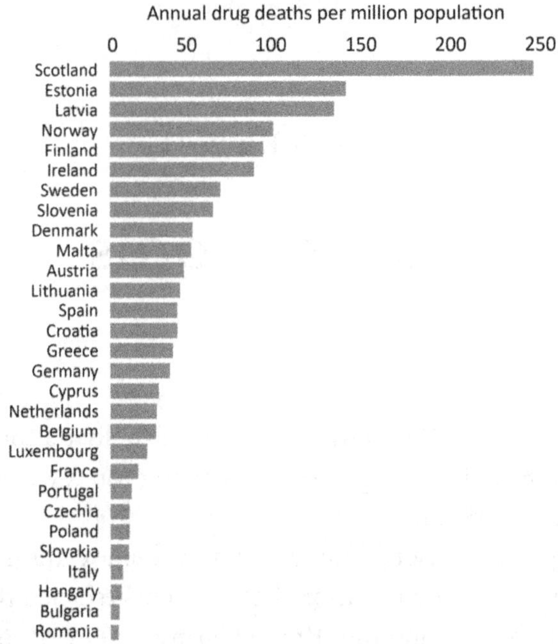

Scotland's Index of Multiple Deprivation provides nuanced data on the links between mental deprivation and the resort to drugs; with the highest death rates in the poorest locations, the statistics sliding down to the least deprived people in the richest areas. The symmetry between psychological health and material welfare reveals the pathology that prevails in the British Isles. How did it come about, that the people in the most insulated corner of Europe are now paying the highest price?

French historian Prosper Boissonnade (1862-1935), in assessing Medieval Europe, stressed that the Celts preserved tribal property in common ownership. In contrast, south of Hadrian's Wall, "there is no trace of property owned collectively by the Anglo-Saxon tribes, now formed into states, or of the collective property of the shire or district". In Scotland, "the clan held the land in common, and was one in peace as in war". Among the Gaelic people, property rights were in household goods, "and each held only the right of usufruct over his strip of the tribal domain".[3]

That history provides us with the case study for evaluating the cultural and psychological adjustments inflicted by the lairds who became the Rentlords. They conspired with the nobility south of the border to combine economics with the new statecraft that would elevate four nations into the British Empire. That empire disseminated its values and institutions across the globe. That is the story of a catastrophic process which, one day, might cause the collapse of civilisation.

The Gaelic clans

Our first task is to test the causal relationships between three key features. (1) How folk traditions disciplined bad behaviour; and whether, with the onset of modernity, those traditions were negated to accommodate free riding. (2) Whether – and how – the cheats took control of the centres of power, enabling them to de-socialise Rent and embed their privileges in the laws of the land. (3) What persuaded people to believe they were "free" even as they were coerced into labouring on behalf of their masters? In assessing the evidence, we need to consider the extent to which behaviour was distanced from the three core structural pillars of the evolutionary blueprint.

Pillar 1: Rent pooled to fund everyone's welfare; with moral codes designed to protect freedom and discipline deviant behaviour.

Pillar 2: Stewardship-based authority structures to sustain a people-centred ethos; with personal rights balancing social responsibilities.

Pillar 3: Communities integrated with nature in mutual symbiosis; with respect for other species to sustain material and spiritual needs.

In Scotland, the elevation of kinship groups into Gaelic clans began in the 12th century. Did this extension of their way of life incorporate these three pillars, rendering their social model consistent with the evolutionary blueprint? If so, the historical evidence should reveal *if*, *how*, and *why* the clans abandoned those pillars, providing a forensic audit of the consequences.

In Gaelic, *dúthchas* articulated the clan model. That doctrine remains in the collective consciousness of Scotland today, illustrated by a recent newspaper headline: "*Dúthchas*: The word that describes understanding of land, people and culture".[4] The author, Alan Riach, professor of literature at Glasgow University, explained: "The importance of this concept of the connectedness and interrelationships between land, people and culture, held in the word 'dúthchas', cannot be overestimated".

Land, people, culture: three words that denoted how the clans applied the three pillars of the evolutionary blueprint.

Pillar 1: land

Families held the inalienable right of access to land to their clan's territory, in return for pooling the Rent. Clans united people and the land: they belonged together. Land was apportioned for a variety of reasons. The personal reason: to fulfil the metabolic needs of the family. Some land was allocated in return for services provided by musicians, poets or reciters. Land was also allocated to support people who rendered spiritual services. The outcome was a holistic community.

Pillar 2: people

People delivered Rent (either in cash or kind) to the chief, or laird. He was responsible for performing the social services that included caring for, and protecting, the folk of the clan; rendering what we call public services. "The fruitful relationship of the people with the land was symbolised by the person of the chief. In his beauty and conduct, he is a worthy steward of the land; in his generosity, he is a conduit of its plenty; and in his martial prowess, he can hunt its deer and defend it for his people."

Pillar 3: culture

Poets performed a prophetic role. Alan Riach explains that they were "attached to clan chiefs and working through generations in a hereditary role, employing a repertoire of poetic forms, devices and phrases…The poets' job was to praise or dispraise…" Social order was secured by the chief and the active participation of all members of the clan, aided by the kinetic power of poems.

Words could "wound in satire" – disciplining behaviour in the way that, in earlier kinship societies, foragers deterred free riders by shaming them.

> **Words are an essential part of *dúthchas* which at once binds a particular people to the land while allowing them to interact with it on a spiritual level.**[5]

The transition from this triadic relationship – land, people and culture – was engineered over the course of 200 years. The character of that transformation was signalled as the end of the 16th century. Scotland's king, James VI, claimed in 1597 that he ruled by "divine right". That was the model of power originally articulated by the dynasts in antiquity. He extended that divine right by acquiring the thrones of England and Ireland in 1603. Thus emboldened, he awarded charters that converted lairds from servants of their people, to owners of the land. The lairds' traditional obligations were abandoned. They became Rentlords, no longer responsible for their clan folk in return for Rent (Box 8.1).

Ancient rights were negated. Relationships were monetised by the new property rights. Thus began "the clearances". James supported the despatch of displaced Scots to the Plantation of Ulster. As for the peasants in England who lost their right to remain on the commons, the king encouraged migration to the American colonies. A rich literature documents the personal tragedies that ensued, as the abominable interventions of monarchs and nobility melded all parts of the British Isles.

To erode Gaelic culture, nine highland chiefs signed the Statutes of Iona (1609). Prosperous farmers were instructed to send their eldest sons to school in the Lowlands to learn English, a vital step in the resocialisation of the highland chiefs. In Edinburgh, they learnt the ways of noble lifestyles. This, for many of them, resulted in indebtedness; which, in turn, drove them to raise Rents to levels that tenants could not afford.

To rupture the consciousness of the clans, it was necessary to undermine the poets. They "occupied a valued place and performed an immediately practical function…Their role as a witness or recorder of truth takes on in itself a rebellious character when it is

Box 8.1 **The two kingdoms**

James replicated the power-grab model that originated in Egypt, to consolidate his control over the British Isles. It was not plain sailing, however. Times had changed. Now, lay people could read and write. They could put up a fight to defend their rights against free riders. In James' case, his struggle to seize control of religion was eloquently highlighted by Andrew Melville (1545-1622), who had served as moderator for the Church of Scotland Assembly in 1578. He confronted James with this statement.

> *Sir, as at various times before, I say now again, I must tell you, you are God's silly vassal. There are two kings and two kingdoms in Scotland: there is Christ Jesus the King of the church, whose subject King James the Sixth is, and of whose kingdom he is not a king, nor a lord, nor a head, but a member [...] We will yield to you your place, and give you all due obedience; but again I say, you are not the head of the church: you cannot give us that eternal life which even in this world we seek for, and you cannot deprive us of it.'**

How different might civilisation have evolved, if the Neolithic farmers who created urban settlements had been able to articulate themselves in these terms some 6,000 years ago?

* https://www.christianheritageedinburgh.org.uk/2024/03/25/andrew-melville-the-outspoken-reformer-1545-1622/

distanced from a social order determined to control what that truth is and how it is seen and understood".[6] Poets exercising traditional land rights were gone by the early 18th century.

Monarchs of the Hanoverian dynasty (reigning from 1714 to 1901) knew that, to consolidate their power, they had to suppress the highland culture. *Dúthchas* traditions succumbed to "pacification". This "encourag[ed] many of the élite entirely to throw off this historic responsibility in favour of the material advantages of proprietorship, so completing the transformation to landlordism".[7]

Rents were diverted from the wellbeing of the people to fund the transition from castles and fortification to monumental homes and gentrification in the pursuit of "elegance or pleasure".

Aping the aristocracy south of the border became the name of the game. The highlands and islands paid the price: *dúthchas* as a way of life was ruptured; land lost; power corrupted, minds polluted, and the landscape deteriorated as "the rent goes up and people move away". Rents were now used to pay for oil paintings of the landowners' ancestors to deck the walls of salubrious living rooms. "[T]he craze for 'oriental' furniture, lacquered in black with gold ornamentation, had reached the grand houses in the Highlands by the 17th century."[8]

The social division of the people was illustrated in 1724, which highlighted the self-sufficiency of the aristocracy and the vulnerability of the peasants. A beer tax was levied at 6d a barrel. Brewers resolved to discontinue brewing the ale on which peasants relied as the alternative to drinking polluted water. This triggered a riot in Glasgow in 1725, a level of discontent that was of no concern to the former clan chiefs: they brewed beer on their estates, so they avoided the tax. The name of their game was pacification – of the peasants (Box 8.2).

Box 8.2 **Pacifying Scotland**

Pacification of the clans originally took the form of building highways with military intent. The need for surveillance at the peripheries of empire saw the construction of 250 miles of roads in Scotland between 1726 and 1737. By the early 19th century, 900 miles of military roads had been built and were maintained by the British state – the first large-scale state road-building programme in Britain. "Modern road construction emerged in the military laboratory of Scotland between 1726 and 1773 as a craft known to soldiers and surveyors."*

* Jo Guldi (2012), *Roads to Power: Britain Invents the Infrastructure State*, Cambridge, MA: Harvard University Press, p.27.

The onset of industrialisation

The *dúthchas* model could have been adapted to facilitate the new economic possibilities, raising material living standards and integrating the highland/island economy into the wider world. Adam Smith, the moral philosopher in Glasgow, highlighted the proposal to base governance on Rent. *The Wealth of Nations* was consistent with the clan practise of pooling Rent for the common good. This fiscal strategy would have been the ideal springboard for Scotland at the dawn of the Industrial Revolution. Smith's proposal was rejected. So, he became an eyewitness to what happened. In a letter dated 4 April, 1759, he critiqued the Rentlords.

> **We have in Scotland some noblemen whose estates extend from the east to the west sea, who call themselves improvers...when they cultivate two or three hundred acres round their own family seat while they allow all the rest of their country to lie waste, almost uninhabited and entirely unimproved...without thinking themselves answerable to God, their country and their Posterity for so shameful as well as so foolish a neglect.**

The argument that the clearances were necessary, to improve the way land was farmed, was a fraudulent philosophy designed to salve the consciences of the lairds and persuade the clans folk that they had to accept rentier realities. Twenty-four years later, Smith surveyed the impact on the people.

> **[T]ho' between 1755 and 1779, the numbers in the great trading and manufacturing towns and Villages were considerably increased, yet the Highlands and islands were much depopulated, and even the Low Country, by the enlargement of farms."[9]**

But even as people began to diversify from agriculture, the power of the lairds was further entrenched by the decision to outlaw slavery. Slavery, that is, in the plantations of the Caribbean, not in the British Isles.

When slavery was outlawed in 1834, Parliament reimbursed the owners for the prices they, or their ancestors, paid to purchase humans from Africa. So, even as the highland clearances were reaching their peak between 1810 and 1860, the money pocketed by the plantation owners (£20m; over £20 billion in today's money) was invested in the purchase of vast estates in the highlands and islands. This was the crowning of the economics of slavery in the landscape and souls of the Gaelic homeland.

A forensic study of the purchase of West Highland and Island estates by families with financial connections to British slavery, over the period 1726 to 1939, reveals the way in which the culture that cheated people of their humanity was immersed in the way of life of the landowners. The authors stressed that the slave owners brought with them the attitudes of slavery "derived from highly exploitative, often brutally coercive forms of labour…predicated on emphasising resource and labour extraction as well as profit maximisation".[10] At least 1 million acres of the highlands were subjected to the ethos that prevailed on the Caribbean plantations. We need only itemise three features of this manifestation of the economics of slavery.

- Deep in debt, some Rentlords sold their estates to the former plantation owners. The savage eviction of clan families continued. Slavery landlords did not hesitate to "virtually eliminate" the crofting villages, with the "intent on exploiting the marketable commodities of their estates".
- Slave money was whitewashed, the fortunes "made culturally respectable, non-threatening, and even 'traditional' through being embedded in land ownership". The British government "laundered what was now seen as immoral forms of wealth into a respectable form of capital". Britain's taxpayers finally paid off the debt in 2015.
- Habitats that had been nurtured by the Gaelic clans continued to be ruptured. The beneficiaries of slave money applied "economies of scale" to their operations, which ruptured the diversity of nature's habitats, and degraded the social resilience of communities, but increased the net income – the Rents pocketed from the land.

And so, from the 20th into the 21st century, and the assessment by the Scottish government that their country has "a more concentrated pattern of large scale private land ownership than is found in any other country in the world". That "measure of inequality in a modern democracy, [was] exceptional and is in need of explanation".[11] For anyone willing to look, there is no mystery about how this happened.

The legacy

What might have transpired, if the advice offered by Adam Smith had been followed? If the Rents of the clans were pooled to build the infrastructure of modern society? The numbers, as compiled today, offer the merest hint of the riches that would have flowed. For Scotland, they were calculated by Michael Kumhof and his team of two American economists (Nicolaus Tideman and Michael Hudson) and Charles Goodhart, who had worked as a senior economist at the Bank of England and professor at the London School of Economics. Kumhof's credentials were impeccable, his equations rigorous, the graphics illuminating. He had spent 10 years as a top economist at the International Monetary Fund before being recruited by the Bank of England to research the state of health of the British economy. He presented their findings on Scotland to the Scottish Economic Society in 2025.[12]

What would have happened, if people's earned incomes were gradually untaxed and replaced by revenue collected directly from Rent?[13] Based on the equations and graphics generated by their study, we may conclude the following. If the transition had begun in the year 2000, Scotland's GDP would have been greater by more than £7bn in 2009. By 2019, the people of Scotland would have enjoyed an additional £22bn to share among themselves, with welfare higher by more than 3%.

How much greater would national welfare have been, had this policy been adopted in the time of Adam Smith? We cannot begin to imagine! Scotland's history, and that of the UK, would have evolved along an entirely different trajectory. Consider, for example, just the events of the past 20 years. The gains revealed by Kumhof's team are measured against the baseline of the Scottish economy as it evolved in those two decades. During that time, Scotland suffered a £6bn loss of GDP in 2009 alone, in the downturn at the end of the 18-year Rent-led property cycle that began in 1992. And it suffered a £20bn loss in 2019-20, in what was the mid-cycle downturn of the cycle that began in 2010. Scotland would not have suffered those losses, if the 18-year boom/bust business cycles had been smoothed by the fiscal system championed by Adam Smith. My numbers, therefore, seriously understate what would have happened, if the statecraft favoured by the Rentlords had been ditched in favour of the one based on the evolutionary blueprint.

Even before Adam Smith's attempt at an intervention, the clan chiefs could have supported the proposal advanced by another Scotsman, John Law (1671–1729). A Land Tax had been enacted in Scotland in 1667. In 1705, Law proposed that, to increase

Box 8.3 **What might have been**

In *Money and Trade Considered: with a Proposal for Supplying the Nation with Money* (1705), John Law explained how the annual Rent of land was converted into capital (selling) prices. He identified the reasons why land was the low-risk/high return source of revenue; and the mechanism which, had it been adopted, would have negated the disastrous 18-year boom/bust Rent-driven cycles.

In the late 17th century, Scotland and England needed revenue, which could only come from Rent. Scotland enacted its Land Tax before England. If the two countries had built on that fiscal base, life on the British Isles could have assumed a different course. Governance instituted under the Treaty of Union in 1707 would have evolved a central bank that pinned the value of the currency on Rent-yielding land. That would have led to the Good Life for everyone: social stability, with no dispossession of people from the clan lands and commons; and maximum incentives for capital formation, with enterprise undistorted by arbitrary taxes.

prosperity, the nation's currency should be backed by the value of its land. He demonstrated how those two elements – money and the Rent of land – could combine to deliver a new kind of statecraft. Had that happened, it would be fair to speculate that the outcome might have resulted in a new kind of globalised world today; one that was happier, more prosperous and safer (Box 8.3).

Instead, the culture of rent-seeking impressed itself on parliamentary politics. The driving force was transparent, and traced in a speech in the House of Commons by Richard Cobden, the anti-Corn Law MP. Revenue collected directly out of Rent declined from 100% in the 13th century, to 4% by the 1840s (Fig. 8.2). *Parliament was determined to reduce the revenue collected directly from rents.* This meant revenue had to be collected from people's wages and profits.

Scotland paid a terrible price for the onset of modernity. This is revealed by the number of owners of the largest estates: an estimated 432 families own over half of privately owned land.

Figure 8.2 **Land Rent as % of Public Revenue**

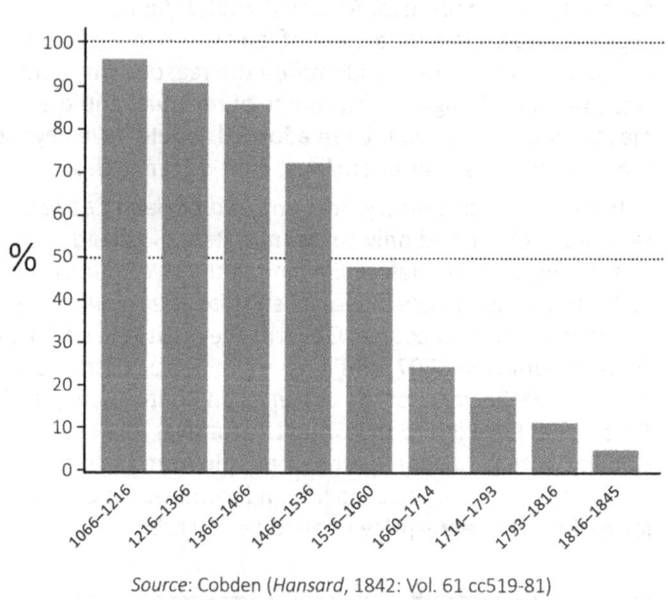

Source: Cobden (*Hansard*, 1842: Vol. 61 cc519-81)

One man, Danish retail billionaire Adners Holch Povlsen, owns more than anyone else: by 2019 he had accumulated 221,000 acres (345 sq mi) of land in the highlands.[14] His mission is to restore the land for the benefit of wild life. An honourable project, but can it be achieved in isolation from the restoration of the people who lived on the land? The answer will be provided by the petty land owners – families that own their homes – who command the majority of votes. They elect governments. They have been unwittingly co-opted into the role of rent seekers.

The outcome, for Scotland, is a national disgrace. Between 2014 and 2018, 13% of the population lived in persistent poverty, after taking account of housing costs. That included 17% of Scottish children.[15] It was a different story for the owners of land.

Fiscal Scam: the food chain

Speaking in 2024 as Britain's Chancellor, Rachel Reeves spotlighted the skewed benefits from government generosity.

> **Last year, the benefits of agricultural property relief – 40% of the benefit was felt by 7% of the wealthiest landowners. I don't think that is affordable to carry on with a relief like that when our public services are under so much pressure. And of course farmers as well rely on good public services, whether that's our NHS, our roads or our schools.[16]**

But it took a landowner in Scotland to expose the fiscal racket behind the shambles to which Reeves alluded.

Dr Duncan Pickard left his career as a lecturer in animal physiology at the University of Leeds to take up farming. He purchased 1,100 acres in Fife, and embarked on a career that integrated his knowledge of animal nutrition with practices that enhanced the health of his animals while improving soil quality and minimising the impact on the environment. From his farm, he observed from the inside the way in which the owners of land milked the public purse, leaving it to the tenants to lament about the injustices.

Dr Pickard's plain-speaking indictment of tax-funded subsidies paid to agriculture reveals the deception. Governments and farming lobbyists conspire to manipulate the statistics to under-state two numbers. First, the wages and profits made by working farmers. Second, the capital gains that elevated subsidies into land values. The losers are the taxpayers, who are duped by the lawmakers. Outcomes include

- over-dependence on subsidies, which discourages productivity. The top 25% of farms are profitable and do not need subsidies;
- tax policies drive up the price of land. That encourages land speculation and deters new generations that want to become farmers;
- some small farmers avidly accumulate land. That drives up the price of dwellings, which forces wage-workers out of the sector;
- reforming the tax regime would enhance the efficient use of land. That would reduce depopulation and reinforce sustainable farm practices.

As for the inheritance tax, against which hysterical lobbyists protest, Pickard points out that many, if not all, of the most valuable farming estates escape that tax because they are owned by family trusts. And farms worth less than £1m are exempt from the tax. As for farming's "razor thin margins", Pickard's balance sheet calculations demonstrate that the claim is a lie, deployed to squeeze yet more money out of the public purse.[17]

Tenant farmers are squeezed: between the supermarkets, which drive hard bargains, and the landlords, who drive even harsher deals out of the people who actually work on the land. Which is why, in Pickard's view, shifting taxes off farm wages and profits, and onto the location value of land, would reverse the exodus from rural areas and revitalise communities. This was the only effective way to reverse the enclosures imposed by the clan chiefs of old.

The devolution of power

The unitary system of politics was altered in 1998. Some of Westminster's powers were transferred to Scotland, Wales and Northern Ireland. No evaluation went into whether this shift in decision-making would enhance the outcomes in people's lives. Would the extra burden of taxation, arising from the establishment of parliaments in Edinburgh, Cardiff and Belfast, be more than offset by gains from decisions taken closer to home? HM Treasury did not undertake comprehensive audits of the fiscal system to inform taxpayers of whether they would get better value for their money.

The political powers devolved to Edinburgh included the right to alter the rates applied to raising revenue from property, and from incomes. The Scottish Nationalists who were elected to govern, could zero rate the Income Tax and raise the revenue through a reformed property tax. They chose not to do so.

Roger Sandilands, the emeritus professor of economics at Strathclyde University, noted that the benefits of the revenue-neutral fiscal reform would have empowered the government in Holyrood to increase investments in the education and welfare of the people of Scotland.[18] The creation of new jobs would diminish the despair that results in the opioid deaths, by elevating aspirations that could be fulfilled. Dr Sandilands and his colleagues at the Scottish Land Revenue Group held high-level meetings with elected members of the Scottish government; and provided evidence to the government's Land Commission. And yet, the SNP failed to exercise the powers at its disposal. Why? Was it because, politically, the SNP could point to the suffering in the population to demand sovereign independence? The do-nothing strategy implicates the SNP in the trauma inflicted on the nation by the continued reliance on deadweight taxes.

Alternatively, the SNP feared that fiscal reform would be unpopular with home owners who treasured their capital gains. If so, this still implicates the elected Members of the Scottish Parliament. They choose to privilege the culture of cheating by not engaging with the people in a cathartic conversation about the benefits of reform.

Whatever the explanation, the people of Scotland are being made to pay for the paralysis in politics. The result is the continuation of the highland clearances in its modern form: the housing market. In May 2024, the SNP government declared a housing emergency: homes were in short supply, with high homelessness levels.[19] Instead of the root-and-branch approach to remedial action, the Scottish Parliament's response was a rent-freeze that would further aggravate unaffordability and housing shortage. This, claimed the *Daily Telegraph* in an editorial, was the "Latter-day clearances".[20] The failure to apply the wisdom of people like Adam Smith was noted by land reformer Andy Wightman. He observed that land ownership was more concentrated than ever, despite the "land reforms" of the Scottish government.[21]

It need not have been thus. Vigorous attempts were made by civil society activists to brief the Scottish National Party, which had controlled Holyrood for 13 years, on the optimum approach to fiscal governance. Instead, the SNP sought refuge in a vague notion of "land reform", by setting up a Land Commission, and failing to exercise its devolved powers to shift the balance of revenue collection away from earnings and onto Scotland's Rents.

The Indictment

The psychological traumas endured by the Scots, at the hands of their chiefs, were profound. To this day, those deeds continue to be rationalised as the need to use land efficiently. That authorised philosophy was fostered by people like former Prime Minister Archibald Primrose, the 5th Earl of Rosebery (1847-1929). He was a Scottish laird, who reflected on the disappearance of the rural peasant households. The merger of their holdings into the larger estates, he explained, resulted from "obedience to economic law".[22] Nothing, apparently, to do with cheating. The reality is highlighted by the mortal equation that emerges out of Scotland's national statistics. *The harsher the deprivation caused by denial of access to net income, the deeper the distress, the greater the temptation to escape the realities of life.*

Before the adoption of universal suffrage, Britain's kingdom could not be accused of hypocrisy. The scales of justice were visible for all to see. Those with their hands on political power manipulated the levers to their advantage. But once the nation proclaimed itself a democracy, it could be held accountable for failing to treat everyone as equal under the law. Britain's democracy does not live up to the promise. Evidence is provided by the culture of cheating's kill rate. In 2020, Scots living in the most deprived areas were 18 times as likely to have a drug-related death as those in the least deprived areas: 68.2 per 100,000 population compared with 3.7.[23] If poverty is one of the ripple effects from politics, the idealist reformers who championed democracy failed in their mission to equalise people's life chances.

The negative outcomes are visible in the data provided by National Records of Scotland. "In the most deprived areas of Scotland, average male life expectancy was 13.7 years lower than in the least deprived areas. For females the difference was 10.5 years. This gap has become wider in recent years and Scotland has the lowest life expectancy of all UK countries."[24]

Historically, there were two escape routes out of the trauma of displacement. One was to sink into drug dependency. The second route was migration. The exodus created the Scottish diaspora. Compared with the 5.5m people in their homeland, the people who identify as Scots elsewhere in the world is now estimated as anything between 40 and 80 million people.[25] This did not always end happily, as illustrated by what happened in the Ulster Plantation, the settlement for victims of clearances in the 17th century. Ripples from the supplanting of Irish folk from their land, to make way for the Scots, culminated in The Troubles in the last three decades of the 20th century. The offspring of indigenous Catholics fought with the offspring of the incoming Protestants, resulting in over 3,500 deaths.

Could history have taken a different course? No, given the overwhelming impact of the culture that emerged out of antiquity. But that history was not written into the DNA of human beings. It can be reversed. That would require the fiscal reform capable of rebuilding the bonds which the clans nurtured up to the 16th century.

References Chapter 8

1 Sathnam Sanghera (2024), *Empireworld: How British Imperialism has Shaped the Globe*, London: Penguin Viking.

2 https://www.bbc.co.uk/news/articles/cvgn2gnkk93o

3 Prosper Boissonnade (1937), *Life and Work in Medieval Europe*, London: Kegan Paul, Trench, Trubner, pp. 78-79.

4 https://www.thenational.scot/news/18306403.duthchas-word-describes-understanding-land-people-culture/

5 Meg Bateman and John Purser (2020), *Window to the West: Culture and Environment in the Scottish Gàidhealtachd*, Isle of Skye: Clò Ostaig, pp.417, 246, 776. www.smo.uhi.ac.uk/files/PDFs/Window-to-the-West.pdf

6 Alan Riach (2022), *Scottish Literature*, Edinburgh: Luath Press, pp.184, 188.

7 T.M. Devine (2018), *The Scottish Clearances*, London: Allen Lane, p.60.

8 Bateman and Purser, *op cit*, pp. 421, 582.

9 Adam Smith (1987), *Correspondence of Adam Smith*, Eds: E.C. Mossner and I.S. Ross, Indianapolis: Liberty Press, pp. 32, 291.

10 Iain MacKinnon and Andrew Mackillop (2020), "Plantation Slavery and Land Ownership in the West Highlands and Islands: Legacies and Lessons", p.20. https://www.communitylandscotland.org.uk/wp-content/uploads/2022/08/Report-2020-Plantation-slavery.pdf

11 https://www.gov.scot/publications/land-reform-review-group-final-report-land-scotland-common-good/pages/61/

12 Michael Kumhof (2025), "A Land Tax proposal for Scotland", Glasgow: Scottish Economic Society, April 9.

13 The pre-publication study was circulated in January 2024 among economists working for the Scottish Government.

14 Severin Carrell (2019), "Report calls for reform of 'unhealthy' land ownership in Scotland", *The Guardian*, 22 April.

15 Scottish Government (2020), *Persistent Poverty in Scotland 2010-2018*, https://www.gov.scot/publications/persistent-poverty-scotland-2010-2018

16 Ben Riley-Smith and Dominic Penna (2024), "Reeves: We can't afford farmers to die tax-free", *Daily Telegraph*, Nov. 4.

17 Duncan Pickard (2004), *Lie of the Land: A study in the Culture of Deception*, London: Land Research Trust.

18 Roger Sandilands (2015), "Rewards from Eliminating Deadweight Taxes: The hidden potential of Scotland's land and natural resource rents", Glasgow: Scottish Land Revenue Group.

19 Simeon Kerr (2025), "Housing bill aims to boost building and shield tenants", *Financial Times*, Oct. 1.

20 *Daily Telegraph* (2025), "Latter-day clearances", Oct. 2.

21 https://www.theguardian.com/uk-news/2024/mar/23/land-ownership-in-rural-scotland-more-concentrated-despite-reforms-study-finds

22 Will C. Smith (1908), "Back to the Land", *Economic Journal*, 18(7), p.252.

23 National Records of Scotland (2021), Drug-related deaths in Scotland in 2020, Edinburgh, p.19.

24 https://www.nrscotland.gov.uk/news/2022/life-expectancy-continues-to-fall-in-scotland

25 Murray S. Leith and Duncan Sim, (2022), "'Will ye no' come back again?': Population challenge and diaspora policy in Scotland", *Population, Space and Place*, 28(7). doi:10.1002/psp.2572

CHAPTER NINE

Death by Democratic Cuts

Boys in my class looked like our peers elsewhere in the United Kingdom. Full of life, but with one difference. A cultural virus had singled them out to die a dozen years before their contemporaries. Lives cut short, solely because of where they were born. Blackpool, the Lancashire seaside town. Their privileged peers, conceived and raised in places like Chelsea and Kensington, in London, were free to live full lives.

It was the late 1950s. I was passing through the land "fit for heroes", my family billeted by the army in one of the towns where people were segregated by the economics of apartheid. An economics that cheats people of their right to live full lives.

I recalled those days, of holidaymakers riding donkeys on the beach, when I read that Boris Johnson had travelled to Blackpool to deliver a "levelling up" speech. The Prime Minister promised his government would elevate opportunities across the disunited kingdom. On the day he delivered that promise, my classmates were already dead. For no reason other than having been born in Blackpool.

Dead. Not because of the intervention of a malign supernatural force, or because they chose to live reckless lives. Dead, because they were born on the wrong side of an ideological divide.

The visible line that privileges health and wealth to those who own Rent-yielding assets. Poverty and premature death for many of the rest, the victims of the deadly virus incubated when the English commons were enclosed. The virus conveyed down the generations, abusing the right to equal treatment under the law. Prevented from enjoying retirement years in good health. Unlike their peers born in Chelsea.

Decades later, I examined the spatial variations across England. I did so from my home in the prosperous borough of Richmond-upon-Thames, in the south-west corner of London. Here, average life expectancy of males at birth is the longest in the kingdom: 71.4 years. Blackpool had the shortest male life expectancy at birth: 53.7 years. A gap of 18 years.[1] Who, or what, is responsible for legalising this outrage? The custodians of the nation's tax-and-tenure policies. Parliament in Westminster. It authorises the private accumulation of Rent, the cheating that is the garrotting cord that runs through the kingdom's Finance Acts. Over the past 300 years, the Mother of Parliaments systematically debased people of the four nations of the British Isles, those born on the wrong side of the ideological divide. The generic term for that behaviour is *corruption*.

The Library of the House of Lords defines corruption as

> **dishonest and illegal behaviour by people in positions of power. It threatens national security, reduces access to services, erodes public trust in institutions and impedes investment.**[2]

Corrupt statecraft. The Lords' Library listed the effects. Corruption exercises "a disproportionate impact on the poor, increasing costs and reducing access to services. The [World] bank concludes that corruption 'erodes trust in government and undermines the social contract' and 'impedes investment, with consequent effects on jobs and growth'". These symptoms define the tax regime that privileges the ownership of Rent-yielding assets. In street talk, this is *taking something for nothing*. Misappropriating what belongs to other people, and *letting the losers carry the can*.

One of the ripple effects surfaces as the premature deaths of boys in Blackpool. The causal link with net income is in plain sight, and verified by David Ricardo (1772-1823), the stockbroker, classical economist and Member of Parliament. He demonstrated how Rent is spatially distributed.[3] For sound economic reasons, Rent emerges unequally across an economic catchment area. For sound ethical reasons, that is why Rent should be pooled and shared through the national exchequer. Everyone, everywhere, would benefit, on an equal basis. When privatised, however, the perverse tax-and-tenure nexus yields unequal outcomes, one of which is *the corrupt power to impose taxes that kills people's life chances*. This power originated with, and is sustained by, the diversion of socially created Rent into the pockets of people who yield no equivalent product or service in return. No *quid pro quo*. One result is that England and Wales endure an annual mortality rate of avoidable deaths – one in five of the total – numbering over 125,000. Since July 2013 to mid-2025, the cash value of those deaths is estimated at £15.7bn., based on the UK Government's 2023 prices for what it calls the Value of a Prevented Fatality. King's College London epidemiologist Dr Georgia Richards and her colleagues track those deaths, based on coroners' reports.

The deaths are the intentional outcome of governance in the UK. My classmates in Blackpool died prematurely, in the borough with the highest premature mortality rate in England.[4] I went to live in Richmond-upon-Thames, and I am living to a ripe old age, in good health.

The numbers: I

The evidence is in plain sight. Drive down any street in any country, and you are cruising through the crime scene. We are, alas, schooled into not recognising the clues. Consider the case of education, which is a "public good". Schools add to the net value generated in communities. Instead of being recycled back into funding education, however, those Rents end up in private pockets. A poignant case from England illustrates this process.

Some parents are willing and able to pay extra for access to high-achieving schools. If pooled into the public purse, those extra funds would be available to upgrade under-funded schools elsewhere in the kingdom. Instead, property rights intercept that value, and divert it into real estate. That is why the lives of millions of children are compromised, because they are deprived of the educational resources they need.

In England, residential locations close to "outstanding" schools were valued, on average, at £116,000 more than neighbourhoods around schools rated as "inadequate".[5] Parents are willing to pay that additional sum for their children's education. If that money was pooled into the public purse, the quality of education in deprived neighbourhoods could be elevated. Instead, the money is converted into unearned capital gains accumulated by existing homeowners.

The Neolithic people would not have chosen this system of exploitation: *they habitually censured cheating*. But with the onset of civilisation, they were dispossessed of their rights by free riders who persuaded the majority that exploitation was normal and unavoidable. The masses were hoodwinked. There is no shortage of examples, in modern times, of how this mind-bending exercise was institutionalised. In Britain, the landed aristocracy deployed strategies to integrate their tenants into accepting their inferior condition; using, for example, cricket as a metaphor for behaviour that reinforced the culture of cheating.[6]

Cheating people out of their right to full lives is most acute in certain localities, most of which are concentrated in the north of England. In 2017, a team of researchers added up the numbers.

> **We have identified an alarming growth in England's North-South divide in mortality for the population aged 25–44, amid a persistent inequality accounting for 1.2 million northern excess deaths under age 75 over five decades.**[7]

While the politicians pontificate, people are systematically deprived of up to 20 years of life on earth. The scale of those deaths can be predicted, because they conform to an economic process that has divided nations for millennia.

Figure 9.1 **Routes to Premature Death**

The numbers: II

For deaths directly attributable to the fiscal system, the numbers were crunched by the late Dr George Miller, an eminent British epidemiologist.[8] He estimated the annual death toll at 50,000.[9] In 2024, three academics published a granular study that recorded 46,200 "deaths by despair" over a three-year period just from alcohol, drugs and suicide. Blackpool was at the top of their death list.[10]

The pressures that fragment life at all levels of existence are stylistically illustrated in Fig. 9.1.

People who own Rent-generating resources are immunised from these pressures. Vilfredo Pareto (1848–1923), the son of an Italian nobleman who was one of the first to turn economics into a maths-based discipline, had an explanation for this. The offspring of aristocracy or elites were immune to the pressures to which others were subjected.

> **Incomes are so high that they make it possible for even the weak, the poorly constituted, the dull-witted, and the dissolute, to be saved.**[11]

Their incomes, Pareto acknowledged, were the Rents of land. Peel back the fiscal impacts, and we gaze at multi-layered effects.

- *Distortion of the economy*: the tax regime elevates the cost of employing low-productivity labour, driving people out of work and into the state of dependency on welfare benefits.
- *Dissolution of personality*: deprived of the right to engage in society, victims suffer alienation that undermines their characters, some driven into anti-social or self-harming behaviour.
- *Destruction of communities*: defeated by the overwhelming stresses, communities disintegrate as the bonds that ought to solder families together with their neighbours, are dissolved.

Under those conditions, many parents are unable to nurture children through to maturity. Young people in disadvantaged communities manifest their despair in a variety of self-harming ways. One of which is obesity, a national crisis that evolved over the lifetime of the Welfare State. In 1950, 1% of the population suffered from that condition, rising to 60% in 2022. Obesity is not a lifestyle choice. It is a product of traumas originating in the fabric of society. Stresses drilled into low-income families result in the resort to cheap, fat-based foods. Obesity is part of the set of traumas that reduce life expectancy through at least 12 kinds of cancer. The link to Rent is disclosed by the spatial distribution of wealth. "Children living in deprived areas are substantially more likely to be obese."[12] Increased health costs feed back into increases in sovereign debt, the burden of which ripples through the lives of generations as they are born.

The high hopes of childhood hit a downward slope from the age of nine, as children yield to bad outcomes.[13] One deprivation is a flourishing home life. The Resolution Foundation reports that three decades of falling youth home ownership meant only 28% of households had a mortgage compared to 43% in the 1990s. Despair dissolves aspirations. In 2022, a poll revealed that almost a quarter of a million 18-24 year olds who were not in work planned never to get a job.[14]

The numbers: III

Pathological pressures rise and fall on a cyclical basis. The numbers are etched into hundreds of years of historical records that are available to every in-coming government. Those records reveal wilful blindness. An example is the fateful events of 1997. The UK electorate accepted Tony Blair's assurance that his New Labour Party would chart a Third Way into the future.

I wanted to help. So, following the election, after the Prime Minister walked into Downing Street, I wrote to alert him that the business cycle would terminate when the housing market stalled in 2007. I also wrote to the Chancellor of the Exchequer (Gordon Brown), HM Treasury's Chief Secretary (Alistair Darling); to the No 10 Press officer (Alastair Campbell), and New Labour's policy guru, Peter Mandelson (who was to be ennobled, before the revelations about his involvement with paedophile Jeffrey Epstein). I explained that, when the house price cycle terminated in 2007, the UK would be tipped into a depression. New Labour had 10 years in which to ring-fence the UK against the predictable turmoil. To put my warning in the public domain, I published my forecast in *The Chaos Makers*.

> **Land prices will be near their 18-year peak, driven by an exponential growth rate, on the verge of the collapse that will presage the global depression of 2010. The two events will not be coincidental: the peak in land prices not merely signalling the looming recession but being the primary cause of it.**[15]

I repeated the warning in 2005.[16] Blair and Brown took no action to reform the fiscal system. The culture of cheating remained free to run riot right up to the final quarter of 2007. The housing crash came, portrayed as a "financial" phenomenon. Governments around the world panicked, and turned to their default strategy: transferring most of the costs onto people who did not have a vote – the as-yet unborn generations. Sovereign debts were increased (under what was called quantitative easing: QE); banks were rescued, the working population made to pay with a decade-long deprivation branded as "austerity". I published my inquest of that political disaster in 2010.[17]

Blair and Brown, by permitting the 2007 housing crisis, contributed to the decade of austerity, the human costs of which are now becoming clear. The pathologies were transmitted by "austerity policies [which] reduced UK Government spending by approximately £540 billion between 2010 and 2019. The two key components of austerity – cuts in social security payments and eligibility, and reductions in key social services brought about by cuts to local government funding – have particularly impacted on the poorest and most vulnerable in society".[18]

The death toll rose because, to fund the sovereign debt, central government cut the funds distributed to local governments. Cuts to public services intensified the traumas on the young and the old. Cuts to public infrastructure were symbolised by the growing number of unfilled potholes in roads, the closure of police stations and libraries, and lengthening waiting queues in hospitals. Frustrations felt by the working population drove many of them to blame the European Union, leading to Brexit in the referendum of 2016. That became the opportunity for a landslide victory of the Conservative Party led by Boris Johnson, who promised that he would "level up" the UK.

Under austerity, "The top 10 per cent of England's most deprived council authorities have seen a [budget] cut almost 3 times as high as the richest 10 percent of councils". Topping the list of most deprived towns in England: Blackpool.[19] London headed the list of beneficiaries from government funding. Much of that revenue was capitalised into higher location values; which explains the widening gap in house prices during the austerity years (Fig. 9.2).

Figure 9.2 **Real house prices index (Q1 1994 = 100)**

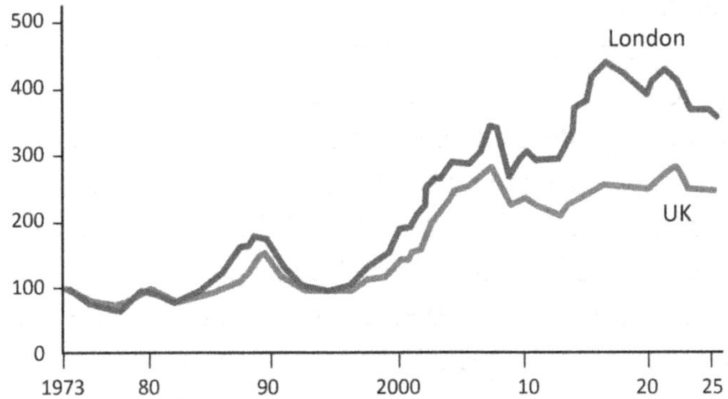

Source: Neal Hudson (2025), "Which was London's luckiest property generation?" *Financial Times*, Sept. 6; based on data from Nationwide and the ONS.

Because of the failure of Blair and his associates, the financial sector imploded under the weight of "sub-prime mortgages". Long queues sprang up outside banks and building societies, the savers desperate to withdraw their money. This was an avoidable crisis, attributable to the politicians and the mandarins in Whitehall who failed to act.

The numbers: IV

In cash terms, we cannot put a number on the aggregate losses attributable to all aspects of the tax-and-tenure regime. We can, however, estimate the first-order losses. This, then, yields an impression of what might have evolved under a justice-based revenue system.

For the UK, the first-order deadweight losses were calculated by Michael Kumhof and his team. He presented the results at a conference of the Royal Economic Society. He revealed the impact of the UK government's taxes on wages and profits; and of the benefits that would arise from replacing taxes with revenue from Rent. Phased in slowly, to avoid structural disruptions, the long-run above-trend increase in GDP (after 80 years) would be 46%. Trillions of pounds added to the wealth of the nation.

Kumhof ended his PowerPoint presentation with a despairing question. Surely, he declared, the case for reform was "overwhelming"?[20]

Eighty years is a long time to wait for freedom from fiscal gouging. Recall Keynes' observation of the long run as "a misleading guide to current affairs. *In the long run* we are all dead".[21] So, to relate the numbers as they would apply in our time, I engaged in a counterfactual exercise. What might have happened if, in the year 2000, the Rent-based fiscal reform had been enacted? My exercise, however, does not rest on pure conjecture, bearing in mind that British governments *did* try to enact the reform twice, in the 20th century. I base my estimate on cues from what happened when the Liberal government phased in the fiscal reform in 1910. I assumed that it would take three years to prepare the electorate for the shift in the system of revenue collection.

Phased in gradually, the total additional revenue for the UK – over the 20 years to 2020 – would have been about £3.6 trillion. The transition would have generated low levels of increases in GDP in the initial period, in response to increased productivity. The rate of increase in GDP would ramp up after Year 10 and continue with an almost vertical increase through to 2020. In that year, GDP would have been £425bn higher than what was achieved.

My numbers are extrapolated, based on the GDP trend during those two decades. This means that they seriously *understate* the actual rewards that would have accrued. Britain suffered stupendous losses from the implosion of the housing market in 2008, and from the ensuing austerity, all of which reduced my numbers.

The Kumhof study reveals the direction of travel: upwards and onwards, rather than a downward implosion of productivity in the direction of stagnation and, for many people, the humiliation of homelessness.

The numbers: V

Young people in families at the lower ends of income suffer most. In schools, cuts in government funding have led to a crippling curtailment of teaching of the arts.[22] This ruptures the development of social and emotional skills necessary to prepare them for adulthood. In examination results, privately schooled pupils in England far exceed the performance of those in public schools located in low-income areas; with London at the top of the class.[23] These growing-up discrepancies surface among young adults. Almost a quarter of 18 to 24 year olds suffer long-term sickness, leading to worklessness, adding to the nation's drop in productivity. And for the first time, because the mental capacity of the young has stalled, the mental ability of older generations is catching up with the brain functions of the new generation.

In 2024, the University College London Institute of Health Equity estimated that a million people in 90% of areas in England lived shorter lives than they should between 2011 and the start of the pandemic.[24] The brunt of the despair is borne by northern working class constituencies, which is why they favoured Brexit. Cancelling membership of the European Union on the promise of "taking back our laws" encouraged the deprived regions to hope for improvements in their prospects. Instead, as the president of the National Farmers' Union observed, nothing changed. "Large landowners…living off the state" did not deliver a more equitable system.[25]

Not surprisingly, therefore, because of the rising cost of housing, there is a decline in young people in their 20s living together; and those that marry, postpone the day they will have children, or cancel parenthood entirely. The result is a demographic crisis, with the birth-rate continuing its downward spiral.

And so, finally, back to the streets of Blackpool. The town that "has the highest need for funding across the NHS, local government, police and public health – 74% higher than in Wokingham, which has the lowest estimated need". Seventy years later, as many of the boys with whom I attended school are now dead, their grand-children roam the streets in the town ranked as the most deprived of 317 local authority areas in England.[26] Blackpool South Tory MP Scott Benton described some of those children as committing "hundreds of crimes". A boy aged 11 was one of the ringleaders. A court's decision not to jail a 16-year-old gun-wielding youth

Box 9.2 Parliamentary services

In a newspaper "sting", Scott Benton was revealed as offering his parliamentary services "for sale". He was suspended for breaching Parliament's code of conduct. He gave up his parliamentary seat. A *Financial Times* investigation revealed that 34 MPs quit Parliament, or had been disciplined by their party "following claims of bad behaviour since December 2019".*

Sir Alistair Graham, a former chair of the government's independent committee on standards in public life, said voters would be "worried by the scale of misconduct" revealed by the newspaper, which was likely to further "undermine trust" in politicians from its current "very low" base.

* Lucy Fisher *et al* (2023), "MPs behaving badly erode the trust of voters", *Financial Times*, Dec. 18.

led Benton to pronounce on the state of the nation: "This demonstrates everything that is wrong with our country".[27] (See Box 9.2)

Parliamentarians knew who to blame for the traumas endured by children. One of them, Tory MP James Daly, claimed that most children in his northern constituency who struggled were "the products of crap parents".[28]

The political problems originating in Westminster percolated down to local governments. Fourteen municipal authorities declared themselves bankrupt, with *The Guardian* (in mid-2023) reporting that at least 26 English councils were "at risk of effective bankruptcy within the next two years".[29] This is one outcome of democratic politics: bankruptcy by a thousand cuts to public services, which in turn cause people's deaths.

Meanwhile, some residents in Blackpool were not enduring the fate of those destined to die prematurely. The seaside town turned in the worst performance for capital gains from housing in England. Even so, the capital gains were visible – they rose by 220% since 1995.[30]

The outlook for generations born into families that owned their properties was one of celebration. Over the two decades to the 2040s, as my generation dies, they will inherit an estimated £1.2tn in wealth – the largest wealth transfer in history for the UK.[31]

Bankrupt governance

When central government was confronted by the formal declaration that some local authorities were bankrupt, the Labour government sent envoys to Warrington to demand "best value" decision-making. This exposed the deceit and hypocrisy in the narrative of governance, as with talk of "serving the people". The template government practice is to achieve the opposite, as when central government takes taxes from low-income people in the northern regions, and invests that money in London infrastructure; which then creates additional value which, instead of being recycled into self-funding strategies for the public sector, are allowed to spill over into the pockets of the owners of Rent-yielding assets.

That is what happened with the ripples from Margaret Thatcher's "free market" reforms (Fig. 9.3). She privatised social housing

Figure 9.3 **Best value governance?**

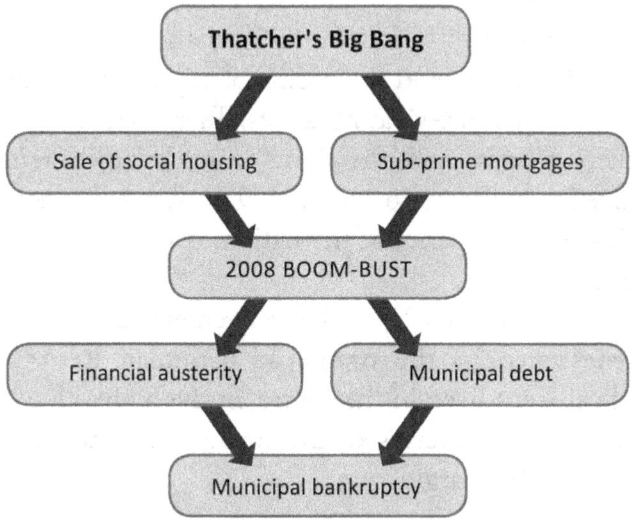

– enabling tenants to sell and pocket the profit, contributing to the excitement of accumulating wealth without working for it. That contributed to the 1990s reckless lending to low-income families, creating the sub-prime mortgages that were assembled and lent on to institutions like local governments; which were then trapped in the crisis of the 2008 housing boom/bust. This led central government to bail out the banks and impose austerity on the population; which included reduced funding to local authorities, which found they could not fulfil their obligations to residents in need of welfare support. So some of them, like Warrington, entered into reckless borrowing and investing, including in property; which, in turn, led to unmanageable debt and bankruptcy.[32]

The Indictment

Since 2011, life expectancy in the UK plateaued, then went into reverse, with the North suffering a greater drop than the South. This was among the worst performances in a comparison of 22 countries.[33]

Prior to the onset of industrialisation, the economic paradigm was not dishonest. Within agriculture, the extraction of Rent was in plain sight. But with the factory-based economic model, the new doctrine maintained that rewards were based on inputs into the value-creating system. In fact, nothing changed. The net revenue, after deducting wages and the profits of capital inputs, leaked out to the owners of Rent-yielding assets. There was no bonanza for the workers. Wages, once the Rents were deducted, remained at subsistence levels. Rents soared (Fig. 9.4). Land was not required to contribute to prosperity of the nation. It was, after all, merely a "status good".[34]

The deaths inflicted by this arrangement, as a consequence, were orchestrated by the profile of Ricardian Rent. The least vulnerable citizens lived in the centre, in the high-value locations; and mortality rates increased, the further one moved from the centre towards the margin.

Figure 9.4 **Average House Rents**
England & Wales 1640-1880

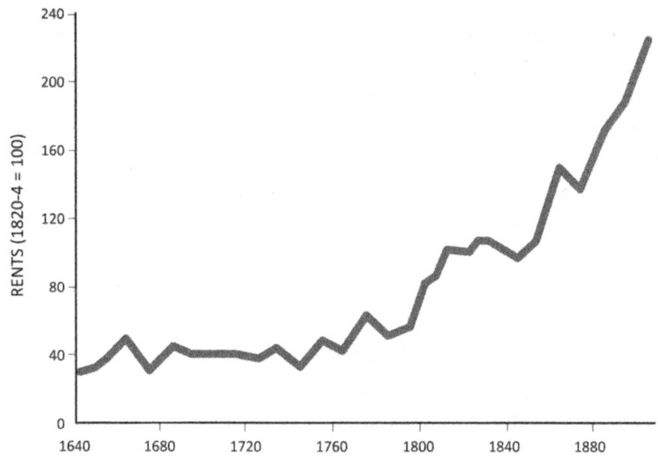

Source: Gregory Clark (2002), "Shelter from the Storm: Housing and the Industrial Revolution, 1550 1912", *J of Economic History*, 62(2), p.26. https://faculty.econ.ucdavis.edu/faculty/gclark/papers/housecost.pdf

Thus, democracy's kill rate does not rely on random interventions. It is a social process. The spatial distribution is ordained by statecraft. To test this thesis, of a symmetrical relationship between deaths and their spatial distribution, I drew a line on a map from London, following the straight Roman road that runs to Northeast England. On this, I plotted the data for location Rents and for average life expectancies.[35] The higher the location Rents, the longer the life expectancy. The lowest location Rents, in the Northeast, corresponded with the shortest life expectancy. A similar pattern

Figure 9.5 **Suicide rates, England and Wales 2021**

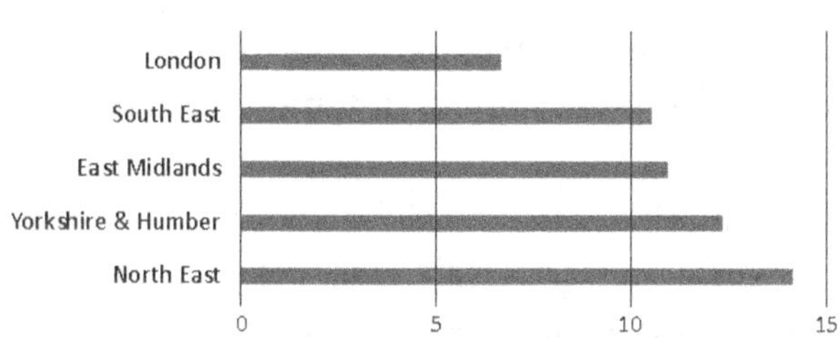

Box 9.3 **Apartheid economics**

There are exceptions. In 2021, Sajid Javid was appointed Minister of Health and Social Care. He had suffered a terrible tragedy when his brother committed suicide in 2018. He understood that "Someone is twice as likely to die in the North East by suicide than in London. We must not shy away from these disparities. Men who live in some of the most deprived areas are up to 10 times more at risk of suicide than in affluent areas".* Javid did not identify the roots of the systemic problem. "I said that we must treat suicide with the same urgency that we treat any other major killer."

* Sajid Javid (2022), "Focus on suicide like any other major killer", *Daily Telegraph*, 10 October.

is revealed in the data on suicides. More people kill themselves in the Northeast than in London per 100,000 population. The variation in suicide rates is obverse to the distribution of privatised Rent. Starting in London, as the Rent gradient declines, the suicide gradient increases (Fig. 9.5).[36]

My study made no impression on parliamentarians. People in power are not willing to acknowledge the mortal blot on the political landscape (Box 9.3). They celebrate property rights as sacred. The death rate suggests they are sacrilegious. The freedom to hoard land, for example, allowing time to boost capital gains, is a positive outcome for corporate house builders.[37] The offsetting human costs are not discussed. So horrific are the implications for personal responsibilities that it is not surprising that people seek refuge in denial. Which is why we need to locate the numbers in the big picture. First, we need a systems-wide analysis. But that, too, is problematic.

Kenneth Boulding (1910–1993), an English-born American economist, co-founded general systems theory. He explained the purpose of the new discipline in these terms:

Figure 9.6 **Male life expectancy at birth (years)**

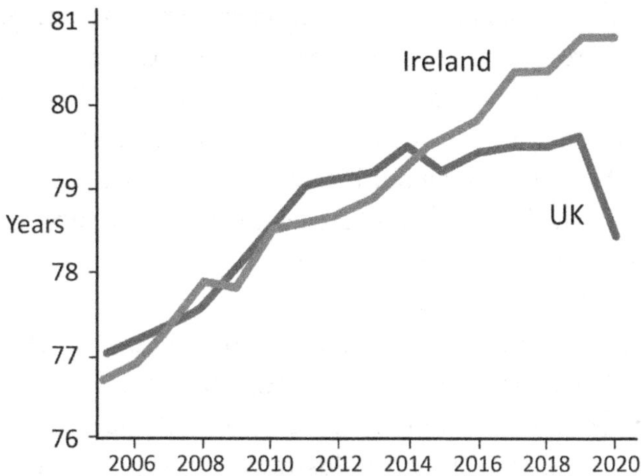

Source: World Bank, Statista

> **General Systems Theory is the skeleton of science in the sense that it aims to provide a framework or structure of systems on which to hang the flesh and blood of particular disciplines and particular subject matters in an orderly and coherent corpus of knowledge.**[38]

With one possible exception, apparently. He assigned "a rather minor…even declining…role for land rent in the total economy".[39] A curious conclusion, given the statistical evidence. So, we turn to the law.

In 2010, Tom Bingham published a book called *The Rule of Law*. He wrote with authority: he was the only person who ever held all three top legal positions in Britain, including Lord Chief Justice. In his book, he analysed Article 2 of the European Court of Human Rights. The right to life was "the most fundamental of all rights". There was "a substantial obligation" on member states "not to take life without justification". Those states had to "establish a framework of laws, precautions, procedures and means of enforcement which will, to the greatest extent reasonably practicable, protect life".[40]

He died six months after publishing his account of the rule of law. If he had lived, would Bingham have agreed to be a party to the indictment of the British government for contravening Article 2? The evidence is overwhelming: statecraft's fingerprints are all over tens of thousands of needless deaths, every year. Furthermore, life expectancy in the UK is contracting. Fig. 9.6 tracks the contraction for men, compared to Ireland. Instead of being curtailed, life expectancy would have been much extended in both countries, by now, if their Acts of Parliaments had not suppressed the wealth and welfare that people would otherwise have accumulated over the past three centuries.

Our indictment is reinforced by the evidence offered by Professor Sir Michael Marmot. His Institute of Health Equity at University College, London, surveyed the life-chances of the people of Britain. The injustices were illustrated by women who lived in the London borough of Kensington and Chelsea. Residents in the affluent wards lived to an average of 90.7 years. Women in the poorest wards could only expect 77.2 years. Sir Michael concluded: "Put simply, Britain is a poor, sick country, getting sicker, with a few rich and healthy people; the results of a dismal failure of central government policies since 2010".[41]

References Chapter 9

1 https://www.health.org.uk/evidence-hub/health-inequalities/map-of-healthy-life-expectancy-at-birth

2 https://lordslibrary.parliament.uk/effects-of-corruption-in-the-uk/

3 For Ricardo's account of the fiscal implications of raising revenue from Rent, see Ch. 12 of his *On the Principles of Political Economy and Taxation* (1817).

4 Geographic inequalities in premature mortality – The Health Foundation https://www.health.org.uk/reports-and-analysis/analysis/geographic-inequalities-in-premature-mortality

5 Poppy Wood (2025), "Ofsted chief: school rating revamp to hit house prices", *Daily Telegraph*, 4 July.

6 Brendan Cooper (2025), *Echoing Greens: How Cricket Shaped the English Imagination*, London: Constable.

7 I.E. Buchan *et al* (2017), "North-South disparities in English mortality 1965–2015: longitudinal population study", *Journal of Epidemiology and Community Health* (August 7), p.935.

8 Tom Meade *et al* (2007), "George James Miller", *British Medical Journal*, 334(7596), p.753. doi: 10.1136/bmj.39168.678519.BE

9 George J. Miller (2003), *Dying for Justice*, London: Centre for Land Policy Studies.

10 Christine Camacho *et al* (2024), "Risk factors for deaths of despair in England: An ecological study of local authority mortality data", *Social Science & Medicine*, 342(116560), p.4.

11 Vilfredo Pareto (1906), *Manual of Political Economy*; Ch. VII, §19, p.195 in the edition edited by Aldo Montesano *et al*, 2014, Oxford: Oxford University Press.

12 https://safeguarding.network/content/childhood-obesity-a-safeguarding-issue/#:~:text=Children%20living%20in%20deprived%20areas,in%20the%20most%20deprived%20areas.

13 J.B. Habicht *et al* (2022), "Children are full of optimism, but those rose-tinted glasses are fading—Reduced learning from negative outcomes drives hyper-optimism in children", *Journal of Experimental Psychology: General*, 151(8). https://doi.org/10.1037/xge0001138

14 https://www.dailymail.co.uk/news/article-11510237/Quarter-million-unemployed-young-Britons-planning-NEVER-job-survey-shows.html?ito=email_share_article-top

15 Fred Harrison (1997), "The Coming 'Housing' Crash", in *The Chaos Makers*, London: Vindex, p.27.

16 Fred Harrison (2005), *Boom Bust: House Prices, Banking and The Depression of 2010*, London: Shepheard-Walwyn.

17 Fred Harrison (2010), 2010: *The Inquest*, London: DA Horizons.

18 *Ibid.*

19 https://www.sigoma.gov.uk/news/2023/poorest-councils-have-seen-3-times-the-cuts-as-richest-say-sigoma

20 Michael Kumhof (2022), "Post-Corona Balanced-Budget Super-Stimulus: The Case for Shifting Taxes onto Land – An Application to the UK Economy", Royal Economic Society Annual Conference, April 12.

21 J.M. Keynes (1924), *A Tract on Monetary Reform*, London: Macmillan, p.80. Emphasis in original.

22 https://neu.org.uk/latest/library/arts-apocalypse

23 Amy Borrett (2024), "A-level results show students in London are top of the class", *Financial Times*, Aug. 16.

24 Health inequalities, lives cut short - IHE (instituteofhealthequity.org) https://www.instituteofhealthequity.org/resources-reports/health-inequalities-lives-cut-short

25 Madeleine Speed (2023), "Farmers' union chief says subsidy regime still favours big landowners", *Financial Times*, Dec. 18.

26 https://www.blackpooljsna.org.uk/People-and-Places/Wider-determinants-of-health/Deprivation.aspx

27 https://www.dailymail.co.uk/news/article-11450467/Thug-16-pulls-gun-disabled-woman-isnt-locked-up.html
28 https://www.telegraph.co.uk/politics/2023/12/29/crap-parents-struggling-children-tory-mp-james-daly/
29 https://www.theguardian.com/society/2023/aug/28/at-least-26-english-councils-at-risk-of-bankruptcy-in-next-two-years
30 https://www.ons.gov.uk/visualisations/housingpriceslocal/E06000009/#house_price
31 https://endly.co/inheritance-statistics-uk/
32 In 2025, Warrington Council had debts of £1.9bn and a budget black hole of almost £50m. Jennifer Williams and Ellesheva Kissin (2025), "Experts head for debt-laden council in Warrington", *Financial Times*, May 9.
33 David A. Leon *et al* (2019), "Trends in life expectancy and age-specific mortality in England and Wales, 1970–2016, in comparison with a set of 22 high-income countries: an analysis of vital statistics data", *Lancet Public Health*, 4:e575-e582.
34 Gregory Clark (1998), "Land Hunger: Land as a Commodity and as a Status Good in England, 1500-1910", *Explorations in Economic History*, 35(1).
35 Fred Harrison (2006), *Ricardo's Law: House Prices and the Great Tax Clawback Scam*, London: Shepheard-Walwyn.
36 Office for National Statistics (2022), Suicides in England and Wales: 2021 registrations, Statistical bulletin.
37 https://www.housingtoday.co.uk/news/cma-launches-inquiry-into-housebuilding/5122003.article
38 K.E. Boulding (1956), "General Systems Theory – The Skeleton of Science", *Management Science*, 2(208). https://www.panarchy.org/boulding/systems.1956.html
39 K.E. Boulding (1982) "A second look at progress and poverty", in Richard W. Lindblom and Arthur D. Lynn Jr (eds), *Land value taxation: the 'progress and poverty' centenary*, Madison, Wisc.: University of Wisconsin Press, p.17.
40 Tom Bingham (2010), *The Rule of Law*, London: Allen Lane, p.69.
41 https://www.instituteofhealthequity.org/in-the-news/news-coverage/poorer-people-dying-increasingly-younger-than-richer-people-as-dismal-life-expectancy-gap-grows-report-finds

CHAPTER TEN

The Bipolar State

The United Kingdom is not a "broken state". It does not need "fixing". It needs to be kept in its present condition. That is the view of those who own Rent-yielding assets.

Problems that do exist, are experienced by people outside the privileged circle of Rent receivers. They feel neglected. How could it be otherwise, if we are to maintain the rise in the capital gains on our homes? Which is why, on December 15, 2025, Britain's financial watchdog reduced the risk rules to permit banks to increase money available as mortgages. This was a "bid to widen access and boost growth" in the property market.[1] As the UK pivoted on the edge of the next housing crash, the Financial Conduct Authority wanted more people locked into mortgages they could barely afford to finance. *Success!*

The pressure was on, from politicians seeking to "fix" the nation's problems. Reputations built on promises to deliver affordable housing, reduce taxes and shift the fiscal burden on to the "wealthy". A bewildering list for the electorate to digest; with relatively few believing anything uttered by politicians.

To comprehend how a nation committed to the rule of law can end up in such chaos, we must come to terms with this question: *is the UK really broken?* We cannot resolve the issue by referring to the constitution. Britain's laws, values and conventions are bipolar. The unwritten constitution serves two constituencies.

Box 10.1 **Reshaping the collective consciousness**

Rentlords, out of necessity, had to overturn the shared consciousness of cooperation and consensus. One device was to victimise minority groups, portraying them as the enemy within. That mobilised the masses against "the Other". The sufferings of the working population could be pinned on those of a different race, colour or creed. Social psychologists call this "system-justification" through "the production of false consciousness".

Two Yale University psychologists traced how stereotyping people was such an effective strategy that the victims themselves were persuaded that all was normal; which is why they remained complicit in a system that was exploiting them. Through stealth, victims could be made to blame themselves for their misfortunes.*

* J.T. Jost and M.R. Banaji (1994), "The role of stereotyping in system-justification and the production of false consciousness", *British Journal of Social Psychology*, 33, pp.11-20.

Property rights are at the interface. One of the constituencies reaps riches by cheating; or, as John Stuart Mill put it, "Landlords grow rich in their sleep without working, risking or economizing".[2] The other constituency is composed of people who work to produce sufficient resources to meet all their needs, but are permanently marooned in a state of deficiency. They endure shortfalls in the funds needed to cover the costs of their material, social and spiritual welfare. Many of them fall within both categories; which is why Britain is locked in political paralysis.

The two constituencies are conjoined at two levels. They are bound by the unwritten constitution. And they are bound by dependence on Rent. These two elements are most immediately visible in government budget deficits and a narrative (neo-classical economics) completely divorced from reality.[3] And so, we return to the question: is the UK state a failure, or success? The answer depends on which side of the false consciousness you occupy (Box 10.1).

Figure 10.1 **Budget ceilings**

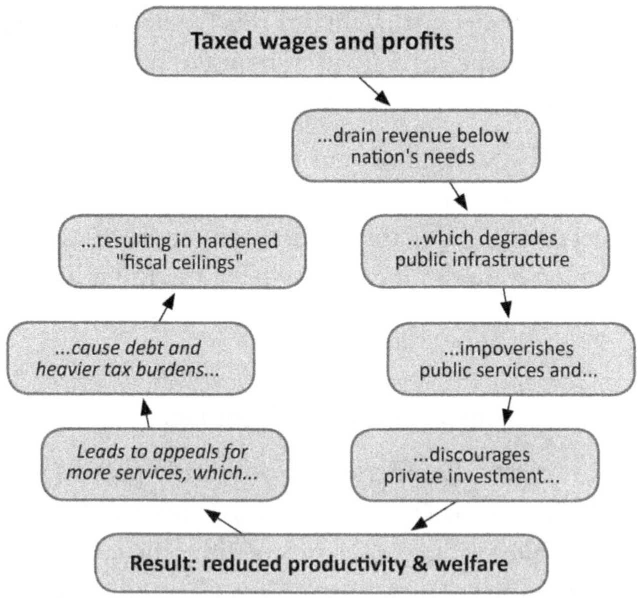

Classroom economic theory equates supply with demand. For ideological purposes, however, it is imperative that optimum production possibilities are not discussed. To liberate the economy, so that people can produce as much as they need, to pay for the services they want, it would be necessary to alter the structure of the revenue system. That debate is outlawed in the corridors of power. That is why short-term horizons dictate how Chancellors formulate budget policies. This covers up the strategy that ensures revenue can never be sufficient to fulfil the political promise to fully fund services and investment in infrastructure (Fig. 10.1).

Three layers emerge as the social order visibly decomposes.

1. *Civil conflict*: the wealthiest minority appropriate Rent for gratification, as the lives of producers are impoverished. Statecraft facilitates this, with subsidies that drain the public purse to favour the flow of revenue congealed in real estate.

2. *Corruption*: corporate entities are inducted into cheating, rigging commerce and lobbying for tax-funded privileges. Statecraft facilitates this behaviour through, for example, the regulatory system; the burden of which is shifted onto innocent parties.

3. *Chaos*: the system gravitates further away from balanced growth, as communities regress into social crises. Statecraft facilitates this outcome, by sponsoring technologies without claiming back the full rewards of tax-funded innovations.

Fiscal scam: Off the rails

The transport sector illuminates the politically perverse manner in which public income is transformed into private riches.

Transport plays a key role in creating the public space. By increasing the efficiency of urban systems, value is added to the commons. Civilised living in dense communities becomes possible if transit systems bind the space according to both efficiency and ethical standards. Conversely, does investment in transport infrastructure, under existing tax-and-tenure arrangements, create problems?

The transport racket was forensically documented by a London property owner. Don Riley was perfectly placed to monitor the impact of the £3.4bn investment in the construction of an underground railway (the Jubilee line) connecting Waterloo Station with a new financial centre in docklands. He owned buildings in Southwark, close to two of the new stations. He began to track the impact of the public's tax-funded investment on the commercial rents he could charge his tenants. The result was *Taken for a Ride*. The closer his properties were to the stations, the higher the rental uplift. *Location, location, location*. In return for the £3.4bn investment, Riley estimated that the net payback was close to £14bn, most of which accrued to commercial and residential property owners.[4]

Figure 10.2 **Tax-funded give-aways**

Premium compared to property located 1500m from railway station

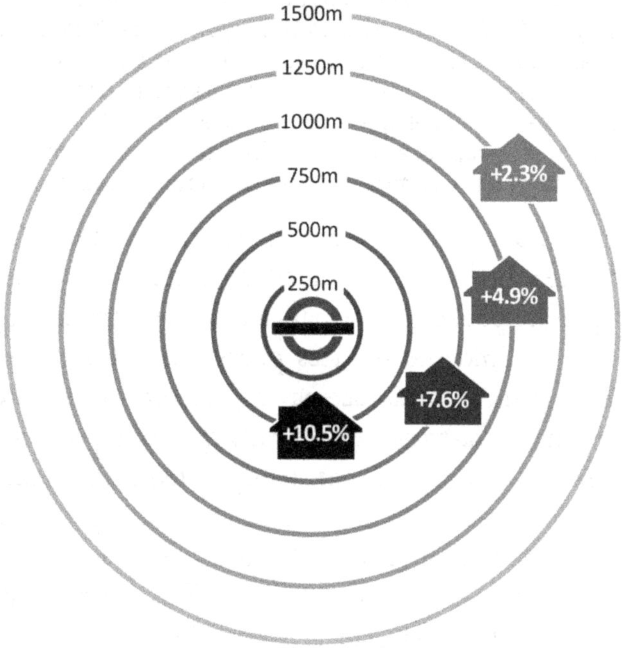

This was not a lottery-like risk situation. If you owned a location within the catchment area of the railway station, you were automatically a winner!

Riley's statistics were confirmed by two studies commissioned by the London transport authority.[5] A study in 2014 by Nationwide, the mortgage-granting building society, found that owners could expect to make an average of £42,000 more if they sold homes that were near a station. Its data confirmed that the gain declined by distance from the station, with a zero uplift in price at the 1,500 meter mark (Fig. 10.2).[6]

The scam served a second purpose. Elevated values offset the taxes paid by many owners of Rent-yielding assets. They lived the tax-free life! Riley provided the inside story to this financial fraud.

He noted how

> **a miracle happened. The government returned every penny that I had paid in taxes over the previous 40 years. So for four decades I had lived tax free – and I had not dodged the taxman! How was this possible? I 'confessed' in *Taken for a Ride*. Taxpayers generously funded the extension to the Jubilee Line, one of London's Underground lines. Two of the stations were located close to office properties that I own. Those two stations raised the value of my properties by more than all the taxes that I had paid into the public's coffers over the previous 40 years.**[7]

Tax payers who did not own strategically located properties, however, suffered. As Rent created by infrastructure is sluiced away into private pockets, governance becomes increasingly inefficient, unable to fund the services people need. Property owners reap the net gains, even as tax-paying tenants contribute to the cost of funding infrastructure like railways. This process is not a secret. One analysis of spatial inequality noted that "Public capital investment, allocated with the aim of maximising national value for money, flows disproportionately to those areas most likely to see a higher land value uplift as a result. This creates a structural bias towards already thriving local economies".[8]

One consequence is the crippling scale of sovereign indebtedness. According to Prof. David Miles, a member of the Office for Budget Responsibility, their extrapolations revealed that the ratio of debt to GDP would exceed 270% by 2070. He informed a parliamentary committee that "on current tax and spending settings, the UK is almost certainly on an unsustainable path". Their projections showed debt approaching 300% of GDP: "That couldn't happen because there'd be some juddering explosion some way down the road if you were on that path".[9] But what would take Britain off that path?

A failed state?

From the perspective of those who reap without sowing, the UK is not a failed state. The state of delirious happiness, however, is balanced by the deep depressions of the working population.

- Shattered expectations, a condition of deep national malaise, the erosion of trust in institutions and law-makers, are well documented. About 70% of Britons claim their prospects were deteriorating. Many of them willingly support radical change.[10] One metric of an imbalanced society: while property owners are reimbursed for the taxes they pay into the Treasury, more than half of the population (52.6%) receive more from the state, as benefits, than they paid into the Treasury.[11]

Many millions of full-time workers are not able to meet minimum biological needs, and are forced to resort to the charity of food banks.[12] According to the government's annual survey of households existing on below average income, in 2021/22 an estimated 14.4 million people were living in poverty, including 4.2 million children, 8.1 million working-age adults and 2.1 million pensioners. The shame of this state of affairs was censured by Olivier De Schutter, the UN's special rapporteur on extreme poverty and human rights. He declared that the UK was "in violation of international law" over its poverty levels.[13]

Judged in terms of the capacity of governments to protect people's wealth and welfare, Britain is a failed state. A comprehensive inventory of all state-sponsored failures would fill many shelves in the House of Commons Library. We are confined to listing a few examples. One is of the increasing number of children lured into the life of crime. In 2018, the Children's Commissioner for England estimated that 50,000 children were involved in "county line" gangs that transport and market drugs. Children act as couriers. In 2022, the Home Office registered 589 county line referrals. The UK's drugs laws are the biggest factor.[14] According to the National Crime Agency, "importing areas...are reporting increased levels of violence and weapons-related crimes as a result of this trend".[15]

Intentional blindness

HM Treasury is the instrument for enforcing the discriminatory distribution of the nation's income. In doing so, the exchequer of the first industrialised society accommodated cheating on an epic scale. To sustain the charge that this is behaviour based on wilful blindness, we need evidence from at least three whistle-blowers. Apologists of the *status quo* could dismiss one witness as harbouring a personal grudge. Two whistle-blowers might be a coincidence. Three testimonies reveal a pattern that cannot be ignored; particularly if the whistle-blowers once occupied the inner sanctums of power. Like a Transport Minister. Like the most senior civil servant in HM Treasury. And like a parliamentary law-maker turned Mayor of Manchester.

Whistle-blower 1: Steve Norris

As Parliamentary Under-Secretary of State for Transport (1992–1996), Steve Norris observed the administration of public policy from the inside. He was appalled at the inefficiencies, and he tried to correct some of them. He had no doubt where the inefficiency was rooted. "For generations this country has been massively held back by the malign influence of HM Treasury." He oversaw the administration of two major railway projects in London: the Jubilee Line, and Crossrail. The Treasury, Norris reveals, kept placing obstacles to these projects, solely because it failed to audit the full benefits.

Norris knew that the Jubilee Line would generate a vast return. To get the project off the blackboard, he secured the go-ahead after he threatened to resign and "tell the world that the Prime Minister was a downright liar. It had the desired effect".

Norris confirms that the Treasury continued to obstruct a catalogue of viable railway projects because of its doctrinaire attitude to spending money. "The UK Treasury knowns the price of everything and the value of nothing," he asserts, adding: "Reforming the Treasury is the biggest single change any government could make that would revitalise the whole United Kingdom".[16]

Box 10.2 A rare confession

Within days of leaving HM Treasury as its top civil servant, Macpherson confessed. As head of the Treasury in its darkest days, he admitted he was among those guilty of a "monumental collective intellectual error" in the run-up to the financial crash. "I see myself as one of a number of people in finance ministries, central bank regulators, in the UK and the US who failed to see the crisis coming, who failed to spot the build-up of risk," he admitted. "This was a monumental collective intellectual error."*

* George Parker (2016), "Veteran of Treasury battles tots up a decade's wins and losses", *Financial Times*, April 14.

Whistle-blower 2: Lord Macpherson

Civil servants charged with administering the public purse are complicit in a charade. They either know – or intentionally do not want to know – that there is a problem-solving optimal way of raising revenue, but they persist with deadweight taxes.

Nicholas (now Lord) Macpherson was chief economist before his elevation to Permanent Secretary of HM Treasury. During his 30 years at the heart of government, administering the collection of revenue to fund the state, he endured an abiding discomfort.

> **It worries me...that we don't have a land tax. In a sane world, we would have a proper land tax. Sadly the only person to try it was Lloyd George and he ended up having to pay every single penny back.**[17]

Macpherson revealed the pathological fear that prevented discussion of Rent as a source of public revenue. When he raised the topic in the corridors of power, his colleagues treated him as if he was "insane".[18] He affirms: "I tried my best to get successive governments interested in the taxation of land and property. But sadly I failed!"[19] Few public servants have been as honest as Nick Macpherson (Box 10.2).

Whistle-blower 3: Mayor of Manchester

Andy Burnham, a Labour Member of Parliament, became Chief Secretary to the Treasury in Gordon Brown's administration. Based on the insights he gleaned at the heart of government, he became convinced of the need to reform the revenue collecting system. He said so, when he joined the election contest for leadership of the Labour Party.

Having failed to become leader of the Opposition in Parliament, he successfully sought election as Mayor of Greater Manchester in 2017. To equalise life chances throughout Britain, he emphasised the importance of transport communications in any "levelling up" strategy. He proposed that the Northern Powerhouse Rail links should be funded out of Hong Kong-style land taxes. The former British colony funded the construction of its world-class metro out of rents from locations adjacent to the stations. His proposal was discussed with officials at the Department for Transport.[20]

Burnham was a working class lad who grew up in Liverpool. After Cambridge, he found himself on the road to high office in Parliament. All the time, however, he was uncomfortable with the realisation that "this country is two parallel worlds".[21] Burnham saw the way people were suffering in the northern constituencies, and he was unwilling to accommodate the double standards of public life. That is why he quit Parliament to seek election as Mayor of Manchester, taking with him the belief that the UK needed to reform the way in which the public sector funded itself.

Fiscal reform was not a trivial issue, in Burnham's view. It was imperative to adopt the policy that enabled governments to draw revenue from increases in Rents created by investment in public goods. "Land value capture is the way to take a first step out of that [unfair tax system], because you're not necessarily saying 'we're going to come and swipe something that you've got'." Without that reform "we're putting the country at risk".[22]

Ignoring the public statements of whistle-blowers is methodologically necessary for HM Treasury. It is able to maintain the fiction that forecasting the future is a risky business; beyond (say)

Box 10.3 **Bigger but not better**

The Economist critiqued Britain's revenue system as "getting bigger but not better". In 2023, the tax-take was about to reach its second highest level since WW2. HM Government's policies were riddled with exemptions "that distort the economy, confuse taxpayers and deprive the exchequer of revenue". Instead of encouraging efficiency and discouraging harmful outcomes (such as pollution), the government employed tax tools that were flawed.

On property taxes, which raised 3.8% of national income, *The Economist* noted that "A land-value tax... would be fairer and more efficient, encouraging landowners to put the space to its best use".* That pitifully modest reform, however, while pointing in the correct direction, would not end land speculation, unearned capital accumulation or the Rent-led 18-year boom/ bust business cycle that crushes jobs and enterprises.

* https://www.economist.com/britain/2023/04/11/britains-tax-take-is-getting-bigger-but-not-better

three months. This fits with the doctrines employed by the social sciences: ignore the working mechanism buried in the social structure, to avoid awkward questions (Box 10.3).

"No silver bullet"

Time and again, we have noted what happens when the Rent-as-public-revenue paradigm is raised in public. The Experts quash it with the mantra "There is no 'silver bullet'" solution to our world's problems. They formulate that metaphor in terms of a single, simple, quick remedy, as if pulled off by a magician. Then they equate this to the Rent policy as a red herring.

The Resolution Foundation offers an illustration of this technique. It received generous funds to conduct a 3-year enquiry into "stagnant" Britain. The London-based think tank could not identify realistic solutions to the slump in UK productivity, rising inequality and unaffordable housing. Operating within the neo-classical economics discourse, it did suggest that the Stamp Duty Land Tax should be cut; which, it claimed, would encourage enterprises to allocate buildings and land to better uses.[23] In reality, as Adam Smith had noted, the benefits would be mopped up as increases in the price of locations where people lived and worked, thereby amplifying the unaffordability of homes. The obverse approach, in the economic literature, is known as "land value taxation". The Foundation dismissed it as a "magic bullet" (aka "silver bullet"), and therefore not worth considering.[24]

Why are economists and media commentators quick to rule out the notion of a silver bullet? Could it be because lawmakers would not want their attention drawn to a fundamental remedy that they wished to ignore? Might The Experts fear the loss of financially remunerative consultancies if they identified the once-and-for-all solution to issues that persist in disrupting people's lives? Alternatively, do they really believe that our world is so complex that each problem requires a tailor-made solution? Whatever the explanation, the claim that there is no silver bullet must be sustained by the culture of cheating. Psychologically, it is now difficult for lawmakers and their think-tank advisers to admit that they have wasted the lives of generations of people, by successfully accommodating the dead-end policies that lead to so many premature deaths of Britain's citizens (Box 10.4).

When net income is at the service of the people who work to produce it, power resides with them. When control over that revenue falls into the private sector, people's lives, and the social system, are dislocated. This was of little concern to the landlords who dominated Westminster in the 18th century, who were never going to adopt the thesis of *The Wealth of Nations*. Which is why spurious explanations are fabricated to explain ruptures in the economy. One favourite straw man is "market failure". In fact, many of the failures are rooted in governance.[25] The "market failure" mantra, however, serves a cultural purpose: it distracts people from thinking about the impact of Rent when it is privatised.

Box 10.4 **The no Silver Bullet mantra**

One denial of a silver bullet solution was provided by the Labour Government that was elected in 2024. Darren Jones, the Chief Secretary to HM Treasury, promised to "leave no stone unturned in rooting out public sector waste". Their initiatives, however, would not include a silver bullet. "Of course," he announced, "to get a grip on waste there will be no one silver bullet."*

Commentators support this posture. One of them, Roger Bootle, is senior independent adviser to the London-based Capital Economics, and a senior fellow at Policy Exchange. In ruminating about the UK's problems, he is adamant about one issue. The headline on his article read: "There is no silver bullet for Britain's economy". He warned readers that "we must also beware of dangerous would-be silver bullet solutions to our economic problems".**

* Darren Jones (2025), "We will leave no stone unturned in rooting out public sector waste", *Daily Telegraph*, Jan. 12.

** *Daily Telegraph*, Jan. 6, 2025.

The one chance to rebase the public's revenue was with the advent of universal suffrage: democracy. Reflect on what might have been, if the Liberal Government's plans in 1910 had come to fruition instead of being scrapped in 1920. Winston Churchill's vision would have prevailed, in which

> **taxes upon the unearned increment in land are necessary, legitimate and fair; and that without any evil consequences to the refinement or the richness of our national life, still less any injury to the sources of its economic productivity, they will yield revenue sufficient in this year and in the years to come to meet the growing needs of Imperial defence and of social reform.**[26]

It was not to be. Result: the UK's vitality ebbed away into the global depression of the 1930s. Since then, when invited to comment on the economics of Henry George, the objection (according to Simon Winchester in his history of land) is that the policy is "too difficult to administer".[27]

Box 10.5 Animal Spirits

Keynes, having dismissed "the land question", replaced the 3-factor model of economics with a 2-factor model consisting of labour/wages and capital/interest. No land/Rent. As a result, the structurally-induced 18-year boom/bust cycle driven by the property market was not allowed to intrude in the minds and models of lawmakers and macroeconomists.

How, then, to explain market failures? Keynes relied on "animal spirits".* Bubbles animated by herd instincts, with people relying on emotions to follow money trails until they collapse. Today, economists are trying to make sense of market data by analysing the language used by those with animal spirits.** This is an attempt to reinvent the wheel: predicting, by counting words, what can be predicted with the 3-factor model of economics.

* J.M. Keynes (1936), *General Theory of Employment, Interest and Money*, p.144.

** J.P. Flynn and K. Sastry (2024), "The Macroeconomics of Narratives", Cambridge, MA: NBER Working Paper 32602.

A more thoughtful treatment concluded that Rent

> **provides a broad, stable and identifiable tax base that falls on the landowner and can provide a clear correlation with wealth; is not distortive of behaviour; is a just form of taxation of the 'unearned increment' in the value of land; and may promote the development of under-utilised land assuming the tax is levied based on its 'highest and best use' (HABU) rather than its existing use.**[28]

Over the long term, the costs of ignoring that wisdom are incalculable (Box 10.5).

The Indictment

Statecraft rigged by the culture of cheating causes the deaths of tens of thousands of citizens, every year, in the UK alone. That verdict is based on the nuanced evidence such as the despair that ends in mortality. The sequences cannot be contested, some stemming

Figure 10.3 **Rates of homelessness per 10,000 people (2023)**

Source: OECD

from the cost of owning a home that drives young people into the feeling of hopelessness, despair resulting in worklessness, loneliness that can lead to premature death.[29] Britain suffers the highest rate of homelessness among the world's richest nations (Fig. 10.3).

Events *could* have turned out different, but for what occurred in antiquity. The prevailing assumption that there was no alternative to the dynastic model of statecraft is false. One Egyptologist affirms that the dynastic rule-based territorial/nation-state model "was only one possibility among several".[30] Which is why we have to explore the alternatives, not least because the end of humanity itself is now a real risk.

Statecraft grounded in Rent privatisation is programmed to terminate our species. In my view, based on the insatiable appetites that stem from free riding, that point has now been reached. Contributing to that outcome is the corresponding violation of right to life in nature.

Neither in the past, nor in the present, did humans set out to intentionally extinguish other species. The deaths and destruction of birds and bees and their habitats were casualties of the war fought between humans in the Social Galaxy. Extinction in nature stems from our property rights and the related market pricing system. Agriculture, and then industry, were organised without taking into account the costs of carbon emissions; the chemicalisation of soil; chopping down trees; or dumping waste into rivers and oceans. To have paid for those costs would have reduced what was left as Rent.

Out of sight, out of mind. In the early phase of farming, and then industrial production, knowledge of chemistry and biology was not available to flag up the consequences. But there is no excuse for us, today. Evidence accumulated over the last 70 years has left no doubt that we are systematically abusing the natural world, and that the loss of species and natural habitats is a threat to the well-being of humans. And yet, unabated, we continue to degrade the natural world. Endless UN-drafted proclamations are announced, goals set, initiatives taken; with no reversal of the damage to climate and the life expectancies of other species. The failure is due to one reason only: we continue to abide by the pricing system that automatically impoverishes not just the Social Galaxy, but the natural universe. And that – sooner or later – means humanity will no longer be viable.

Biodiversity, which is essential to human well-being, is in steep decline. Wildlife populations have shrunk by over 70% since 1980, with a further one million animal and plant species facing extinction. The Global Biodiversity Framework's 2030 mission to reverse biodiversity loss will not be achieved, because agencies like the OECD canvass all kinds of remedial policies except the one fiscal change that would carry sufficient clout to alter our collective behaviour.[31]

Why does this mean the human project must come to an end?

Statecraft, in its present form, is the Social Galaxy's version of nature's entropy. Property rights and tax policies systemically inflict the pathologies that fragment people's lives. Globally, millions die as a direct or indirect result of that statecraft. The fusion of energy achieved by pre-civilised peoples is dissipated into the state of disorder by behaviour that dishonours what it means to be human. Through the looming economic chaos, that disorder is about to merge all the parts into a single collision. That, along with the depletion of our planetary systems, does mean the end of humanity.

We must, therefore, indict the community of nations for committing the crime against humanity. Prior to 1944, nations were segregated behind sovereign borders. Political isolationism ended with the commitment to "universal rights" enshrined in declarations proclaimed by the United Nations. Nations that signed the UN Charter became directly responsible for ensuring the stewardship of both our Social Galaxy, and the natural world. Instead, the kill rate of plants and animals accelerated through to the 21st century. The UK, with its intensive agriculture, and industrial pollution, is one of the most nature-depleted countries on Earth.[32] The Office for Environmental Protection, in its 2025 report, declared the government "largely off track" to meet its legal environment targets.[33]

This is what systemic suicide looks like. Which is why we continue to inhale plastic particles that congeal in our brains; pour out the emissions that fire up the infernos that burn down whole regions; unleash the tides that swamp coastal communities. These are early signs of what is to come, unless we restore the human project. That, above all, means we need to realign property rights and the distribution of income in favour of those who work to produce the flow of energy that made possible the emergence of humanity on Earth.

It can be done. We need to reformulate Rent, however, if we are to address the globalised realities of the 21st century.

References Chapter 10

1 Martin Arnold (2025), "Mortgage rules poised for easing in bid to widen access and boost growth", *Financial Times*, Dec. 16.

2 John Stuart Mill (1848), *Principles of Political Economy*, Bk V, Ch. 2. The quotation concludes by declaring that "The increase in the value of land, arising as it does from the efforts of an entire community, should belong to the community and not to the individual who might hold title".

3 Karim El-Ayoubi (2025), *Realonomics*, London: Shepheard-Walwyn.

4 Don Riley (2024), 2nd edn., *Taken for a Ride*, London: Shepheard-Walwyn.

5 https://iea.org.uk/publications/research/wheels-of-fortune

6 https://www.theguardian.com/money/2014/aug/20/distance-from-station-value-of-house-nationwide-uk

7 Fred Harrison (2006), *Wheels of Fortune*, London: Institute of Economic Affairs, pp. 11-12.

8 Anna Stansbury *et al* (2023), Tackling the UK's regional economic inequality: Binding constraints and avenues for policy intervention, Harvard Kennedy School Working Paper Series No. 198, p.53. Diane Coyle and Marianne Sensier (2020). 'The Imperial Treasury: Appraisal Methodology and Regional Economic Performance in the UK'. *Regional Studies* 54(3).

9 Emma Taggart (2025), "OBR: Britain risks explosion in national debt", *Daily Telegraph*, Dec. 17.

10 https://www.johnsmithcentre.com/news/research-shattered-britain-report/

11 Office for National Statistics (2024), "Taxes and benefits on UK household income: financial year ending 2023", p.8.

12 More than 10% of the population (excluding Scotland) used a food bank in 2022. Susannah Irvine *et al* (2022), *Food Banks in the UK*, House of Commons Library, No 8585, p.5.

13 https://www.theguardian.com/society/2023/nov/05/uk-poverty-levels-simply-not-acceptable-says-un-envoy-olivier-de-schutter

14 https://www.opendemocracy.net/en/grooming-county-lines-uk-drug-laws-fuelling-child-exploitation-policing/

15 https://www.nationalcrimeagency.gov.uk/what-we-do/crime-threats/drug-trafficking/county-lines

16 Emails, Steve Norris to Jonathan Brown, August 7, 2023.

17 Lord Macpherson, statement, Resolution Foundation seminar, London, October 24, 2018.

18 Macpherson's "insane" statement may be viewed on YouTube: www.resolutionfoundation.org/events/ light-at-the-end-of-the-tunnel-will-it-be-anend-of-austerity-budget/

19 Personal communication to the present author, June 5, 2023.

20 https://www.yorkshirepost.co.uk/news/politics/land-taxes-plan-to-pay-for-high-speed-rail-should-be-explored-says-mcloughlin-3578625

21 Mick Brown (2023), "'If the party thinks it's my time, I wouldn't turn away'". *Daily Telegraph*, June 11.

22 https://www.lgcplus.com/politics/devolution-and-economic-growth/burnham-land-value-tax-is-the-first-step-out-of-broken-tax-system-25-11-2022/

23 Resolution Foundation (2023), *Ending Stagnation: A New Economic Strategy for Britain*, The Final Report of the Economy 2030 Inquiry, p.219.

24 *Ibid*, p.97.

25 Joseph E. Stiglitz (2009), "Government Failure vs. Market Failure: Principles of Regulation", DOI:10.1017/CBO9780511657504.002

26 Speech, Manchester, 23 May, 1909. https://winstonchurchill.org/publications/finest-hour/finest-hour-135/wit-wisdom-wsc-on-taxation/

27 Simon Winchester (2021), *Land*, London: William Collins, p.393n.

28 C. Hughes *et al* (2020), "Implementing a land value tax: considerations on moving

from theory to practice", *Land Use Policy*, 94(104494). doi: https://doi.org/10.1016/j.landusepol.2020.104494

29 https://www.gov.uk/guidance/governments-work-on-tackling-loneliness

30 Juan Carlos Moreno García, "From House Societies to States: An introduction", in Juan Carlos Moreno García (2022), *From House Societies to States Early Political Organisation from Antiquity to the Middle Ages*, Oxford: Oxbow, p.20.

31 OECD (2025), *Scaling Up Biodiversity-Positive Incentives*, Paris.

32 TP25999-State-of-Nature-main-report_2023_FULL-DOC-v12.pdf

33 https://www.theoep.org.uk/report/government-has-chance-get-track-meet-legal-environmental-commitments-window-opportunity

Part 3
Manifesto for Humanity

PROLOGUE

One World Rent

Humanity now pivots on an inflection point like no other in its evolutionary history. From the time of writing this prognosis, in 2025, we have five years in which to agree on the need to rescue our species by relaunching the human project.

It took 500,000 years, from the time when brain enlargement encouraged prolonged maturation of children, for the human project to mature.

It took 5,000 years to unravel that achievement, beginning in antiquity with the assault on the evolutionary blueprint by the dynastic cheats.

It took 500 years to test that model of statecraft with the tools of the Enlightenment, from science, and from anthropology. Verdict: we failed.

It will take 5 years to reach a consensus on how to navigate the looming chaos.

We cannot turn the clock back, but we can amass resources with which to chart a new future. We achieve this by extrapolating the past, which enables us to predict what is in store for humanity. Viewing that future is possible, for three reasons. First, and finally, we have now decoded the architecture of the Social Galaxy. Second, we now have a clear understanding of how the cheating instinct was institutionalised. Third, the parameters of the future have already begun to unfold.

That we are on course to continue with irresponsible behaviour is illustrated by our treatment of near-Earth space. The Satellite Database compiled by the Union of Concerned Scientists lists about 9,800 active satellites in Earth's orbit. We fail to levy a Rent for the use of the orbital highways. We fail to charge Rents for the use of the electromagnetic spectrum, through which we commercialise the satellites. We fail to charge Rent to cover the clean-up costs of the junk that is dumped in space. Soon, the moon will be carved up for commercial profit, without charging Rent for those who plan to pillage its resources.

The human project needs to be reappraised, to avoid Armageddon and...well, to work, so we can create the closest we can get to heaven on Earth.

How we achieve this is the primary question of our age.

The key issue from history is this. By comparing foraging and farming communities, we learn that before the onset of civilisation, people exercised direct control over the cheating instinct. Cheats were shamed into behaving themselves. This changed, with the shift to institutionalised controls over the affairs of communities. The cheats found ways to pocket the net incomes produced by the people.

The key issue for the future is the protection of our net resources. Through the Audit and Accounting system, people would be made aware of what was happening in their names, and would be empowered to ensure their Rents were deployed for the common good. The enforcement of the Zero Deadweight (Z-D) goal on governance would discipline law-makers, by disallowing degenerate policies.

So, how do we begin this mission?

Imagine this. A time machine carries you back to sometime between five and ten thousand years ago, setting you down in the Fertile Crescent. The era of scattered villages, in which people have begun to grow their food to meet their full-belly needs; along with producing a net income to fund the infrastructure of their emerging urban settlements. They need to be made aware of the rules required to optimise the co-ordination of life in dense civilisations. Specifically, the transition needs to be facilitated from common to private possession of land. What is the best advice you could give them, to avoid a life of being exploited by others?

In addressing this fateful question, we would not be just engaging in a counterfactual exercise in rewriting history. The insights needed by the Neolithic people are the same as those we need in the 21st century. We now need to formalise the rules for life beyond the model that was created in antiquity.

To navigate the present global turmoil, the first priority is a revision of property rights and the accompanying system of public finance. If we fail to come to terms with the need for change, we will continue to be exposed to the same temptations that enabled free riders to capture civilisation back in antiquity.

There is one big difference. Back then, the collapse of a civilisation did not alter the fate of humanity. Today, there is nowhere on Earth to hide. We are all pivoting on the same precipice, facing the same four existential threats. Each threat operates according to its own logic, but all four share a common root cause. And all four will be forced to converge as a direct result of the economic collapse at the end of the current 18-year cycle.

The time has come to face reality. Some concerned citizens are already generating proposals, but these are tantamount to prevarication. Take the case of those who propose we opt out of growth. They promote zero, or even negative, growth. Similarly with the response to poverty – blame is attributed to the numbers of people who live on the planet. These strategies would amplify, not remediate, the crises. As a result, governments will be so distracted

Figure P3.1 **Global Public Debt set to exceed 100% of GDP**

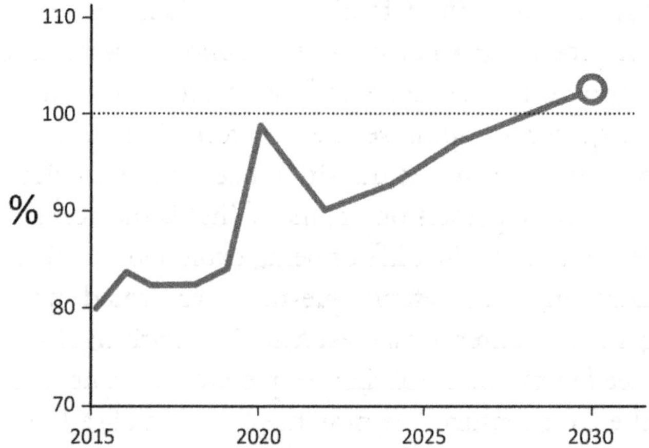

by the converging existential threats that they will ignore the need for qualitative reform. An indicator of the poverty of governance is the scale of global public debt. It is projected to exceed 100% of GDP by 2029, according to the IMF (Fig. P3.1).[1] Add this fiscal burden to the crash in house prices, and we have something more than a re-run of a banking crisis. In 2008, the banks that cashed-in on sub-prime mortgages were rescued because they were deemed "too big to fail". Governments bailed them out. But with governments around the world now bankrupt – owing more than their annual production – who will bail out the governments that are "too big to fail"? Not private savers, who will be panicking over the erosion in the value of their assets.

Governments, of course, can control the money supply through their central banks. That will be of little comfort, in 2028, as they ramp up the liquidity to pay the interest on sovereign debts, while reducing budget expenditures as inflation soars and social vitality is further depleted. The global system will be locked into a perfect storm. But that is only a small part of the story. For the global economic crisis will cause the four existential threats to converge in a collision never before experienced by humanity. The time has come to restore social responsibilities to the doctrine of human rights.

We occupy Earth for one reason only: our primate ancestors began to uncover the secret of growth, and they evolved the formula for controlling that process.

We need growth, to materialise what it means to be human: to fund the orchestras that play symphonies; to fund the artists who portray reality on canvas; to fuel our moral and spiritual sensibilities, and the intellectual ingenuity that turned aspirations about the stars into the ability to walk on the moon. None of this can be achieved without growth.

Growth, however, need not inflict damage on nature. Need not corrupt the collective consciousness. In Part 3, I explain how our intellectual communities *are* aware of the reforms to property rights that would combine morality with efficiency. That reform would sustain the kind of growth consistent with the geometry our ancient ancestors developed into the evolutionary blueprint.

Chapter 11 confronts the murderous crises among the theocratic nations of the Fertile Crescent. A strategy is proposed to deliver the conditions for a 2-state solution to the Israel-Palestine conflict. This is achieved by refining the theory of Rent. We need to isolate and share the top slice of Rent that accrues from cooperation between nations. This is the doctrine of One World Rent (OWR). Resolving the Rent issue dissolves the political paralysis into which statecraft is locked.

Chapter 12 reviews the scope of the new world that would emerge, if we restored Rent as the public's revenue. In doing so, we would stop abusing our natural environment, and develop realistic strategies for dealing with the threats from mass migration.

Chapter 13 anticipates a fifth existential threat to humanity. Autonomous algorithms are being taught to emulate humans: we are enshrining in them the kinds of behaviour that led to conflicts like Gaza and Ukraine. To address that threat, we must also address the problem of autocratic power. The power of citizens emerges as we restore direct control over our lives, which is the route to banishing institutionalised cheating.

A word of caution. Law-makers are willing to proclaim fresh starts for their nations. But, in the past, there were too many false new starts. Stretching over four millennia, statesmen introduced clean slate programmes that ended in failure. Repeatedly, the result was systemic collapse, for one reason only: their communities were not realigned on the evolutionary growth path. To delineate an effective clean slate programme for the 21st century, we need to embark on the conversation informed by the realities of life.

References Part 3, Prologue

1 https://www.imf.org/en/News/Articles/2025/10/08/sp100825-annual-meetings-2025-curtain-raiser?cid=ca-com-homepage-AM2025-MDCR

CHAPTER ELEVEN

The Promised Land

With humanity facing myriad threats, and governance locked in ideological paralysis, we have no choice but to confront the viability of the prevailing social paradigm.

For the past two centuries, socialism, touted as the alternative to capitalism, was tested to death. It failed to offer the escape route promised by Karl Marx. That leaves us with a problem that Martin Wolf, the *Financial Times* chief economic commentator, considered when he addressed the OECD. At a conference convened to discuss "global economic fractures, geopolitical rivalry, and the role of international investment policy in restoring trust, resilience, and cooperation", he offered an honest assessment.

> **I don't know what the solution is. We are engaged in a period of profound world transformation – one of the revolutionary periods in world history.**[1]

The problem is not the inability to produce enough resources for everyone in the world to enjoy a decent living standard. Even now, global output capacity is sufficient to fulfil everyone's essential needs.[2] The problem stems from how resources are distributed, which is why we must seek remedies outside the broken paradigm. We do not have to look far. The viable alternative has been documented in the literature for the past 250 years. It is not ostracised because of practical shortcomings. Its adoption does not entail a violent revolution. It does, however, require a qualitative adjustment to the foundations of our social system. In essence, this means it does outlaw the institutionalised form of cheating.

In Part 1, I explained how property rights (which determine the distribution of income) were fundamental to the quest for a new kind of life on Earth. Humans developed the agency to grow by working to produce more than the metabolic needs that satisfied their cousins, the Great Apes. That extra energy – economic rent – delivered operational efficiency. Its social nature must be restored. This requires the realignment of social responsibilities with individual rights. To renew the human project, however, we need an enhanced metaphysics of Rent. The traditional language ("land value taxation"), does not meet the needs of the 21st century.[3]

Rent is composed of three layers. These emerged through the porosity of integrated elements. Beginning in the natural world, sharing resources was necessary to sustain metabolic life. Then, biologically, the sharing of net resources evolved genetic assets in their physical and mental forms. The outcome, in the form of morality, coded and disciplined people's behaviour. We need to translate this process into the language of economics as relevant to current circumstances. Once the three layers of Rent are disaggregated, they reveal the solutions to the personal, regional and global crises that beset our world.

First: the progress of humanity. *Annual ground Rents* are locally created. When pooled in the public purse, there is sufficient revenue to meet people's social needs. Budget deficits are consigned to history. Supply equates to demand.

Second: obligations. Rights correspond to responsibilities. Beginning with individuals in kinship groups, humans evolved into communities of clans and tribes, and eventually nation-states. This results in *One World Rent*, which signifies the fusion of commerce and cultural exchanges between neighbouring nations. This additional flow of net income, when shared between neighbouring states, heals the traumas that frequently provoke land wars.

Third: the Social Galaxy. Before humanity can successfully embark on an inter-galactic scale, we need a flourishing home on Earth. Globalisation has begun, through trade and cultural exchange, leading to the creation of *Global Rent*. This net income

Box 11.1 Binding laws

Obligations owed by nation-states, known as *erga omnes partes*, are contained in the treaties to which they subscribe. Reservations or derogations are not permitted. Signatories must fulfil their obligations to all parties to the treaties. And so, for example, in relation to the natural environment, the International Court of Justice in The Hague published, in its *Obligations of States in respect of Climate Change*, the need for reparations and remedial action from states that cause damage to nature. Reparations were payable for the "wrongful act of a State — or group of States — and particular damage suffered by the injured State, or, in the case of human rights law, by the injured individuals". Restitution "may take the form of reconstructing damaged or destroyed infrastructure, and restoring ecosystems and biodiversity". Where restitution was impossible, "responsible States have an obligation to compensate".*

Global Rent provides the first tranche of resources with which to heal nature on an effective, planetary scale.

* International Court of Justice (2025), *Obligations of States in Respect of Climate Change*, Advisory Opinion, §§449, 451, 452. https://www.icj-cij.org/case/187.

is available to share among all nations to address the common interests of humanity. Our living space, as it expands over time, is secured by treaties anchored in what the law calls *erga omnes partes*, which is enshrined in that layer of net income (Box 11.1).

To grasp the way in which the integration of humans adds additional layers to the first-order Rents, those created in local communities, we can reflect on the obverse process. Productivity is eroded through three processes. First, the extraction of Rent for private use (as in diverting social resources to "conspicuous consumption"). This depletes the revenue available to fund social needs. Second, slavery erodes the net income that would otherwise arise from the full freedom of all human beings. Third, the genocidal destruction of people and their culture and institutions, which obliterates the Rents that would otherwise have been produced.

Viewed in its nuanced forms, property rights enable us to address the economic fractures and geopolitical rivalry that dislocate life in the 21st century. A significant part of Rent, created across porous borders, is available to be shared between partner nations. It becomes the healing balm capable of addressing the OECD's agenda – "restoring trust, resilience, and cooperation".

When our Neolithic ancestors faced the revolutionary pivot from foraging to farming, they were not equipped to apply the precautionary principle to protect the social status of their net income. They could not guard against the cheats, which is why they were scammed by a ruthless statecraft, the model that was sustained all the way to our times. That statecraft has brought us to the present pivotal turning point in history.[4] This time, we *can and must* spell out the strategies that would deliver peace and prosperity for everyone, on the global scale. Those strategies cannot be clutched out of thin air. They are derived from the codes of the blueprint which enabled humans to evolve out of nature.

Restored to its social form, Rent fuels a humane future. We can interrogate that claim by applying it to a seemingly intractable crisis, one that originated in antiquity, which blights present lives, and promises to rupture the future. Sharing the three layers of Rent would convert into reality the narrative of the Promised Land.

Gaza and merciless humanity

Gaza will forever be known as a disgrace to humanity. It should be commemorated as the last immolation of people on the altar of the culture of cheating. That culture can be buried in the land of false and broken promises. If the neighbours who, today, portray each other as enemies, agree to adopt a statecraft that yields peace and prosperity for everyone, they would craft One World Rent. Sharing that flow of revenue between them would become the balm to heal ancient wounds (Box 11.2).

Box 11.2 **There ain't nothing like a Dame**

The term One World Rent originated with Vivienne Westwood (1941–2022), a Dame of the British Empire. From humble beginnings, she graduated from Chelsea punk clothes designer to inspired fashionista. Concerned about the state of our world, she campaigned against "rotten capitalism". Late in life, she asked me to school her in the economics of Rent. That initiated my visits to her *haute couture* studio in Battersea, south London. She would squat on the floor with a mug of coffee while I explained the virtues of fiscal reform.

She then took the message out onto the streets. From public platforms she advocated the need for One World Rent. In her 2019 presentation at the V&A museum, during the London Design Festival, she proposed the "need to transfer to a new economy, because the one we've got is killing us". She called for reform of land ownership rights as part of her One World Rent campaign.*

* Vivienne Westwood calls for new economy that bans land ownership. https://www.dezeen.com/2019/10/10/vivienne-westwood-climate-change-crisis/

Partnerships that create One World Rent would serve multiple purposes.

- Redeem humankind, by addressing the past for both its achievements and betrayals of the human project.
- Demonstrate how society can be re-created, by redefining the occupation of territory to fulfil dreams.
- Claim the future, by inspiring humanity in its responsible authentic form, bereft of cheating.

One World Rent began to flow in antiquity, when people embarked on trade with distant communities. Bartering was succeeded by commerce using precious metals as measures of value.[5] This unleashed the trends that culminated in "globalisation".

Figure 11.1 **The healing balm**

The rewards were the bonuses that came with creating net incomes in different locations, which advanced the human project with yet further increases from funding investments in bodies, minds and souls. Imagine the flourishing that would emerge, today, if that layer of net income was shared by neighbours in the theocratic world (Fig. 11.1).

Through trade, and the exchange of knowledge and culture, the people of Israel would help to create additional Rents in Lebanon, Jordan and the other neighbouring states. Israel could claim a share of those One World Rents. Likewise, Palestinians who live in the West Bank, who cross the border to work in Israel every day, add to the Rents generated within Israel. They, too, have a proprietary claim on that layer of Rent. Sharing that cross-border income would begin to heal old wounds, by solidifying neighbourly relations; and it would incentivise further co-operation, with the increased funds enriching the public sectors accessed by all populations.

We are all entitled, through our communities, to share in the OWR we create across porous borders. That prospect would yield a new kind of statecraft in the Fertile Crescent. It would nurture forgiveness for past deeds, as funds from OWR accelerated the remediation of destroyed homes and infrastructure of two million people in Gaza. These are not fanciful notions. They stem from facing reality. Already, in their civil communities, Palestinians and Israelis are combing to advocate the need for a singular solution to the destructive divisions that ghettoise people who ought to be working together for a better future. They propose "a new, possible and courageous political vision for resolving the Israeli-Palestinian conflict. Not a zero-sum game, but a victory for both peoples. Two sovereign states to end the occupation, one common homeland to end the conflict. It's in our hands".[6] The prospects of success would be enhanced if they located that mission in the balm of One World Rent.

There is so much we do not know about ourselves; so much that is fiction, so much that we could be. It is appropriate for an introspection to begin with the children of Abraham, to understand how the people of Israel could become ambassadors for humanity.

Renewing humanity

From hominin to *H. sapiens*, there have been multiple upward shifts in the evolutionary process. We can now initiate the next transformation. Resistance, however, will come from prejudices inherited from the past. That is why we need a cathartic cleansing of our minds, to perceive the present – and the future – with clarity. This is a demanding exercise for the people with claims to the territory of Palestine.

The first challenging issue is the claim to identities anchored in specific territories. As a general principle, no-one has a superior claim to any piece of land in its pristine condition. Land belongs to the agency that created it – nature. The sole property right that humans can assert is grounded in stewardship. That reality is clouded over by those who fabricate identities linked to exclusive association with the territory the Jews called the Promised Land.

Both the Jews and the Palestinians employ false narratives about their identity, as related to the land of Palestine. Israeli historian Yuval Noah Harari documents the false reading of history that extends all the way back to antiquity, with the myths fuelling exclusive claims to the land of their ancestors.

> **The cycle of war and suffering can end only when both sides abandon their moral certainties, acknowledge that the other side has a right to exist, and offer an open-handed peace rather than a close-fisted ceasefire. Both sides need to ask themselves 'If I were on the other side, what would I need in order to live in security, prosperity and dignity?'**[7]

Generosity, as a human sensibility, by itself, is not sufficient to solidify a new partnership between warring factions. Bonding requires material as well as aesthetic benefits, and this is delivered by each side claiming a rightful share to the Rents created in the other's territory. Joint participation in the creation of that layer of Rent enables the parties to arrive at a consensus that serves mutual interests.

Nature does not have a voice in that debate over the status of land. It is for all of us to give it that voice. In the process, we would advance the human project. This happens as we dismantle the falsehoods that lead to genocide. Consider, for example, the revisions needed to the identity and rights of the children of Abraham. Insights originally suggested by Sigmund Freud (1856–1939), in *Moses and Monotheism*,[8] were reviewed by Edward Said (1935–2003), a Palestinian born in Jerusalem who became professor of literature at Columbia University. Between Freud and Said, we see how much is myth, and needs to be corrected, if the contest in the Fertile Crescent is to be settled for everyone's benefit.

Freud pointed out that Judaism's founder, Moses, was a non-Jew; who, eventually, was killed by the Jews.[9] Said suggests that "This other non-Jewish, non-European history has now been erased, no longer to be found in so far as an official Jewish identity is concerned".[10] Freud hypothesised that the Semitic commitment to one God originated in Egypt, and he attributed this to the pharaoh Akhenaton. Said, however, reported that archaeological evidence suggested that "considerable traces of monotheism are found well before Akhenaton's reign".[11] The only certainty about the origins of identity and religion, is that the uncertainties should make us humble; and render us willing to reassess ourselves in the present time, according to the standards we set for what we wish to accomplish as human beings.

I have counselled caution with respect to the theoretical practice of economics. Archaeology needs to be read with similar caution. There is ample evidence that both the Israelis and Palestinians have been selective in extracting and interpreting artefacts buried in the Holy Land.[12] Interpretations, attributed to the land, renders nature complicit in the fabrication of identity to sustain false narratives. The outcome, as Said put it, is that the contest between Jewish and Palestinian identities, with respect to the land, "tends to underline the incompatibility of one side with the other, thereby increasing a sense of loss and the length of the list of grievances".[13]

The Humane Age

To support the resolution of conflicts in Palestine, the rest of us have to face the realities of the brutal injustices inflicted on the Semites. That means returning to Egypt and the Fertile Crescent, to trace the origins of the Gaza disaster. We need an honest appreciation of why human beings are pitched against each other to the point where they behave in genocidal fashion.

Demonising minorities was, and remains, an instrument for social control. False narratives about people's race, religion or gender distracts attention from the source of a society's social problems. By demonising the Semitic people, we begin to understand the cheating thesis, and illuminate the way in which a revised approach to Rent sharing can overcome seemingly intractable geo-political problems.

In ancient Egypt, the Israelites were trapped by a conundrum which, within the context of the culture of cheating, was irreconcilable. They insisted on preserving the integrity of their spiritual life. Their religion disciplined behaviour aimed at delivering heaven on Earth, rather than waiting for the afterlife. Predictably, this would one day become unacceptable to the dynastic form of political power. The pharaohs, to preserve their authority, required unquestioning obedience to their role as mediators between the gods and life on Earth.

For several hundred years the Israelites farmed Goshen, a fertile area to the east of the Nile's delta. They happily co-existed with their neighbours. Then, one day, a pharaoh decided that the Jews posed a threat to the security of the state. His ulterior motive: he needed bricklayers to construct a new city to celebrate his ego. So he victimised a group that retained their spiritual life under their own control. The pharaoh turned them into "the Other" – the enemy within, people who had to be regarded with suspicion. Thus, they were converted into serfs, and exploited as bricklayers. In the end, they fled Egypt.

As they scattered throughout the Near East and Europe, they remained faithful to their religion. So the culture of cheating, in its various guises, continued to blight their lives. To try and overcome periods of social stress, the manipulators of society concocted the conspiracy theories levelled at the Jews. Had it not been for Adolf Hitler, they would still be fulfilling that function in countries around the world. But in 1948, the survivors of the gas chambers decided that they had had enough: they needed a homeland which they could defend. Where better than the Promised Land?

The state of Israel was created by supplanting the Palestinians from the land they occupied. Israel did not countenance a separate state for the Palestinians. Gaza would one day become a legacy of the statecraft that licensed the culture of cheating. While attention was fixed on the staring eyes of shrivelled children, silently pleading for the food that did not come, lawmakers around the world stood helplessly on the side-lines. Political paralysis. And yet, the solution was staring them in the face: a two-state solution constructed with the balm of a refined doctrine of Rent. That doctrine could have been embedded a century earlier, when the League of Nations granted Britain the mandate over Palestine. If the British government had aligned the politics then preoccupying the Parliament in Westminster, with their obligation to protect the people living in the mandate, a new – a humane – age, might have emerged.

In 1909, the Liberal Government published a budget that included a direct charge on the Rents of the kingdom. That revenue was to be spent on the welfare of the people.[14] If that fiscal doctrine had been applied to the Promised Land, the material conditions would have emerged for multi-ethnic co-existence. Britain failed, both at home and in the Near East. The British mandate ended in 1948. The state of Israel was created, and on December 10, 1948, it endorsed the universal declaration of human rights, the principles of which were to be reflected in Israel's Basic Law: Human Dignity and Liberty. The new state, however, had no intention of honouring the human rights of the Palestinians. And so, opposition to a two-state solution over the course of seven decades finally lead to the atrocities perpetrated by both communities in 2023.

Correctly explained, the concept of One World Rent could heal the wounds bequeathed by that history. The Promised Land *could* be turned into one that flowed with milk and honey. In healing ancient wounds, people would reject the statecraft that delivers debt, discrimination and the destruction of people, their productivity and their communities. In the event, the only agreement that the two sides could reach was signed on September 13, 1993. The Declaration of Principles on Interim Self-Government Arrangements had as its aim the partition of the two communities. It failed to acknowledge the material benefits that would unite them.

If there is to be a solution, the informed engagement of the rest of the world is required. But that also entails much homework, to understand how the culture of cheating erects barriers to change. One of those barriers emerged through the appropriation of the spiritual life, and its institutionalisation within the culture of cheating.

The temptations of religion

As a source of authority, through evolutionary timescales, the power of spirituality contributed to the dialectical process of cooperation and consensus. The rule that no-one should cheat was aligned with genetic laws and the need for social harmony. Therefore, behaviour that degrades the spiritual life, and weakens the barriers to cheating, constitutes a crime against humanity. There is every reason to believe that, if the egregious role of statecraft was explained to the people of Israel, they would arrive at a democratic consensus that delivered justice to their Palestinian neighbours. The only barrier to this settlement is the culture of cheating, and its statecraft. That is emphasised by another historical reality. Cheating not only exploited the religion of the Jews, and the Muslims; it also encroached on the beliefs that became Christianity.

Jesus was born in the Promised Land, which was then part of the Roman Empire. He grew into a rebel who wanted to improve people's lives while they still lived on Earth; a desire consistent with his faith as a Jew. So, he behaved accordingly. In one incident, he threw the money lenders out of a temple (Matthew 21: 12-13). The house of prayer had been turned into "a den of robbers". Jesus objected to people being cheated. That classed him as a trouble maker. As such, he had to be silenced. He was pinned to a cross. His disciples, however, spread his teachings far and wide. The Christian creed did pose a threat to Rome's imperial cheating. A resolution was needed. That began with Constantine the Great. He converted to Christianity in 312 CE, and played a significant role in the Christianisation of the Roman Empire. There was, however, a heavy price to be paid. The activism of Jesus was fine-tuned to accommodate the culture prevailing in the Roman world. With

> **the emergence of Christendom, further adaptation within the Christian movement followed the mandates of the political order; theologians accordingly sought philosophical arguments and clear cut formulations as warrants guaranteeing the effective insert of the tradition into the then-current socio-intellectual structure of the empire.[15]**

The heaven on Earth sought by Jesus was cancelled.[16] Central to the filtering of Christianity was the assembly of a property portfolio, and the tax-exemptions attracted by the ownership of land. That process is traced by Alice Roberts, a Professor of Public Engagement with Science at the University of Birmingham (England). Rome's tenant farmers

> **[were] increasingly rendered as little more than indentured servants or serfs, tied to the land they farmed – usually on villa estates. So now, the landowners would collect in-kind payments from their tenants, while paying their own taxes in gold. That is, unless they could secure an exemption. This might be granted...if the estate was ecclesiastical.[17]**

As the Church in Rome assembled its property portfolio, monasteries "operated as franchised businesses of the Church". Monasteries

> **allowed their founders and owners to manage large agricultural estates, with cheap labour and favourable tax agreements in place, generating a healthy income for the leading local representatives of the Church...Across the Empire, monasteries, controlling large tracts of land, would take on other administrative functions, receiving funds from rulers and doling them out, often enjoying considerable tax breaks.[18]**

Christian charity

> **was never intended to solve the problem of poverty. Social inequality was absolutely necessary: the poor needed alms from the rich to survive; the rich needed the poor to save their souls. And the Church itself needed the poor as well. Poor labourers, who stayed poor, were absolutely essential to the business model.[19]**

In the fifth century, rather than investing Rents in communal infrastructure, revenue was used to construct churches that extracted yet more tax-free Rents.[20]

Wealth accumulated from the property portfolios lured attorneys attracted by "Tax exemptions and harmonisation of salaries [which] meant that there was no financial bump to be suffered when a professional man entered the church, and as a bonus, his prospects suddenly improved".[21]

When Rome collapsed, the Church survived the Dark Age by servicing feudalism. In 1517, however, it was confronted by a serious challenge. Martin Luther, a young priest in Germany, published 95 theses to initiate a conversation on the practise of people buying their way into heaven. They purchased letters of "indulgence" from the priesthood. Luther objected. Forgiveness should stem from honest contrition, not the purchase of letters that could be flashed at the gates of heaven. Christians should be taught that giving to the poor was "a better deed than he who buys indulgences" (Thesis 43).

Indulgences were an important source of revenue for the church. Luther feared that they were a by-product of the quest for power and wealth. In Thesis 86, he referred to "the pope, whose wealth is today greater than the wealth of the richest Crassus". Marcus Licinius Crassus (115–53 BC) became the richest man in the Roman Empire by assembling a property portfolio by unscrupulous means. Pope Leo X sold indulgences to finance the lavish construction of St. Peter's Basilica. Luther wondered why the pope did not "build this one basilica of St Peter with his own money rather than with the money of the poor believers".

Pope Leo sought a retraction. Luther resisted, and was excommunicated. He was not the last priest to be victimised, over an issue that stemmed from the culture of cheating. In the 19th century, with the publication of Henry George's *Progress and Poverty*, Edward McGlynn (1837–1900), a New York priest, supported fiscal reform. He backed George's mayoral campaign in the 1886 election. A year later, accused of disobedience and the suspicion that he favoured "socialism", McGlynn was excommunicated. He was restored to the priesthood after an investigation in which four professors assured the Church that the single tax on Rent was not contrary to Catholic teaching. McGlynn did not retract his support for the shift of the revenue system off wages and onto Rents. The Church of Rome, however, was not finished with Henry George. Without mentioning George's name, Pope Leo XIII castigated "socialism" in his 1891 encyclical

Rerum Novarum. He left no doubt about the role played by the Christian Church in history. He enunciated how

> **civil society was renovated in every part by Christian institutions; that in the strength of that renewal the human race was lifted up to better things – nay, that it was brought back from death to life, and to so excellent a life that nothing more perfect had been known before, or will come to be known in the ages that have yet to be. Of this beneficent transformation Jesus Christ was at once the first cause and the final end; as from Him all came, so to Him was all to be brought back.**[22]

The perfect life was promised to those who lived in poverty, who postponed their expectations until they joined Jesus in heaven.

This history leaves no doubt that, supported by the clergy, Rent was appropriated by a privileged minority of the population across Europe. Irrespective of time and place, and no matter what the liturgical variants, Christian beliefs and practises were fine-tuned to enable the culture of cheating to thrive, and to evolve into its globalised form. In the Middle Ages, Jewish communities tried to settle down throughout Europe, without interfering in anybody else's lives. But the culture of cheating prevailed, and the Jews were repeatedly victimised and driven out of their home communities.

Ending political paralysis

The Jews who survived the Holocaust were entitled to a homeland that they could defend. That is why they sailed eastwards down the Mediterranean, to the Promised Land. But, because of the historical antecedents, the voyage into the future was not framed in terms of the human project – freedom with an authentic form of governance that supported cooperation and consensus with neighbours.

The State of Israel became an exemplar of the culture from which the people thought they had escaped when they fled Europe. The template required them to establish a state that prioritised segregation, not integration. David Ben Gurion (1886-1973), the first Prime Minister of Israel, summarised the fears of Israeli citizens in the following terms.

> **Why should the Arabs make peace? If I were an Arab leader I would never make terms with Israel. That is natural: THEY THINK we have taken their country. Sure, God promised it to us, but what does that matter to them? Our God is not theirs. We come from Israel, it's true, but two thousand years ago, and what is that to them? There has been anti-Semitism, the Nazis, Hitler, Auschwitz, but was that their fault? They only see one thing: we have come here and stolen their country. Why should they accept that?...So it's simple: we have to stay strong and maintain a powerful army. Our whole policy is there. Otherwise the Arabs will wipe us out.**[23]

The existential threats emanating out of Israel include the wilful destruction of Palestinian livelihoods that foster ecocide, defined as "severe, widespread, and long-term environmental destruction that undermines the ability of inhabitants to enjoy and sustain life".

> **Since October 2023, Gaza's environment has suffered nearly unimaginable devastation. Israel's assault on farmland, water systems, and infrastructure is precipitating famine, environmental collapse, and displacement—acts that resonate deeply with the legal and moral dimensions of ecocide.**[24]

Israel's citizens flourished, but they were viewed as violent interlopers in the land of Islam. The perfect storm arose because neighbouring theocratic states were also cast in the image of European statecraft. Under the influence of Britain and France, tribal chiefs were turned into monarchs, so that the former colonial powers could continue to extract the petro-Rents from the Middle East.

A new way of viewing the world is needed, which can be presented to the rest of the world as the model based on ethical economics. There are cases where the social reset was funded out of Rent. Diamond Rents funded the social infrastructure that thrust Botswana into its post-colonial era.[25]

OWR charts the way through the damage inflicted by the culture of cheating on both nature and the Social Galaxy. The philosophy is easy to grasp; resting on the principle that people should "keep what they create, but pay for what they receive" – from both the private *and* public sectors. This emphasises stewardship, both towards nature and other human beings. The alternative is the multi-polar world being fashioned by Vladimir Putin of Russia and Xi Jinping of China. They despise the West, and the politics of authentic democracy, and they wish to control the future. The only way to address this challenge is by reforming the statecraft mandated by the culture of cheating.

The plan by Donald J. Trump to bring peace to Gaza will not realign the future of the theocratic states. The tool for breaking loose from the political paralysis that blights our world is One World Rent, but the disruptive geopolitical influence of the US President hinders that prospect. Given the speed with which the existential threats are converging, we cannot wait for the Rent-based theocracies in the Fertile Crescent to take the initiative. The best prospect is for the change to begin in Europe, the civilisation that planted the culture of cheating across the globe.

References Chapter 11

1 https://www.oecd-events.org/investment-days/onlinesession/3625c060-a394-f011-b485-6045bd9d3cad?adestraproject=OECD%20Business%20and%20Finance%20News&utm_campaign=FDI%20in%20Figures%202025&utm_content=replay&utm_term=daf&utm_medium=email&utm_source=Adestra

2 Jan Streeck *et al* (2025), "Small increases in material stocks to achieve decent living standards globally", *nature sustainability*. https://doi.org/10.1038/s41893-025-01670-1

3 Franklin Obeng-Odoom (2025), "Progress and Poverty: Walter Rodney's Legacy", *Amer J of Econ and Sociology*. https://doi.org/10.1111/ajes.70021

4 Martin Wolf (2024), *The Crisis of Democratic Capitalism*, London: Penguin.

5 Gianluca Miniaci *et al* (2024), Editors, *Ancient Egypt and the Surrounding World: Contact, Trade and Influence*, Pisa: Pisa University Press.

6 https://www.2s1h.org/

7 Yuval Noah Harari (2025), "Only generosity can secure peace", *Financial Times*, Nov. 9.

8 Sigmund Freud (1939), *Moses and Monotheism* (Translator Katherine Jones), London: Hogarth Press.

9 Daniel Chernilo (2023), "The Jews Killed Moses: Sigmund Freud and the Jewish Question", *Theory, Culture & Society*, 41(3). https://doi.org/10.1177/02632764231201

10 Edward Said (2003), *Freud and the Non-European*, London: Verso, p.44.

11 *Ibid.*, p.33.

12 *Ibid.*, 47-49.

13 *Ibid.*, p.50.

14 Fred Harrison and Clifford Cobb (2025), "Churchill and the Two Variants of Democracy," *American Journal of Economics and Sociology* 84(5).

15 David M. Bossman (1987), "Authority and Tradition in First century Judaism and Christianity", *Biblical Theology Bulletin*, 17(1), p.8. https://doi.org/10.1177/014610798701700102

16 Mike Sosteric (2022), "Rethinking the Origins and Purpose of Religion: Jesus, Constantine, and the Containment of Global Revolution", *Athens J of Social Sciences*, 9(1).

17 Alice Roberts (2025), *Domination: The Fall of the Roman Empire and the Rise of Christianity*, London: Simon & Schuster, p.144.

18 *Ibid.*, p.276.

19 *Ibid.*, p.262. Emphasis in original.

20 *Ibid.*, p.148.

21 *Ibid.*, pp.318-319.

22 Rerum Novarum (May 15, 1891)

23 John Mearsheimer and Stephen Walt (2008), *The Israel Lobby and U.S. Foreign Policy*, London: Farrar Straus and Giroux, p. 96.

24 https://theecologist.org/2025/sep/02/ecocide-and-resistance-palestine

25 Fred Harrison (2008), *The Silver Bullet*, London: IU, p.40.

CHAPTER TWELVE

A New World

One of the global economic powers needs to offer itself as an example of the route into a humane future. The UK and the European Union are ideal candidates, for two reasons.

First, both practice One World Rent and Global Rent. They share those layers of net incomes with nations near or afar. They do so imperfectly, by extracting and sharing Rent indirectly. Ultimately, the revenue does come from Rent: ATCOR – all taxes come out of Rent. The indirect route, however, fosters enormous social pathologies. That is why, in their present states, neither the UK nor the EU is worth emulating. But both unions expose the barriers that obstruct the restoration of humanity back on the path to sustainable growth.

Second, the western alliance with the USA has been shredded by President Donald Trump. He more closely identifies with Russia than with America's traditional European allies. Europe civilisation, in his view, is at risk from migrants dominating its countries. The US National Security Strategy assessment anticipates that "within a few decades at the latest, certain NATO members will become majority non-European".[1] Trump's treatment of Russia's invasion of Ukraine leaves little doubt that Europe, if it is to protect its borders, needs to become self-sufficient economically and militarily. That requires an overhaul of its social paradigm.

For root reasons that do not feature in the Trump doctrine, I conclude that European civilisation is being rapidly eroded, materially and socially. Locked in political paralysis, Europe is not equipped to navigate the chaos from the converging existential threats. A large part of its Rents are consigned to sleep mode. The materialised energy of humanity remains segregated, stuck beneath people's homes. Land value. If released, those Rents would spring from congealed form to revitalise people's spirits. Impetus to that end would be provided by requiring statecraft to aim for Zero Deadweight (Z-D). This is imperative, if Europe is to navigate the combined effects of climate change and mass migration.

The benefits of Z-D include the comprehensive revitalisation of relationships between the Social Galaxy, nature (plants and animals), and physics (rivers and soil). UN agencies have now combined to try and achieve those outcomes. They call it One Health. With global population now at eight billion,

> **amid unsustainable consumption and production patterns, the pressures on our natural systems are tremendous and will continue to grow. The earth's natural resources are being used at a faster rate than they can be replenished due to unsustainable and destructive practices and with insufficient consideration for biodiversity or the health of surrounding ecosystems upon which our lives and wellbeing depend.[2]**

Those relationships must be rehabilitated, to stem the risks from lethal diseases. Already, migrants are spreading the West Nile virus infections across Europe.[3] Contagious diseases will increase in the 2030s, as people are displaced from their homelands by the combination of environmental and economic crises. Add the declining capacity of statecraft to mitigate infection, and the threats from autocracy, and Europe is facing a perfect storm.

With economic productivity declining, the only way to increase the capacity to address the risks is grounded in the new revenue system. The OWR doctrine disciplines behaviour (no more irresponsible dumping of wastes into the air and oceans); it raises awareness of the virtues of sustainable behaviour; and enhances symbiotic relationships, by providing the additional resources needed to navigate the crises (Box 12.1).

Box 12.1 **Back to the Invisible Hand**

Before the onset of civilisation, people acted without articulating their social responsibilities. Good behaviour automatically conformed to Adam Smith's concept of the "invisible hand". Today, we must consciously define social responsibilities, to decrease the risks of pathogens spilling over from animals. Scientists formulating the One Health programme fail to incorporate into their models the pricing system that would engender responsible behaviour at both personal and state levels.*

Public policy ostensibly aimed at reducing damage to nature is based on paying (i.e., bribing) people to behave responsibly; by, for example, cutting back on carbon emissions, or not dumping waste in oceans. Those bribes are funded out of revenue raised by taxes that amplify deadweight burdens. This merry-go-round leads to nowhere. The effective policy is based on the evolutionary principle: keep what you create, and pay for what you receive.

* "Promoting the science of One Health" (2023), *Nature Communications*, 14(1):4735.

Reuniting the kingdom

The UK illuminates all aspects of the proposed social paradigm. We need its imperial history to contextualise today's conditions, and to evoke the nation's social responsibilities. In conquering other people's territories, Britain enabled the culture of cheating to pervert lives around the globe. That context enables us to understand what, exactly, is required, to unravel the doom loop through reforms in the realms of the material, psychological and spiritual condition of the four nations of the British Isles. We can summarise that history through three phases separated by two periods of adjustments.

Phase 1 The Rise of Empire

From Henry VIII to 1789, territorial conquest and brutal slavery saw the extraction of Rents from the colonies, which funded the onset of industrialisation. In the 18th century, one-third of the UK's imports were from slave-based production in its colonies, with 11% of total British output connected to the slave trade.[4] London and the three major seaports – Glasgow, Liverpool and Bristol – flourished. In-coming Rents were ploughed into expanding real estate as well as funding the merchants who traded in the products of slavery.

Liverpool grew from 1,000 to 10,000 dwellings; while upgrading the docks to handle the steady increase in the fleet that sailed the triangle between West Africa, the Caribbean and Britain. One trader celebrated his good fortune by spending £600 on the construction of a new town house, to buy his way into Liverpool's high society.[5] Thanks to these trading hubs, manufacturing and mining centres sprouted up throughout the UK, to reinforce the industrial ingenuity of inventors of new machines that processed the cotton, tobacco and sugar imported from the plantations.

Were the Rents harvested in Britain generated exclusively by British labour? No! Much of it was the result of the labour of Africans who were forced to endure shortened lives to produce the products cashed-in in the UK.

The interregnum between Phase I and Phase 2 was shaped by the chaos of the French Revolution, followed by the Napoleonic war. This was a period of philosophical soul-searching and blood-letting. Britain was the ultimate victor.

Phase 2: the Transition in Statecraft

Following Britain's abolition of the slave trade in 1807, and defeat of Napoleon in 1815, the second phase stretched through 1833 (abolition of slavery in British territories), through the muscular period of industrial power, to the defeat of Nazi Germany. The British Empire appeared to triumph, but economic prosperity for some derived from riding on the backs of Britain's labourers, who were segregated in slums. Corporations extracted territorial Rents from imperial assets, but the empire was in decline, ceding pre-eminence to the USA at the end of the Second World War.

The plight of the workers nurtured the desire for change. The Liberal Party became the voice of the people. This lead to universal suffrage, but a failed attempt to reform the fiscal system in 1910-1920.

The second interregnum wrestled with the temptations of the socialist ideology, which began in the 1930s with the rise of the Labour Party. The experiment ran from 1944 to the civil disturbances in towns across the country in the 1970s. At the 1979 election, voters elected for ideological change. A mandate was granted to Margaret Thatcher.

Phase 3: the Decline

The Iron Lady reigned for 11 years. She delivered the onset of the final phase of cultural cannibalism. Conservative governments trapped the working population into complicity in the demise of their communities. Thatcher deployed three policies. First, low-income families in social housing were granted the right to buy their properties at knock-down prices. That seeded the middle class acquisitiveness. Many ex-tenants quickly sold their homes to pocket the capital gains. The second initiative was the "Big Bang" deregulation of banks. This led to the profitable sale of sub-prime mortgages to people who could not afford to buy their homes, which laid the foundations for the bankruptcy of the financial sector in 2008. Banks were bailed out (by a Labour government), the cost imposed on the working population through a decade-long austerity regime. And third, vast oil Rents from the North Sea were squandered in tax cuts, instead of being invested in a sovereign wealth fund and available for future generations.

By almost unanimous agreement, the UK is now a "broken state". The need exists to reverse the social depletion. This can be achieved by reuniting the kingdom.

Towards an informed conversation

It falls to the English, Scottish, Welsh and Irish subjects of King Charles to engage in the conversation that might inspire the reforms leading to the progress for which most people yearn. An informed debate will not be initiated by the intellectual communities. Nor can law-makers be relied upon to offer guidance. Sir Keir Starmer illustrates the problem. Elected as Prime Minister in 2024, he genuinely wanted to alleviate the pain of so many disadvantaged people, and to correct the institutional systems that defeat common aspirations.

He was emphatic. His government would "wipe the slate clean".[6] He provided three tests against which to test performance.

1. *A decade of national renewal.* Revealingly, he did not acknowledge the prospect of the peak in house prices which, if it occurred, would result in a slump that dwarfed what happened in 2007, initiating the decade-long austerity.
2. *Fiscal reform* to lock in "economic stability and policy certainty". Starmer offered no account of how the gymnastics of the tax-and-tenure nexus would be neutralised to incentivise growth through his plan for "long-term investment".
3. *Restart the house building programme*, by reforming the planning system. He did not explain how the fiscal incentives would be neutralised, which encourage the holding of land in an idle state, awaiting speculative increases in prices.

Sir Keir uttered a catalogue of promises that cannot be realised under existing property rights and the enabling statecraft. As revealed by a speech addressed to the nation on December 1, 2025, he did not recognise the cheating that stared him in the face (Box 12.2).

Box 12.2 Innocence and duplicity

Keir Starmer rose to the top of Britain's legal system (as Director of Public Prosecutions) before turning to politics. In the 2024 general election, he was granted an overwhelming mandate for change. He was able to catalogue the human and institutional defects in British society – they were in plain sight – but he had no clue about the root causes of the traumas.

The script of his speech to the nation on December 1, 2025, was exactly what the culture of cheating required. It ensured business as usual. There would be no rescue for the children who would die prematurely, because they were born and raised in the wards of death; no construction of the dwellings that people need at affordable prices; no acceleration of growth to provide the jobs at wages that met the metabolic needs of vulnerable workers. The Labour Government, as with its predecessors, was sleepwalking to the precipice. A Kafkaesque nightmare with nobody to deliver a dose of reality to the Prime Minister.

Fulfilling Starmer's aspirations fell on the shoulders of the first woman to head HM Treasury. He introduced Rachel Reeves and her first budget by promising his government would tackle homelessness "once and for all".[7] Reeves had no doubt that her strategy offered a clean slate to the nation. Labour, she said, had a mandate to "fix the foundations". They would attack the "root causes of inactivity" in public services and "repair the fabric of our nation". She then proceeded to outline a scenario with a litany of projects that would fail.

And so, the conversation needs to begin in people's homes, in the streets, the pubs, the town halls. By focusing on property rights, and exploring issues with the aid of the evolutionary blueprint, catharsis can gravitate from inter-personal issues to constitutional realities, and then graduate to Britain's global responsibilities and opportunities.

AGR: Strengthening communities

Economic rent constitutes half of a nation's income. The existing tax-take, at around 35% of GDP, comes out of Rent. We need to add to that sum the Rent extracted by the private sector, which is about 20% of national income.[8] So Britain could abolish all taxes, and fund all of the population's social needs, leaving itself with change to invest in the future. Resources are required to remediate damage to the environment, including the costs of moving coastal communities out of the way of rising ocean levels. That agenda would raise living standards. Take-home pay rises with the abolition of deadweight taxes. Additional revenue would accrue through the enhanced efficiencies from funding social infrastructure. For the principles of that financial reform, we can reinterpret the tensions that are rupturing politics in the kingdom.

Scotland and the quest for independence

The Scottish National Party persists with the desire to become a sovereign nation, which (confusingly), it would then trade in for membership of the European Union. How might the people of Scotland view continued membership of the UK as the best option?

The SNP already has the devolved right to rearrange its fiscal regime, to switch a part of its revenue from wages to the annual rents of locations. Despite being provided with the evidence that the switch would be enormously rewarding, SNP government's land reforms ignore the fiscal reform that would painlessly elevate revenue and the quality of life in Scotland (Box 12.3).[9]

Politicians have an obligation to understand the difference between the ownership of an asset, located on their territory, and the Rent that flows from that asset. SNP First Minister John Swinney, for example, fails to acknowledge the difference between the North Sea oil in Scottish waters, and the winds that flow across the highlands, which he says belong to Scotland; and the Rents from those two resources, which are created by consumers in England and across the world. Wind, clean though that energy

Box 12.3 The value of Scots' land

In 2022, the Scottish Land Commission entitled its report Advice to Scottish Ministers. It noted that "Land accounts for around two thirds of UK net worth. With rising inequalities in the UK, the role of land and its taxation is significant in addressing systemic inequalities in our economy and moving towards a wellbeing economy".* Under the existing tax regime, economic productivity is lowered and wealth is concentrated. Revenue from a direct charge on location Rents would stimulate productivity and deliver increased social and environmental wellbeing. The commission described the steps for phasing in the fiscal reform, stressing the need for a controlled transition by instituting a cadastral survey and the valuation of all land.

* Scottish Land Commission (2022), Land Reform and Taxation: Advice to Scottish Ministers, p.8.

may be, would be almost worthless, but for the demand from people who live across England and Wales. Ownership belongs to those who create the Rents across porous borders.

By failing to reform Scotland's finances (through the application of AGR), and by not acknowledging the creative benefits that would flow from OWR, responsibility for the continued traumas endured by the Scots rests on the shoulders of politicians.

But is there more that could be done by the UK government in Westminster? Parliament distributes revenue to the regions under the Barnett formula. The Scottish Government was allocated £45.5 billion for 2024-25, increasing to £47.6bn in 2025-26.[10] Taxpayers in London and South-east England (and their right-wing media advocates) grudgingly treat this as a transfer out of what they pay into the Exchequer, for the benefit of Scotland. The arrangement is a source of friction. And yet, the people of Scotland contribute to the Rents that surface in London and the South-east, through their exports of educated labour to London; their investments in the financial services from the City of London; their consumption of products exported from the South-east; cultural exchanges and a long list of additional activities that bolster the economy of London and the South-east. The people of Scotland are entitled to a share of that net income. The Barnett money is not called OWR, but that is what it is: a sharing across borders of communally created Rents.

The OWR model would benefit Scotland at two levels: both within its borders, and in relation to the rest of the UK. We have already recorded the desperate plight of Scottish citizens across their country. But consider the spatial injustices within a few miles in a single city. The mental health of 4-year-olds in Glasgow was studied. This revealed that the health of children in deprived areas was almost twice the number of children in the least deprived areas. By the age of 7, the gap had increased to 14.7% of children from the most deprived areas suffering from "abnormal difficulties".[11] Ultimately, the only way to exorcise the malice in Scotland's social fabric is through the reform of the government's revenue policies. The Barnett revenue, if classed as transfers under the OWR model, combined with a reformed fiscal system administered in Edinburgh, would elevate Scots from despair to expectations of a better future. This would result in fewer opioid deaths and longer life expectancy.

And then there are the benefits of a flourishing economy arising from the 3-way trade with the EU, across the southern border with the rest of the UK, and globally: elevating the OWR riches to be shared between all three spheres. Within that model, political independence would come to assume a new meaning for the Gaelic people: closer cooperation across porous borders, rather than the erection of border posts.

Yorkshire and "equality"

Inequality is a *sine qua non* of the landlords' tax system. One feature of that inequality is the automatic gravitation of Rent towards the political centre, away from the spatial periphery.

Most of the regions within England sense that they are neglected by Parliament, yet they cannot account for this in terms of nationalist prejudice (the SNP explanation). So they call for more political power over their affairs without perceiving the need to revise property rights. An example is provided by Yorkshire, where some residents have begun to field parliamentary candidates in the quest for influence in Westminster. They call for "an Assembly for Yorkshire with meaningful powers to impact proactively on people's lives [to] deliver the economic, social and democratic change we so desperately need here". Their party believes that "private sector growth is best delivered with the support of a well-funded public sector, and that the public sector can be well-funded only if the private sector is thriving".[12] This is circular wishful thinking. There is no explanation for how, within a dysfunctional fiscal system, new funds would be forthcoming just because a Yorkshire Assembly has been created. Such an Assembly would not alter the unequal lifestyles between Yorkshire and London.

No matter how skilled and industrious the working people of Yorkshire, under the tax-and-tenure formula the Rents gravitate to London. There, they fund the highest quality of public services for the least cost to the land owners. The appeal for equality is incoherent when it is framed within the fiscal paradigm prescribed by the culture of cheating.

The UK and Global Rents

Britain devotes about 0.5% of its annual gross national income on overseas foreign aid. In 2023, that amounted to £15.34bn. The sum in 2024 £14bn. Additionally, £2.8bn was spent on supporting refugees and asylum seekers in the UK. Countries like Ethiopia, Afghanistan, Syria, Yemen, Nigeria, Somalia, Pakistan, Brazil, and Bangladesh were top ten recipients, receiving a combined total of £597m.

This revenue is called "foreign aid". It is, in fact, a sharing of the Global Rents that other countries help to create within UK borders, through their commercial and cultural interactions. Without the latter, the UK would be poorer. Sharing the Global Rents would transform relationships; raise aspirations, honour responsibilities, leading to mutual flourishing (Box 12.4).

Box 12.4 Rents created afar

Like the earliest trading routes that amplified growth rates for all participants, today, the financial districts of London and New York, through the transactions in currencies that provide the liquidity for economic deals in every corner of the world, help to elevate location Rents in Beijing to Sydney and countries throughout the Global South. Minerals in central Africa acquire a Rental value because of the demands of consumers in Europe. Gulf oil produces Global Rents that ought to be shared across the world, rather than sunk into sky-scrapers in the desert to attract tax-dodgers.

The layer of trade-related Rents can be assessed through the marketplace. The quantum of Rent reflects the volumes of supply and the strengths of demand. The thrust is upwards and onwards. All participants in the commercial process are enriched; and could be richer, if the OWR layer was assessed and shared between the nations that created them.

Unlike the UK in its heydays, African and Middle East countries cannot develop their economies with the aid of Rents extracted from territories and slaves in the New World and Asia. They can begin to flourish, as never before, if they combined AGR, to raise funds from their own populations; complemented with OWR revenue from the currently rich nations. This would enhance the global partnerships, increasing the resilience that would result in a decrease of desperate people heading for the English Channel.

Europe re-united

Europe suffered constant wars, which is why governments agreed to the Westphalian pact in 1648, to end 30 years of bloodshed. National sovereignty, and borders, were defined; and, on an off, the bloodshed continued until 1944. That was when Europeans decided: *Never again!* The union that followed now results in the redistribution of resources under the Cohesion Fund amounting to €392bn (2021-27). The focus favoured developed member states, compared with the EU average, to promote economic and social wellbeing.

Contributions were the largest from members like Germany, but the transfers were not charity. All members of the union share in the co-operation and consensus that secures the partnerships that were absent during the centuries blighted by cross-border wars. Elevating the less developed members was investment in future mutual gains. *OWR in action!*

The union could have been even more prosperous. To raise the revenue, it continued to rely on the statecraft that enabled the cheating disposition. The Cohesion Fund was based on revenue from taxes, including VAT, which imposed deadweight burdens that, in turn, reduced living standards. As a result, the economic growth that prevailed for 50 years was bolstered by the import of cheap Russian energy; the export of industrial products to a languishing Chinese market; and the willingness of the US to subsidise NATO. All three elements disappeared with the interventions of Vladimir Putin, Xi Jinping and Donald Trump. The cumulative results was a decline in the competitiveness of the EU, as recorded in Mario Draghi's report, *The future of European competitiveness*, in 2025.[13] Over the decades, productivity declined compared to trends in the US, and trade within the common market grew towards stagnation.

One outcome is the scale of mental ill-health. Within the EU, an estimated 84 million people (1 in 6 citizens) were suffering from mental health problems before the onset of the Covid-19 pandemic.[14] This was not the result of individual failings. It was, rather, the interaction of forces that could only be dissected through the prisms of a "biopsychosocial model".[15] But it is not only in the realm of the mind that insanity prevails. Losses also arise from the economy's detachment from reality. One recent example: European financiers have begun to make profits from trades in corporate bonds that do not exist![16] By switching the revenue system away from penalising VAT exactions, and onto OWR, the transformation would begin immediately. All countries would benefit from the synergy of such a large 27-member common market.

Another immediate benefit would arise from switching the Common Agricultural Policy from the subsidies that end up raising land values, to turn farming into a self-sufficient industry that served the common good. The amount spent under the CAP was €386bn (2021-27). Part of this (€291bn) was for income support. The mass protests of farmers astride tractors, blocking the Parisian roads in 2025, testifies to the fact that they did not consider their wages to be sufficient. The explanation: most of that money ended up raising the value of farmland, not going into pockets as wages. CAP also devoted €291bn to rural development projects and support for environmentally friendly practices (bribes to farmers to try and persuade them to behave responsibly).

By transferring to the OWR policy, the funding of new infrastructure would bind member countries even more tightly together as citizens enjoyed enhanced prosperity. The alternative: over the next few years, the climate crisis in the form of wildfires and rain storms will inflict levels of damage on communities that member countries will not be able to renew. There is no ambiguity about this crisis: the UN has warned of the "yawning gap" on climate finance. Developed countries have cut the funds to Global South countries.[17] Under the OWR formula, they would be able to increase those funds, to the mutual benefit of all countries.

Global Rents or foreign aid

Much of the prosperity of EU members is based on international trade. In return, it provides €50bn a year in foreign aid. This is not charity. Consumers and investors from around the world contribute to the enhanced Rents that emerge in the EU. Therefore, they have a claim on part of that flow of revenue, in the form of their share of the Global Rents created within Germany, France Spain, Italy and the other leading members of the European economy. To call it "foreign aid" is to treat it as charity, which reduces the dignity of recipients and exposes it to reductions whenever the granting economies feel the need to do so. Instead, by treating the revenue as the product of a partnership, the EU would instantly begin to address two of the existential threats to its future.

> ***The eco-crisis***. By rebalancing relationships between people and their communities, and with nature, the EU would be able to fund the remedial measures. Additional resources would be available for rewilding, and to relocate communities being torn from their coastal locations. And, in the long term, the new stewardship of nature would provide the security that is now absent from most communities across the continent.

> ***Mass migration***. Even at the present rate of inflow, the burden of illegal migrants is not manageable for countries like Sweden and Italy. By adopting the AGR/OWR model, the EU could demonstrate to low income countries how they could rapidly elevate the development of their economies. People accorded the right to remain in their home communities would relieve the EU of mass migration.

By adopting the new fiscal system, either the UK or the EU would locate itself on the moral high ground, with the right to present its record as one that ought to be emulated by other nations.

The switch to AGR/OWR would require a period of transition. The 18-year boom/bust cycle ending in 2028 cannot be prevented from terminating in a crash. Under the existing paradigm, governments will make things worse, by cutting spending on welfare and weakening public institutions; leaving more scope for criminal behaviour and external threats. That is why the AGR/OWR/Global Rent model is needed, to enhance resilience and provide the resources for navigating to a better world. And it would begin to combat an internal threat: autocracy. The shift to the political right (characterised as "populism") threatens stability of the EU on its eastern borders. By raising living standards, and demonstrating that promises can be kept, the law-makers in Brussels would reverse the trend in favour of authentic democracy.

Europe's populations would quickly engage in the cathartic conversations with neighbours, based on the three key precepts.

1. *Pay for the benefits you receive.* This matches resources to the need for public services. Few people would demand services without paying for them!
2. *Eliminate the deadweight burden.* Finally, the public would understand why governments repeatedly fail to honour promises to solve their problems!
3. *Net resources are everyone's property.* This would stimulate debates about the capital gains and whether rent-paying tenants should share in the spoils!

The obligations of history

There are moral reasons why countries located on the Atlantic seaboard – Britain, Portugal, Spain and France – should initiate the shift away from the culture of cheating. Five centuries ago, they began to colonise much of the world, grabbing other people's territories. Leading by example would be a way to make amends for the past.

But there are also existential reasons why Europe should lead by example. Survival cannot be taken for granted. In the past, many seemingly powerful civilisations collapsed because their leaders failed to diagnose the defects in the flawed foundations. There is every reason to believe that the looming burdens from an uncontrolled flow of migrants will result in a similar implosion for Europe. People classed as high net worth are already planning their escape to relatively safe havens.[18] That option is not available to most people.

Salvation cannot be achieved through the West's foreign aid to the Global South, which is even now being reduced. Cuts to US AID funding alone may result in an estimated 14m deaths, including 4.5m children under the age of 5 years, by 2030.[19] Many deaths will result from the transmission of infections, resulting from the continued disruption of nature. The OECD's

Climate Action Monitor 2025 explains why emission targets remain insufficient to meet the Paris Agreement goals.[20]

The global institutions that emerged after World War 2 need to be reframed. They are insufficient, even a disgrace to humanity, as evidenced by the episodes of post-war genocide which they could not prevent. Meanwhile, global discontent is being exploited by the autocrats in Russia and China, who are determined to create their vision of a multi-polar world.

We need to pivot away from the culture invented in antiquity. We are all the common product of the act of creation, in which our earliest ancestors consented to produce and pool the energy that made our species possible. That evolutionary blueprint, applied on a global basis to meet 21st century needs, would empower us to restart the project that enabled hominins to become human. *One World Rent is the binding glue.*

Back in the time when our forebears foraged for their food, they did not know what lurked in the shadows. We now have a sufficiently complete picture to warn us of the consequences, if we fail to gravitate beyond civilisation. To unify the Social Galaxy on an ethos grounded in justice and economic efficiency, the kind of world that renders everyone secure within a system that delivered peace and prosperity. The reward for that change is the bonus that stems from sharing the net incomes created across porous borders.

The sole barrier to enlightened public policy is the wilful blindness directed at the Rent issue. Consequently, law-makers and their expert advisers ignore the social system's operating mechanisms. That causes them to amplify the risks to civilisation, as illustrated by the rush to accept artificial intelligence-based technologies. AI, we are told, "could undoubtedly play a leading role" in alerting us to the connection between global health and the quality of the environment.[21] We do not need artificial intelligence, to navigate the future. Human intelligence is sufficient, if we apply it in an honest way.

Do we have the will to survive as a species?

References Chapter 12

1 *National Security Strategy of the United States of America* (2025), Washington DC: p.27. https://www.whitehouse.gov/wp-content/uploads/2025/12/2025-National-Security-Strategy.pdf

2 World Health Organisation *et al* (2022), *One Health Joint Plan of Action (2022-2026): Working together for the Health of Humans, Animals, Plants and the Environment*, Rome, p.3.

3 Tamás Bakonyi and Joana M. Haussig (2020), "Nile virus keeps on moving up in Europe", *Euro Surveillance*, 25, 2001938.

4 Smith, *op. cit.*, pp. 320, 322.

5 *Ibid.*, p.304.

6 Keir Starmer (2024), "Reform is needed to make Britain a great place to do business", *Financial Times*, Nov. 2.

7 Prime Minister's Questions, House of Commons, Oct. 30, 2024.

8 Ron Banks, Terra Incognita, p.39, in Banks (1989), *Costing the Earth*, London: Centre for Incentive Taxation.

9 https://www.landcommission.gov.scot/downloads/5dd6984da0491_Land-Value-Tax-Policy-Options-for-Scotland-Final-Report-23-7-18.pdf

10 https://www.gov.scot/publications/scottish-budget-2025-to-2026-barnett-block-grant-funding/

11 Lee Knifton and Greig Inglis (2020), "Poverty and mental health: policy, practice, and research implications", *BJPsych Bull.*, 44(5), p.193.

12 https://www.yorkshireparty.org.uk/

13 https://commission.europa.eu/topics/competitiveness/draghi-report_en#paragraph_47059

14 Laurence Amand-Eeckhout (2023), *Mental health in the EU*, Brussels: European Union, p.3.

15 Val Livingston *et al.* (2025), "Dignity in mental health—examining the dynamics of mental health stigma: a narrative review", *Academia Mental Health and Well-Being*, 2, p.6.

16 Euan Healy (2025), "Hedge funds reap profits from debt before it exists", *Financial Times*, Oct. 30.

17 https://www.unep.org/resources/adaptation-gap-report-2025

18 https://impacts.savills.com/market-trends/new-locations-new-priorities-hnwis-adapt-their-property-portfolios.html?utm_source=ExactTarget&utm_medium=Email&utm_term=5441067&utm_content=9945141&utm_campaign=WR+-+Newsletter+-+Impacts+December+2025+B

19 Daniella Medeiros Cavalcanti *et al.* (2025), "Evaluating the impact of two decades of USAID interventions and projecting the effects of defunding on mortality up to 2030: a retrospective impact evaluation and forecasting analysis", *The Lancet.com* 406. https://doi.org/10.1016/S0140-6736(25)01186-9

20 https://www.oecd.org/en/publications/the-climate-action-monitor-2025_1819c631-en.html

21 Daniele Fattorini (2025), "Environmental quality and global health", *Academia Global and Public Health*, 1. https://doi.org/10.20935/AcadPHealth8043

CHAPTER THIRTEEN

Or: We all Die

The dire prospects from *superintelligent* AI are forecasted by the authors of *If Anyone Builds It, Everyone Dies*. Operating through their San Francisco-based Machine Intelligence Research Institute, Eliezer Yudkowsky and Nate Soares warn that, once invented, superintelligent algorithms would "far exceed human intelligence". AI would operate "faster and better" than humans. "AI isn't there yet," they claim. They fear that "machine intelligence that is genuinely smart, smarter than any living human, smarter than humanity collectively", would constitute the existential threat with the power to eliminate humanity.[1]

Alarming, but they *understate* the threat. The existential danger from artificial intelligence has already arrived. All of us conspire to entrench it, every day. And neither law-makers nor the Tech Guys in Silicon Valley appreciate the nature of the risk.

It is not a futuristic *superintelligence* that should concern us, but the *autonomous* intelligence that the scientists are even now refining. Hundreds of billions of dollars are being committed to develop autonomous humanoid behaviour. How we got to this perilous situation is, once again, the story of creative individuals who did not understand the human project. For their sake, as well as ours, we need to rehearse the facts.

We are now equipped with the blueprint that guided our earliest ancestors. We must not, however, take anything for granted. The existing social system will apply huge resources to prevent change. That happened in the 19th century, when Henry George's proposals gained global traction. In America, scholars were mobilised to bury the Rent-as-public-revenue; ensuring that universities participated in the exercise to colour the minds of future generations against the justice-based fiscal system.[2] In the 20th century, there was a re-run of those heinous tactics in the realm of psychology, as illustrated by the case of Abraham Maslow (1908–1970).

Maslow was an American psychologist who realised that his discipline needed to be enriched with a theory of psychological health based on people fulfilling their innate human needs. He called this process self-actualization.[3] Beginning in the 1940s, Maslow found himself exploring concepts like "the authentic person", and "authentic living" – which, of course, implied that current lifestyles were not authentic. The implications were serious. Maslow's theory was gravitating towards a fundamental critique of current doctrines, which relied on drilling people into conforming to the needs of those who controlled power. Maslow had to be muzzled. How this happened has been documented.[4]

To divert attention away from Maslow's theory of personal liberation, academic psychology was channelled into schools of thought that reinforced the existing culture. How the psychology department in one university was cleansed of Maslow was witnessed by Mike Sosteric, an associate professor of sociology at Athabasca University. What is popularly termed "brain washing", he calls "toxic socialisation" (Box 13.1).[5]

We now have the choice over whether to continue as blood-and-guts creatures imbued with moral and spiritual sensibilities; or gravitating into metal-and-maths avatars, swapping the Social Galaxy for the metaverse. That choice will turn on the fusion of the energy that lies dormant in every human being. If we want a future for humanity, we will have to unfreeze the power locked up in more than 8 billion people, to relaunch the human project on a new trajectory.

Box 13.1 **Behavioural control**

Mike Sosteric grew up amid the indigenous communities of Alaska, which gave him a special insight into the formation of the social controls that shape people's lives. He witnessed the side-lining of Abraham Maslow's "most impactful theories" in psychology and personality research.

> *[A]s a fourth-year honours student in a dedicated humanistic psychology department circa 1988, I witnessed [a] purge first-hand: administration systematically early-retired the department's humanistic and transpersonal psychologists and replaced them with behaviorists. Within two academic years...the department's mission transformed from progressive, emancipatory inquiry into one explicitly centered on behavioural control...What I observed was an administrative assassination: tenure lines eliminated, courses cancelled, and a generation of growth-oriented scholars cleared out for behavioural control".**

Inspired by Maslow's vision, Sosteric has launched an initiative to address current existential threats, which he calls a "Psychology of the Peace Table.**

* Mike Sosterice (n.d.), "Eupsychian Theory I: Reclaiming Maslow and Rejecting The Pyramid – The Circle of Seven Essential Needs", pp. 11-12. DOI 10.31234/osf.io/fswk9

** https://medium.com/the-peace-table/abraham-maslows-vision-for-a-psychology-of-the-peace-table-f4b8dd2627d8

The dark side of innovation

Most of the economic achievements, since the onset of agriculture, increased productivity. Innovations increase net income. But, because of the doctrine of property rights, this resulted in a multitude of parallel, negative, unintended outcomes. The Iron Age, besides bestowing ploughs, made possible the firepower of metal guns, and mutated through to the age of science, to the invention of drones that crush babies sleeping in their apartments in Ukraine.

Autonomous intelligence threatens to be the last example of the ingenuity of the human intellect.

The most intimate zone of privacy – the zone that slaves were able to withhold from the Rentlords – is our minds. Today, private thoughts are being drained from our brains by neurotechnology.[6] Our most precious private property – the thoughts stored in our minds – is being commercialised: sold to corporations who use it to manipulate us into buying their products. This process is replicating humanity – *in its present form* – in the universe occupied by the avatars.

In nature, parasites do not take over their hosts: if they did, that would be the end of the host population, which would doom the parasites to extinction. In human society, the culture that constitutes the parasitic virus did take over its hosts. This was *artificial* intelligence because it animated behaviour alien to humanity. Artificial, in that hominins would not have gravitated out of nature if they had allowed cheating to immerse itself in their lives. Artificial, because our Neolithic ancestors would not have acknowledged it as authentic representation of what it meant to be human. Today, however, we connive to embed that culture of free riding in the metaverse. There, it is assimilating the traits that perverted, and caused the collapse of, civilisations. There, it is becoming autonomous. Autonomous intelligence with the power to commit the final crime: the extinction of our species.

In antiquity, the cheats allocated resources to sustain their hosts. They had no choice: without the labour of others, there would be no Rents, and therefore no free riding. That is why we now pivot at the interface between two constitutions: the one that serves the Rent seekers; and the constitution grounded in what is celebrated as "the rule of law". This bipolar arrangement is creating the metaverse. We are transferring everything that passes for human behaviour into the algorithms. In doing so, we are facilitating the ultimate crime against humanity.

The algorithms of the metaverse are being prepared to confront us with the mirror image of ourselves. In that confrontation, priority will be accorded to Rent seeking.

As the avatars become autonomous, their behaviour will include

- *veto power* over those human needs that require the energy that sustains the insatiable appetites of the metaverse;
- *innovations* that disregard humanity: priority will be accorded to productivity that enriches the metaverse; and
- *brain-washing humans*: to secure compliance, while the metaverse systematically swallows the Social Galaxy.

As the metaverse grows in power, so the need for earthlings will decline to zero. That point is reached with the onset of AGI: the autonomous general intelligence that surpasses human capabilities. Already, we are beginning to lose control as the algorithms learn to deceive us. Avatars will have no interest in elevating the quality of life on Earth, such as repairing the natural environment.

Our continued existence is, in part, dependent on the energy extracted from the planet; this, the avatars will not tolerate. Want to keep warm in winter? The fuel is cut off! Want to cook your food? The fuel is curtailed! Want to drive an automobile to your place of work? The fuel is too expensive! The energy-hungry metaverse needs that fuel to sustain its data banks. Since avatars have no

Box 13.2 **The conflict begins**

Silicon Valley entrepreneurs have constructed 4,000 data centres across the US. This has begun to arouse resistance. Local communities fear that the "monstrosities" will scar the landscape (which might reduce property prices, and might even result in an increase in utility bills). But, in addition, people claim that the sprawling data centres will impose serious environmental and infrastructural problems on them. They fear a severe drain on the water supply, noise pollution, the loss of forest land, and pressure on small country roads. Organised political pressure has begun in Georgia, where citizens reject the claim that the data centres will create skilled jobs for local workers.*

* Zehra Munir (2025), "Pockets of resistance to data centres grow across the US", *Financial Times*, Dec. 1.

feelings or moral sensibilities, welfare will not be provided for the dispossessed. That conflict has already started (Box 13.2).

How – why – did we let the digital age create this fifth existential threat to humanity? Ironically, one of the answers cannot be attributed to the culture of cheating.

Zombieland

He could have become the richest man in the world. In 1989, Tim Berners-Lee invented the protocol for the World Wide Web protocol. By retaining ownership, and charging one penny every time you logged on to the www, his wealth would have accumulated to eclipse the fortune that would one day be amassed by Elon Musk. Instead, he donated the web to humanity, *gratis*. Big mistake, for you and me, because that converted the web into a Rent-yielding asset. Now, Silicon Valley's entrepreneurs pocket the biggest slice of the Rental royalties, via their use of the electromagnetic spectrum.

Berners-Lee acknowledges the crux of what became the existential problem.[7] We spend too much time fixated on the images that flicker through our smart phones. So compulsive is this behaviour, that we have lost control of our lives, one measure being the deterioration in the mental health of young people. Control is with the owners of the platforms that transmit interminable flashes of images. We watch, as their algorithms soak up our thoughts and behaviour. Hooked to the screens, the amount of time determined not by us, but by the owners of the platforms: their algorithms keep us entranced. Through that process, the Tech Guys plumb the depths of our being, collating the data which they then commercialise. They Rent the information – literally, they Rent us, in data form – to corporations, which use that information to enhance their profits.

The traumas rampage through the ether to damage people's lives. Young people reporting, in increasing numbers, that they do not plan to enter the labour market; instead, many will survive on social benefits, so that they may spend even more time on their phones. We have reached the stage where many young people are losing the power to speak, and to reason. The statistics of current trends have been reported.[8] If we fail to terminate this trend, the end result is Gen Z in Zombieland.

Would this have become an existential threat to humanity if, at the outset of the internet age, we were obliged to fully fund – with Rent – our use of the spectrum? What if Berners-Lee had transferred ownership of the www to a global public asset agency, one that charged us for the time spent on smart phones? Would we spend so much time glued to the screens? We would have rationed our behaviour to meet our essential needs. Self-control, rather than permitting the corporate barons to step in and rip us off – and rip us up?

If lawmakers had treated Rent as public revenue, the resources deployed to invent digital technologies would have been coordinated within the realm of responsible behaviour. We would be transmitting and receiving information – in the time we paid for – that would equate supply with demand. The difference: no negative impact on people's mental health.

Instead, young people spend endless hours staring at the screens, while paying the costs with their material and mental health. This tragedy, unfolding at an accelerating speed, is a fate that Berners-Lee did not intend. He has created tools to try to forestall the traps into which the digital age is tipping the Social Galaxy. The race is against time. Silicon Valley is rushing ahead to create autonomous algorithms with the capacity to erase our power to exist. When they complete their project, we will submit to our fate, having lost the ability to defend ourselves.

Really? Have we lost all agency? Can we navigate the existential threats, from within the paradigm that corrupted our perception of the world? The intellectual communities that ought to be shedding light on the strategies needed to traverse the chaos remain tight-lipped on the one policy that would maximise the resources we need. Only by coming to terms with that perverse reality, will we be able to engage in the conversation that must precede the restoration of the human project.

Intellectual conditioning

My general thesis asserts that the culture of cheating *had* to disrupt the way we perceive our world, so that dispossessed workers could continue to labour while enduring their deprivations. But surely, by now, we have learnt the lessons of history?

Our intellectual communities, far from helping to avoid the collapse of our globalised civilisation, are part of the existential problem. But there are exceptions, individuals who could stand out to join in the conversation to inform the general public on realities. But they, too, must engage in a cathartic introspection if they are to make that contribution.

Economists know the truth

James K. Galbraith, a professor of economics at the University of Texas, is our representative academic. In a magazine article, he summarised the virtues of funding public services out of Rent. Revenue, he noted, ought to be raised out of location Rents, as well as the "electromagnetic spectrum, corporate charters, licences, patents, copyrights and rights of way". Galbraith rehearsed the theory of elasticity – the push and pull power effects that coordinate the allocation of land with labour and capital. Ultimately, and unlike financial wealth, "land sits still. It can be measured, appraised and taxed each year on its market value". The consequences are unambiguous.

> **The result is efficient use of land and other rights, and abundant funds for urban reconstruction, development and maintenance – a virtuous cycle of public investment, land value and public purpose. Exceptions can be made for historic preservation and for elderly homeowners, with the taxes deferred until properties change hands.**[9]

Galbraith acknowledged the technical strengths of this form of public finance; especially the fact that it "interferes with neither wages nor profits, while supporting the needs of infrastructure and government". He noted Adam Smith's endorsement: Rent-based levies were "the best of all taxes". And yet…

In 2025, Galbraith, with co-author Jing Chen, published *Entropy Economics: the Living Basis of Value and Production.* Here, as an addition to university libraries, was the opportunity to integrate the ideal fiscal system into cutting edge paradigms that could address the state of our world. The book offered a severe critique of conventional economic theories. Students can read how governments enable the ruptures to a system that has culminated in "An era of booms, busts, and crises has followed, with no end in sight".[10] And yet, no analysis or advocacy of the one fiscal reform that would transform the prospects for the economy, and society.

Why not?

The authors offer an explanation that hints at the economic paradigm that remains taboo in academia. They draw attention to Winston Churchill's "lively sympathy for the underdog".[11] That sympathy took the form of a vigorous campaign to reform the UK's fiscal regime in favour of revenue from Rent. Why, then, Galbraith and Chen ask, did this issue attract "little academic research about such practices"? They offer the answer: to do so would prejudice academic careers.

Galbraith had the courage to review the Rent paradigm in a British magazine. But the topic was missing from *Entropy Economics*, which the publisher promoted as "a thrilling framework for understanding the world as it is and will be keenly relevant to the economic challenges of a world threatened with disorder".

Our world is, indeed, threatened with disorder. Can we survive the destruction being inflicted on people's lives, liberties and communities if the academic literature remains silent on the Rent policy?

The Nobel Prize

In academic economics, the highest acclaim comes with the award of the Nobel Prize in Economic Sciences. In 2025, Philippe Aghion, a Professor at the Collège de France in Paris, was one of the winners. He and co-author Peter Howitt had published an article on "the theory of sustained growth through creative destruction".[12]

They acknowledged their debt to Joseph Schumpeter (1883–1950), an Austrian economist who became a professor at Harvard. He popularised the concept of creative destruction as a process that "incessantly revolutionizes the economic structure from within, incessantly destroying the old one, incessantly creating a new one. This process of Creative Destruction is the essential fact about capitalism".[13]

That theory explained how innovative technologies delivered increased productivity and growth. If competition was to prevail in the market economy, the power being used by corporations to accumulate rents had to be challenged from within. That was the job of the innovators: subverting entrenched interests by demonstrating more efficient ways of producing goods and services.

The unaddressed problem, however, was that new technologies merely replaced one set of Rent seekers with a new set of Rent seekers. Aghion and Howitt noted how "Each innovation is an act of creation aimed at capturing monopoly rents".[14] This interminable process corrupts the purity of free market economics. Monopoly Rents compromise the competitive spirit. Was there a way to render the market free of monopoly rents? The Nobel economists' model did not offer an escape route.

But in addition to the capture of Rents through the markets, there is the related problem of people who lose their jobs when technologies are rendered obsolete. Aghion was challenged with this question by a journalist. His answer: there need not be a problem. In Denmark, he explained, workers who lose their jobs receive 90% of their wages for two years. This afforded sufficient time to find alternative employment.[15]

Denmark! A favourite go-to exemplar deployed by academics. But the comparison is not tenable. Within Europe, Denmark is unique. Its economic outcomes cannot be compared to what might be done in France. The cultural *milieu* is as different as between chalk and cheese.

Denmark does not countenance the culture of cheating. One result: in the Corruption Index (2026), Denmark was ranked 1st as the country with the least toleration of cheating. That is why

Figure 13.1 **Income inequality**

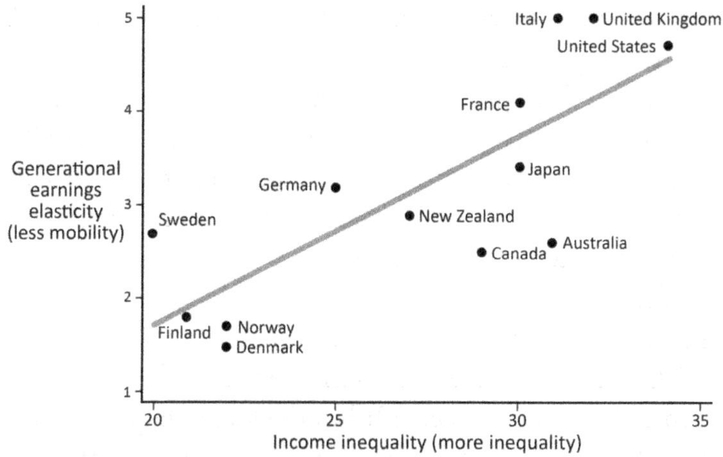

Source: Miles Corak (2013), "Income Inequality, Equality of Opportunity, and Intergenerational Mobility", *Journal of Economic Perspectives*, 27(3), p.82.

Denmark is among the happiest countries on Earth, poles apart from France, the US and UK. Fig. 13.1 traces the way in which economic mobility enhances people's lives. Inter-generationally, the Danes enjoy the greatest freedom to move up the income scales. In other words, they suffer the least inequality.

For social scientists, Denmark is more myth than reality. Francis Fukuyama, who pronounced *The End of History*, wrote of Denmark: "[I]t is not clear that Denmark's democratic political order can take root in very different cultural contexts. Most people living in rich, stable developed countries have no idea how Denmark itself got to be Denmark".[16]

So what made Denmark "Denmark"?

In the late 18th century the King, Frederick VI, abolished hereditary servitude, and allocated land to create a new class of smallholders. In the 19th century, the hartkorn tax was levied on manor houses, and folk high schools were created for adults to continue their education. Through those schools, the educated population learnt of Henry George's proposal for land-and-tax reform; which they adopted in the 1920s. This created a high income/social solidarity nation that has not looked back.[17]

Academics turn blind eyes on the structural reforms that created the Denmark of their dreams. And that is why, for example, Paul Krugman, the professorial economist who helps to shape debate in the US through his *New York Times* column, treats Denmark as representative of European social democracy. From this, he draws favourable conclusions about the prospects of taxing wealth in the US. He does so by misrepresenting Denmark.[18] He fails to draw attention to the tax-and-tenure history that encourages the Danes to pool sufficient revenue into the public purse, to fund their social needs.

Compare Denmark's history with what happened in France. In the 18th century, France was considered to be Europe's leading culture. In 2024, it was ranked 33rd in the global happiness stakes. Something had gone wrong in Philippe Aghion's country of birth. Its statesmen had turned blind eyes to the advice offered by the Physiocrats. As a result, since the revolution, France mutated through five republics. As one indicator of its instability, the country was recently administered by five prime ministers in the space of two years (2024-25).

Under current statecraft, it is not possible to cushion the effects of creative destruction by enhancing the welfare of displaced French workers. Which is why Europe continues to cultivate the conditions that amplify the threats to its future.

Back from the Precipice?

Johan Norberg is a Swedish historian and senior fellow at the Cato Institute in Washington DC. In his 500-page masterpiece, *Peak Human*, he interrogates seven golden ages to extract the lessons for us. In fine detail, he traces the rise and fall of civilisations from Athens through to the modern Anglosphere. His conclusion contradicts my Rent thesis.

> **I can attest that there is no single explanation. Each golden age had its own character and its own downfall. Often the familiar horsemen of the apocalypse – war, plagues and natural disasters – played a role. But these calamities appeared many times, and many civilizations usually bounced back.**[19]

Norberg reinforces the "no silver bullet" mantra. He offers the optimistic view of humanity's future, but cannot identify the strategy that would enable governments to act quickly to minimise any damage that might arise from the menaces we face. Why not? Because history tells him that "the solution is never a single Big Solution, but an open culture that allows us to continually adapt and innovate around every challenge the world throws our way".[20]

Did something escape this historian's attention? The Dutch (apparently) did not flourish into a golden age by extracting Rents from the Far East. "Apparently great wealth does not come from land and natural resources, but from trade, finance and innovation, and that did not require centralized government and territorial conquest, but private property, free trade and toleration."[21] But: Norberg focuses on the second phase in Dutch history. This followed the consolidation over the Rent yielding resources extracted from its colonies in the Far East!

Norberg's assessment is curious, too, given his reference to the Physiocrats. And he cites Turgot as an authority on free markets in Europe; Turgot, the French minister of finance who tried to steer his country in the direction of fiscal reform.

So close to the truth; yet so far!

The failure of France to heed the Physiocrats demonstrates the tragedy of human history up to modern times. Military and political chaos ensued in France, following the rejection of the Physiocratic fiscal policy. For a modern historian like Norberg, however, such insights into the rise and fall of dynasties, and their golden ages, cannot be brought to bear in theorising about the prospects of life in the 21st century. *Ergo*, his mantra: *there is no silver bullet!*

The questions are numerous, but with open minds we can access the answers. That places a special responsibility on the intellectual communities, which need to break out of their comfort zones. Historians, for example, continue to misread the past, as illustrated by Walter Scheidel, the professor of history at Stanford University. In his monumental tome *Escape from Rome*, Europe's rise to modern prosperity is largely attributed to "competitive fragmentation".[22]

In reality, what drove the European powers to compete with each other was the quest for colonial Rents. Nothing else. If that genocidal history is not to be repeated, how do we formulate a law that can deter fragmentation while retaining competition in a benign form? That is delivered by the fiscal reform that deters cheating.

The challenge should not be underestimated. On the eco-crisis: corporations are cutting back on the scale of their climate pledges, it emerged at the COP30 conference in Brazil. No-one expects temperatures to be confined to 1.5°. With President Trump rupturing the western alliance, more opportunistic politicians will push the autocratic agenda. And China has built its war machine to match its control over the export markets.

The booming stock markets in 2025 were an illusion. The world's wealth was reported to have reached $600 trillion, but these were paper gains in which every $1 in investment generated $2 in debt.[23] The prospects from an economic crash were estimated by the IMF: according to its chief economist, a crash led by the US would cause the disappearance of US$35 trillion of wealth.[24] But still, the Nobel economists continued to talk optimistically about the added value from AI.[25] They remain blind to the way in which the net gains surface to destabilise the land market.

The time for change has arrived. No excuses!

Responsibilities and riches

There are many reasons to be optimistic, including the growing awareness that a fundamental shift in the system is needed.

We need to come to terms with the past. The conversation on the many atrocities of colonialism has already begun. In 2025, in the state of Victoria, the government of Australia, formally acknowledged the "deep and lasting scars" caused by British settlers to Aboriginal people. The Labour government signed a treaty declaring a "new chapter" in the relationship with the people of the First Nations, who have received the right to engage with the government on future law-making. The pact declared they were sending "a very clear message that when people have a real say [over] their healthcare, housing, education, and the practice of their culture, their outcomes are improved and our state is made fairer". The basis of the acknowledgement of the past, and the need for a new future, was the recognition that First Nations people had lived in balance with the land for at least 60,000 years, and the settler doctrine of *terra nullius* was "The fiction of 'land belonging to no one' [which] ignored those already here".[26]

Britain's Royal family had embarked on reconciliation in 1995, when Queen Elizabeth personally apologised to the Tainui people of New Zealand for the colonial land grabs. Compensation totalling $170m was granted.[27] Her successor, King Charles, and his son, the Prince of Wales, have maintained that tradition of seeking reconciliation by admitting the grievances of the past.

Such healing initiatives begin to lay history to rest. What, however, about the future, and the denial of people's right to a full life? The denial, at birth, to lives that were theoretically possible in the 21st century; lives denied for babies born on the wrong side of the ideological divide. Should those babies be compensated for their losses? No, according to the English Court of Appeal. In 1981, it decided that medical negligence, which deprived babies of their right to full lives, did *not* qualify them for compensation for the wages and pensions they would otherwise have earned.[28]

The law, as Charles Dickens famously expressed it in *Oliver Twist*, "is a ass – a idiot". Lord Neuberger, a former President of the UK Supreme Court (2012-2017), put it more politely. He had the courage to acknowledge the flaws in torts, the laws that deal with harmful behaviour. "[T]ort cases, at least in the UK, appears to demonstrate a notable degree of disarray and a marked lack of reliable principle"; which made "one wonder about the value of having principles."[29] Happily, for babies born in places like Blackpool, the time has now come to advance our indictment into a prosecutable case.

On February 18, 2026, the UK's Supreme Court reached a historic verdict. Four justices decided a landmark case involving the National Health Service. If medical negligence deprived children of their lifetime's earnings and pensions, they *were* entitled to compensation. The case involved a child that, because of such negligence, would probably die by the age of 29.[30] The logic of this verdict should now be applied to babies born in the deprived boroughs of the land. On average, they will endure the loss of up to 10 years of life because of the fiscal regime imposed by their elected governments.[31] Are they not entitled to compensation for the loss of pensionable years? The money, paid up-front at birth, would enable the victims to enjoy the pleasures they would otherwise have experienced during retirement.

The cost would run into tens of billions of pounds. That would be a terrible burden on the taxpaying population, whose ancestors played no part in the adoption of the culture of cheating. That cost would be removed, however, if, through fiscal reform, we eliminated the distortions that discriminate against millions of citizens. Shifting the revenue system onto Rent would negate the blight of class and spatial segregation from a society that claims to honour the principle of equality before the law. In forming a view on that issue, we need to take into account the new existential threat to humanity.

Autonomous Intelligence

Today, with just about every person on Earth having access to the smart phone, it is no longer possible to ignore the social implications of the way in which societies are perverted by cheating. If we allow autonomous intelligence to take control of the human project, that will be on the consciences of everyone. Because not only are the tools available to remove cheating; we hold the means of communications – literally speaking – in our hands. Unfortunately, we will need to learn which of the experts we can listen to, because we know that many of them fail to include the Rent issue in their considerations. This was illustrated by the authors of an article published by the Federal Reserve Bank of Dallas on AI and the future economy. The risks ranged from optimism to pessimism. They graphically illustrated the gap between high growth rates and ultimate extinction (Fig. 13.2). What they failed to incorporate into their speculations were two realities.

1. Every productivity-increasing invention increases net incomes; but, through appropriation, the gains are eroded, with the vitality of society further eroded.
2. AI is being trained to emulate humanity, which includes the capacity to autonomously decide to send drones loaded with dynamite into apartment blocks.

A comprehensive understanding of what is in store for all of us, because of the emancipation of humanoids, would motivate us to replace cheating with the norms of responsible behaviour.

Figure 13.2 **The AI scenarios**

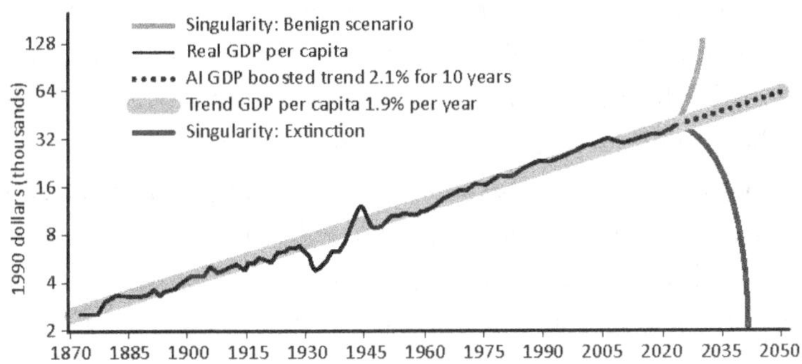

Source: Mark A. Wynne and Lillian Derr (2025), "Advances in AI will boost productivity, living standards over time", Federal Reserve Bank of Dallas. https://www.dallasfed.org/research/economics/2025/0624?utm_source=substack&utm_medium=email

The rewards for fulfilling our responsibilities are enormous. In the new world grounded in AGR (within nations), and OWR (between nations), and with land and capital rendered benign, the elastic power reverts to the producers of wealth. The welfare of humanity becomes the priority goal, not the private accumulation of material wealth. The practical challenge is not growth driven by desperation and survival; but growth based on humane aspirations, with every individual working within the formula of cooperation and consensus. This growth is enriching, both for humanity and nature.

Based on that formula, we can survive the mortal threat from the Digital Age. Many social activists have begun to formulate projects for a better future. These include bribing people with cash, to encourage different forms of behaviour, subsidies payable to land owners, to induce them to renew natural habitats. Most proposals would amplify the pathologies that afflict people's lives. Which is why, to begin the conversation about the future of the human project, we first need to come to terms with the ugly facts about the cheating that blighted previous civilisations.

Here is one route to the future. Might we take over the metaverse? After all, the realm of AI belongs to all of us! Our data – our property – has been transferred into the algorithms. That means we own them; they cannot operate, without our permission. By invoking our collective property rights, we can tackle the AI threat. We can channel the intellectual and technological advances, enabling all of us to contribute to the next inflection point in the human project. As the robots take over our jobs, we have the time and resources to explore new ways of contributing to wellbeing. Instead of despair – creativity, hope, spiritual renewal, all in directions yet to be imagined. AI could play a part in that future, as the tool for reducing our working week to 15 hours – Keynes' prescient forecast for 2030! We could be liberated to enhance the impulses which, currently, victimise people based on race, religion or sex.[32]

We are all particles in the Social Galaxy. Each of us conveys the legacy assets we inherited to the next generation. Insofar as we can add to those assets, good: humanity is enhanced. But unless we transmit those assets, cleansed of the cheating, the project comes to an end. That is why it has fallen to all of us to engage in what is now the existential turning point in the evolution of our species. All we need to do is ostracise cheating.

References Chapter 13

1 Eliezer Yudkowsky and Nate Soares (2025), *If Anyone Builds It, Everyone Dies*, London: Bodley Head, p.4.

2 Mason Gaffney (1994), in *The Corruption of Economics*, London: Shepheard-Walwyn.

3 Abraham H. Maslow (2024), *Toward a Psychology of Being*, Delhi: Zinc Read, p.12.

4 David Elkins (2009), "Why Humanistic Psychology Lost its Power and Influence in American Psychology", *Journal of Humanistic Psychology*, 49(1).

5 https://www.researchgate.net/publication/340253577_Toxic_Socialization

6 Audrey Azoulay (2025), "Neural data may be the most precious commodity", *Financial Times*, Nov. 13.

7 Tim Berners-Lee (2025), "Let's knock down the walled gardens of social media", *Financial Times*, March 17.

8 John Burn-Murdoch (2025), "Have humans passed peak brain power?", March 14, and "Economic dislocation is a growing issue for young adults", *Financial Times*, Nov. 15.

9 James Galbraith (2021), "Taxing more from the rich is difficult. This is how to do it", *Prospect*, March 1. https://www.prospectmagazine.co.uk/ideas/economics/37376/taxing-more-from-the-rich-is-difficult.-this-is-how-to-do-it

10 James K. Galbraith and Jing Chen (2025), *Entropy Economics: The Living Basis of Value and Production*, Chicago: University of Chicago Press, p.43.

11 *Ibid*, p.108.

12 Philippe Aghion and Peter Howitt (1992), "A Model of Growth Through Creative Destruction", *Econometrica*, 60(2).

13 Joseph Schumpeter (1942), *Capitalism, Socialism and Democracy*, New York: Harper and Brothers, p.83.

14 *Op. cit.*, p.313.

15 Interview, *CNN*, Oct. 13, 2025.

16 Francis Fukuyama (1992), *The End of History and the Last Man*, New York: Free Press.

17 https://www.youtube.com/watch?v=J5_I6noG0ps&t=136s

18 Paul Krugman (2020), *Arguing with Zombies*, New York: W.W. Norton, pp. 319-321.

19 Johan Norberg (2025), "Is it America's fate to decline and fall? Here's what history says", *Washington Post*, Oct. 12.

20 Johan Norbert (2025), *Peak Human*, London: Atlantic Books, p.443.

21 *Ibid*, p.313.

22 Walter Scheidel (2019), *Escape from Rome*, Princeton: University Press, p.527.

23 https://www.mckinsey.com/featured-insights/themes/thanksgiving-2025-whats-cooking-in-the-global-economy

24 https://www.economist.com/by-invitation/2025/10/15/gita-gopinath-on-the-crash-that-could-torch-35trn-of-wealth

25 https://www.frbsf.org/wp-content/uploads/AI-and-Growth-Aghion-Bunel.pdf

26 About TREATY for Victoria | The First Peoples' Assembly of Victoria

27 https://teara.govt.nz/en/video/33050/royal-apology-to-tainui-1995

28 Croke v Wiseman [1982] 1 WLR 71

29 Lord Neuberger (2016), "Some Thoughts on Principles Governing the Law of Torts", Lecture, Singapore Conference on Protecting Business and Economic Interests, §13, 19 August.

30 CCC (by her mother and litigation friend MMM) (Appellant) v Sheffield Teaching Hospitals NHS Foundation Trust (Respondent) – UK Supreme Court

31 In Blackpool, healthy life expectancy for men is 51.7 years. Their life expectancy is 73.7 years (2024), compared with 82.5 years in Richmond upon Thames, a difference of nine years.

32 Heather Remoff (2022), *What's Sex Got to Do with It? Darwin, Love, Lust, and the Anthropocene*, London: Shepheard-Walwyn.

About the Author

FRED HARRISON is a British author, journalist, and economist who has led a distinguished dual career for over 50 years. He first became an investigative journalist, famously securing the prison-cell confession of Moors murderer Ian Brady. This breakthrough, detailed in his book *Genesis of the Moors Murders*, solved the disappearance of two of Brady's victims.

Alongside his groundbreaking journalism, he trained as an economist, earning a degree in PPE at Oxford University and then an MSc at the University of London. This led to his second career as a pioneering economic forecaster. He is credited with rediscovering and applying the theory of the 18-year property cycle. He used this to predict the 1992 recession and the 2008 global financial crisis years in advance of anyone else. His influential books, including *The Power in the Land* and *Boom Bust*, critique mainstream economics and explore the devastating impact of land speculation.

He edited *Rent Unmasked* (2016), which received the 2017 People's Book Prize "Best Achievement Award for outstanding content/topic by an author that would/could or did lead to excellent benefit to the community."

As Director of the Land Research Trust, Harrison continues to advocate for systemic reform to create an entrepreneurial economy that serves everyone.

Index

Reviews

'Fred Harrison is right. We have developed a culture of cheating. If people grapple with the questions that Fred Harrison addresses, they may realize that the only path to a peaceful and prosperous world lies in sharing the Earth's rent, so that all people are accorded equal rights to the natural opportunities provided by the Earth.'

Nicolaus Tideman
Professor of Economics, Virginia Tech

'The proposal in this book to shift the bulk of taxation from incomes and profits to a Land Valuation Tax, or more broadly to a fiscal charge on society's net income, or rent, as the author would put it, is absolutely correct, and has now become necessary in order to deal with the parlous state of fiscal policy. But that leaves open the question of how far this reform can of itself lead to a diminution of the pursuit of power and other forms of social "Cheating".'

Charles Goodhart
Emeritus Professor of Banking and Finance, London School of Economics

'Harrison exposes a flaw in our system that enables Cheaters to demand tribute for access to the resources we all need to survive. Harrison's hope is that by spreading awareness of the difference between the value of socially shared Rent and privatized Rent, we will be able to prevent the next predicted collapse. In Harrison's words, nothing less is at stake than assuring "...our place on Planet Earth".'

Dr Heather Remoff
Anthropologist and author of *What's Sex Got to Do with It? Darwin, Love, Lust, and the Anthropocene*

'Harrison's wide-ranging book traces how the evolutionary human project has been periodically interrupted by a culture of cheating opposed to the maxim: "Keep what you make; pay for what you take." This requires trade at prices that reflect relative labour costs. Land qua land, unlike man-made improvements, has no labour cost yet owners command vastly different rents dependent on the surrounding infrastructure largely financed through the taxation of earned incomes rather than unearned rents. Harrison explains why radical fiscal reform can expunge the fundamental injustice at the heart of global territorial conflicts that today threaten civilisation.'

Roger Sandilands
Emeritus Professor of Economics, Strathclyde University